MINORITY STUDENTS AND PUBLIC EDUCATION

Black and American Indian Students

Also by Michael Holzman

Lukács's Road to God

Writing as Social Action (with Marilyn Cooper)

James Jesus Angleton:
The CIA, and the Craft of Counterintelligence

Transgressions (novel)

Guy Burgess: Revolutionary in an Old School Tie

The Black Poverty Cycle and How to End It

MINORITY STUDENTS AND PUBLIC EDUCATION

A Resource Book

Volume One

Black and American Indian Students

Chelmsford Press

Note: All attempts were made to contact copyright holders prior to publication. The publisher apologizes for any oversights and will correct these in subsequent printings.

Chelmsford Press
Briarcliff Manor, New York
ISBN-13: 978-0615930954
ISBN-10: 0615930956

Wisdom, and knowledge, as well as virtue, diffused generally among the body of the people, being necessary for the preservation of their rights and liberties; and as these depend on spreading the opportunities and advantages of education in the various parts of the country, and among the different orders of the people, it shall be the duty of legislatures and magistrates, in all future periods of this commonwealth, to cherish the interests of literature and the sciences, and all seminaries of them; especially the university at Cambridge, public schools and grammar schools in the towns; to encourage private societies and public institutions, rewards and immunities, for the promotion of agriculture, arts, sciences, commerce, trades, manufactures, and a natural history of the country; to countenance and inculcate the principles of humanity and general benevolence, public and private charity, industry and frugality, honesty and punctuality in their dealings; sincerity, good humor, and all social affections, and generous sentiments among the people. *Chapter V, Section II, Constitution of the Commonwealth of Massachusetts.*

Table of Contents

Acknowledgments

All data in the following pages are from or estimated from public sources, chiefly the National Center for Education Statistics of the United States Department of Education and the Bureau of the Census. Other data has been provided by staff of state and local education departments, whose exemplary helpfulness is gratefully acknowledged.

Errors are, of course, my own. I would be grateful to have them brought to my attention so that they might be corrected.

Preface

Public education is under attack today from those who do not believe with John Adams that "opportunities and advantages of education" should be available "in the various parts of the country, and among the different orders of the people." Adams specified that the provision of the "opportunities and advantages of education" is a public duty, not a source of private profit, and that those opportunities and advantages should be available to everyone, not only to the privileged, and everywhere, not just in wealthy suburbs.

The data presented here shows that in general the opportunities for a good education vary with race, ethnicity and economic status. Educational opportunities for all students vary with location. The variation between states and school districts within states is striking. And almost everywhere the opportunities available to the descendents of slaves are fewer than those for others, with the exception of some American Indian tribes.

This resource book is primarily intended to be of use to those in the general public interested in the education of minority students. Educators in schools, in local district offices and in state departments of education may find it useful. It may serve as a convenient reference for journalists and policy makers.

It would be gratifying if these volumes were of some help to those who are working to spread "the opportunities and advantages of education in the various parts of the country, and among the different orders of the people."

BLACK STUDENTS AND PUBLIC EDUCATION

National Summary

The descendents of American slaves remain the largest group of residents of the United States whose opportunities in life are institutionally restricted. (This is also the case for the relatively few descendents of the genocide of American Indians.) This section includes data demonstrating the effects of those limited opportunities in elementary and secondary education. It provides estimated graduation rates, National Assessment of Educational Progress (NAEP) grade 8 Reading and Mathematics proficiency for the nation, for each state and for districts enrolling 20,000 or more Black students. For those districts it also includes enrollment in Gifted and Talented programs, classification of students with Intellectual Disability, out-of-school suspensions and enrollment in Advanced Placement Mathematics. Data is compiled or, where necessary, estimated, from federal, state and district departments of education and other public sources.

Graduation Rates:
The national public school graduation rate for male Black students has now reached 53%. This is a significant increase in a decade from the rate of 41% for the 2001/2 school year. The graduation rate for male White, non-Latino, students has also increased, from 70% to 77% over that period (while decreasing from one percent from 2010). The gap has therefore narrowed in a decade from 29 percentage points to 24. At this rate, it will be eliminated in fifty years.

Of the seven states enrolling more that 200,000 male Black students, four (Georgia, Florida, New York and Illinois) have lower than average male Black graduation rates. Montana and the other four states with higher male Black graduation rates than the White, non-Latino, national average have very small Black minorities. Only Montana achieved a higher male Black than male White, non-Latino, graduation rate in 2010-11. Arizona, South Dakota, New Jersey, Idaho and Vermont currently have higher male Black graduation rates than the national male White, non-Latino, graduation rate in the 2001/2 school year. This relationship between relatively high male Black graduation rates and relatively low concentrations of Black students is supportive of the idea that integrated school systems better serve Black students than segregated systems, perhaps because schools oriented toward the education of White, non-Latino, students are likely to provide teachers and facilities superior to those to which majorities of Black students are consigned. New Jersey continues to show particularly significant outcomes, as it has a large African-American population and one district (Newark) with more than 10,000 Black male students. The exceptional performance of New Jersey is attributable to the challenge-based allocation of resources in that state consequent to the Abbott school funding decision.

Among *districts* enrolling 20,000 or more Black students, ten have higher male Black graduation rates than the national average. Two—Montgomery County (MD) and Newark (NJ)—exceed the 2001/2 male White, non-Latino, graduation rate. Philadelphia, Clark County, Detroit and Rochester, on the other hand, graduate less that a quarter of their male Black students. Six other districts graduate less than one-third.

National Assessment of Educational Progress
The National Assessment of Educational Progress (NAEP) provides percentages of students at or above "proficient" in grade 8 in a variety of subjects for states and selected districts. Reading is the essential skill for education (and life) and by grade 8 schools and school systems have had time to provide that basic skill to students without regard to the socio-economic status of student families. Grade 8 Reading proficiency is, therefore, a good indicator of school quality. The national averages on the NAEP grade 8 Reading assessment are 10% for male Black student and 35% for male White, non-Latino, students. In other words, 90% of male Black students and 65% of male, White non-Latino, students are not proficient readers by grade 8. The range among states for male Black students is from 4% in California to 19% in Connecticut. The range for male White, non-Latino, students is from 19% in West Virginia to 48% in Connecticut. Connecticut, then, can educate its grade 8 male Black students as well as West Virginia can educate its grade 8 male White, non-

Latino, students, but educates less than half the proportion of its male Black students as well as it educates its male White students.

It appears in general that the percentage of male Black students reaching proficiency in each state parallels that for male White, non-Latino, students. That is, the higher the proficiency rate for male White, non-Latino, students, the higher the rate for male Black students. It could be inferred from this that a key variable for Black student educational achievement is the overall quality of the state school systems.

Among large districts, New York City, Charlotte and Miami-Dade have male Black grade 8 reading proficiency levels above the national average, while the lowest rates are found in Detroit, Cleveland and Milwaukee. The percentage of male Black students scoring at the level of proficient or above on grade 8 Mathematics shows quite a different distribution among cities than that for reading. By this measure Boston is at the first rank, with 22% of male Black students, while New York City is tenth, at 10% proficient or above.[1] Here again Detroit, Cleveland and Milwaukee have particularly low percentages of male Black students achieving proficiency.

Gifted and Talented, Intellectually Disabled, Out of School Suspensions and Advanced Placement

The U. S. Department of Education Office for Civil Rights (OCR) had not yet aggregated 2009-2010 data by state or nationally.

United States Department of Education Office for Civil Rights (OCR) district-level data shows that the ratio of male Black to male White, non-Latino, students in Gifted and Talented programs ranges from 9 to 1 in Memphis and Nashville to 1 to 1 in Montgomery County (MD) and Milwaukee.[2] That is, Black students have an equal chance of receiving the increased resources characteristic of Gifted and Talented programs as White, non-Latino, students in Montgomery County and Milwaukee, and barely more than one-tenth that opportunity in Memphis and Nashville. As decades of research have shown that intelligence and talent are evenly distributed in the population these differences are most likely attributable to district policies and practices.

The ratio of male Black to male White, non-Latino, students classified as Intellectually Disabled (replacing the Mentally Retarded category) varied from 8 to 1 in Atlanta and 6 to 1 in Wake County to 1 to 1 in many northern urban districts. As decades of research have shown that such disabilities are evenly distributed in the population these differences are most likely attributable to district policies and practices.

Male Black students were assigned to Advanced Placement Mathematics at less than a tenth the rate as male White, non-Latino, students in two Louisiana districts, while being assigned to Advanced Placement Mathematics at approximately the same rate as male White, non-Latino, students in the predominately Black districts of Newark, Atlanta and Cleveland. Disparities in access to courses like Advanced Placement Mathematics are traceable to district policy decisions, as the College Board has repeatedly advocated an "open admissions" policy for its Advanced Placement program.

Out-of-School suspension ratios vary from approximately 8 to 1 in Newark and Atlanta (and 6 to 1 in two other Atlanta metropolitan area districts) down to less than twice the percentage of male Black as compared to male White, non-Latino, students being given these punishments in districts such as Boston. Disparities are most extreme for students with disabilities and for female Black students both with and without disabilities. The absolute percentage of students give out-of-school suspensions also varies widely. Research has shown that out-of-school suspensions are highly detrimental to student learning and are strongly influenced by racial attitudes of teachers and school administrators.

[1] This is one of the indications that recent NAEP data for New York City is questionable.

[2] OCR data from New York City was incomplete and/or inaccurate.

Conclusion

Some progress is being made, notably in graduation rates, but that much more needs to be done. The large gaps in basic skills achievement levels are particularly troubling. Unless students are proficient in basic skills by grade 8, there is little chance that they will do well in high school or complete further education. There is strong evidence that students, particularly male Black students, who do not finish high school will find themselves incarcerated as young adults and that their children will grow up in poverty in neighborhoods with inferior schools, thus perpetuating the cycle that is limiting all too many American lives.

Comparative Estimated High School Graduation Rates

The percentage of high school students in grade nine graduating with a regular diploma four years later varies widely between racial/ethnic groups and within those groups by state. Asian students graduate at rates from 38% for Asian males in South Carolina to 100% for males and females in a number of states. Black students graduate at rates from 40% for male Black students in Nebraska to 86% for female Black students in Hawaii and 100% in Montana. Latino students graduate at rates from 44% for male Latino students in New York to 100% for Latina students in Maine. White, non-Latino, students graduate at rates from 50% for male White, non-Latino, students in Hawaii to 100% for female White, non-Latino, students in Maine. The variations within race and ethnicity by state may point to the dominance of school factors over home factors in influencing success in high school. Male Black students graduate at the highest rates in states with low Black populations, such as Montana, South Dakota and Idaho. Latino students graduate at higher rates when they are few in number and therefore well-integrated into the general school population and in some districts where there are few, if any, non-Latino students. New Jersey, which has a large Black population, graduates its male Black students at a relatively high rate, most probably due to the "needs-based funding" of schools in place there in accordance with the Abbott decision. State where the Asian student group includes a large percentage of students of Southeast Asian origin tend to have lower graduation rates for Asian students.

On average, the gap between female and male students is four percentage points for Asian and White, non-Latino, students, nine percentage points for Latino students and ten percentage points for Black students. In some states, however, the gender gap is reversed.

Despite recent progress, there is as yet no universally agreed method of calculating high school graduation rates. The method used here estimates graduation rates in the common sense, "apples to apples" method familiar to most parents: the number of regular diplomas awarded at the end of the 2009-20010 school year divided by the number of students enrolled in grade 9 four years earlier.

	Asian		Black		Latino		White	
State	**Male**	**Female**	**Male**	**Female**	**Male**	**Female**	**Male**	**Female**
Alabama	*74%*	*81%*	53%	63%	*57%*	*62%*	*71%*	*75%*
Alaska	*84%*	*90%*	69%	*61%*	62%	*63%*	77%	*77%*
Arizona	88%	*86%*	77%	73%	68%	*67%*	81%	*79%*
Arkansas	92%	*90%*	62%	75%	71%	82%	*75%*	*80%*
California	91%	96%	58%	67%	65%	75%	83%	89%
Colorado	*69%*	*76%*	54%	*62%*	*56%*	*65%*	*74%*	*80%*
Connecticut	100%	99%	59%	69%	*55%*	*60%*	86%	88%
Delaware	94%	92%	58%	71%	*58%*	74%	*73%*	*79%*
District of Columbia	*40%*	*63%*	*43%*	*53%*	*53%*	*55%*	100%	90%
Florida	*81%*	*86%*	*47%*	*60%*	62%	74%	*64%*	*72%*
Georgia	87%	93%	*49%*	*61%*	*53%*	*63%*	*66%*	*73%*
Hawaii	*64%*	*70%*	63%	86%	*46%*	*48%*	*50%*	*51%*
Idaho	87%	94%	72%	69%	73%	75%	78%	*80%*
Illinois	90%	*89%*	*48%*	*59%*	63%	70%	80%	82%
Indiana	100%	93%	57%	63%	70%	77%	77%	*80%*
Iowa	*86%*	*85%*	62%	*60%*	76%	85%	86%	87%
Kansas	*79%*	*84%*	59%	67%	66%	77%	81%	85%
Kentucky	100%	100%	61%	69%	78%	82%	*72%*	*78%*
Louisiana	96%	100%	*50%*	64%	*49%*	*55%*	*66%*	*75%*
Maine	90%	*87%*	68%	*59%*	100%	100%	94%	100%

Maryland	91%	93%	59%	72%	67%	79%	80%	83%
Massachusetts	*86%*	92%	56%	70%	*48%*	*59%*	82%	87%
Michigan	89%	94%	*49%*	*57%*	64%	*68%*	78%	81%
Minnesota	91%	92%	65%	65%	63%	*62%*	93%	94%
Mississippi	*71%*	*82%*	*52%*	63%	*55%*	*59%*	*63%*	*69%*
Missouri	94%	91%	58%	67%	78%	85%	81%	85%
Montana	100%	100%	91%	100%	89%	89%	80%	81%
Nebraska	92%	93%	*40%*	*44%*	71%	78%	86%	85%
Nevada	*71%*	*76%*	*43%*	*47%*	*50%*	*56%*	*65%*	*70%*
New Hampshire	100%	100%	-	-	-	-	80%	83%
New Jersey	99%	100%	73%	78%	74%	80%	90%	90%
New Mexico	*80%*	*78%*	56%	*58%*	*57%*	*63%*	*66%*	*73%*
New York	*84%*	95%	*43%*	*48%*	*44%*	*49%*	*73%*	*75%*
North Carolina	*78%*	*81%*	59%	74%	*47%*	*58%*	*73%*	82%
North Dakota	-	-	-	-	-	-	92%	93%
Ohio	87%	93%	*42%*	*51%*	*56%*	*66%*	*69%*	*73%*
Oklahoma	100%	100%	63%	70%	71%	79%	*76%*	81%
Oregon	*82%*	*82%*	68%	*62%*	78%	78%	78%	*78%*
Pennsylvania	96%	99%	59%	70%	*60%*	71%	86%	90%
Rhode Island	*64%*	*67%*	57%	*62%*	*57%*	*67%*	*75%*	*79%*
South Carolina	*38%*	*41%*	*48%*	*61%*	*45%*	*55%*	*63%*	*72%*
South Dakota	93%	100%	75%	71%	*59%*	79%	83%	85%
Tennessee	92%	97%	67%	76%	66%	71%	81%	83%
Texas	90%	93%	54%	63%	61%	70%	*76%*	*79%*
Utah	*85%*	*84%*	64%	*61%*	*55%*	*54%*	79%	*79%*
Vermont	97%	100%	72%	85%	66%	74%	80%	81%
Virginia	93%	96%	55%	68%	74%	91%	*76%*	84%
Washington	*78%*	*81%*	*50%*	*48%*	*51%*	*55%*	*71%*	*72%*
West Virginia	93%	*90%*	65%	68%	69%	88%	*70%*	*74%*
Wisconsin	88%	100%	*47%*	*50%*	64%	70%	89%	89%
Wyoming	*77%*	97%	56%	64%	74%	81%	78%	*79%*
USA	**87%**	**91%**	**53%**	**63%**	**61%**	**70%**	**77%**	**81%**

"100%" indicates estimate of 100% or higher, usually because of low numbers and relatively high mobility rates.

Italics indicate below national average.

Black Educational Achievement

Estimated High School Graduation Rates (2010-11)

Sorted by State

State	Black		White, non-Latino	
	Male	Female	Male	Female
Alabama	53%	63%	*71%*	75%
Alaska	69%	*61%*	77%	77%
Arizona	77%	73%	81%	79%
Arkansas	62%	75%	*75%*	80%
California	54%	65%	81%	87%
Colorado	54%	*62%*	*74%*	80%
Connecticut	59%	69%	86%	88%
Delaware	58%	71%	*73%*	79%
District of Columbia	*43%*	*53%*	100%	90%
Florida	*47%*	*60%*	*64%*	72%
Georgia	*49%*	*61%*	*66%*	73%
Hawaii	63%	86%	*50%*	51%
Idaho	72%	69%	78%	80%
Illinois	*48%*	*59%*	80%	82%
Indiana	57%	63%	77%	80%
Iowa	62%	*60%*	86%	87%
Kansas	59%	67%	81%	85%
Kentucky	61%	69%	*72%*	78%
Louisiana	*50%*	64%	*66%*	75%
Maine	68%	*59%*	94%	100%*
Maryland	59%	72%	80%	83%
Massachusetts	56%	70%	82%	87%
Michigan	*49%*	*57%*	78%	81%
Minnesota	65%	65%	93%	94%
Mississippi	*52%*	63%	*63%*	69%
Missouri	58%	67%	81%	85%
Montana	91%	100%	80%	81%
Nebraska	*40%*	*44%*	86%	85%
Nevada	*43%*	*47%*	*65%*	70%
New Hampshire	-	-	80%	83%
New Jersey	73%	78%	90%	90%
New Mexico	56%	*58%*	*66%*	73%
New York	*43%*	*48%*	*73%*	75%
North Carolina	59%	74%	*73%*	82%
North Dakota	-	-	92%	93%
Ohio	*46%*	*56%*	80%	85%
Oklahoma	63%	70%	*76%*	81%
Oregon	68%	*62%*	78%	78%
Pennsylvania	59%	70%	86%	90%
Rhode Island	57%	*62%*	*75%*	79%
South Carolina	*48%*	*61%*	*63%*	72%
South Dakota	75%	71%	83%	85%

Tennessee	67%	76%	81%	83%
Texas	*42%*	*49%*	*62%*	65%
Utah	64%	*61%*	79%	79%
Vermont	72%	85%	80%	81%
Virginia	55%	68%	*76%*	84%
Washington	*50%*	*48%*	*71%*	72%
West Virginia	65%	68%	*70%*	74%
Wisconsin	*47%*	*50%*	89%	89%
Wyoming	56%	64%	78%	79%
USA	53%	63%	77%	81%

* Approximate: too few students to accurately estimate graduation rate.

Italics indicate below national average.

Estimated High School Graduation Rates (2010-11)

Sorted by Black Male

State	Black		White, non-Latino	
	Male	Female	Male	Female
Montana	91%	100%	80%	81%
Arizona	77%	73%	81%	79%
South Dakota	75%	71%	83%	85%
New Jersey	73%	78%	90%	90%
Idaho	72%	69%	78%	80%
Vermont	72%	85%	80%	81%
Alaska	69%	*61%*	77%	77%
Maine	68%	*59%*	94%	100%*
Oregon	68%	*62%*	78%	78%
Tennessee	67%	76%	81%	83%
Minnesota	65%	65%	93%	94%
West Virginia	65%	68%	*70%*	74%
Utah	64%	*61%*	79%	79%
Hawaii	63%	86%	*50%*	51%
Oklahoma	63%	70%	*76%*	81%
Arkansas	62%	75%	*75%*	80%
Iowa	62%	*60%*	86%	87%
Kentucky	61%	69%	*72%*	78%
Connecticut	59%	69%	86%	88%
Kansas	59%	67%	81%	85%
Maryland	59%	72%	80%	83%
North Carolina	59%	74%	*73%*	82%
Pennsylvania	59%	70%	86%	90%
Delaware	58%	71%	*73%*	79%
Missouri	58%	67%	81%	85%
Indiana	57%	63%	77%	80%
Rhode Island	57%	*62%*	*75%*	79%
Massachusetts	56%	70%	82%	87%
New Mexico	56%	*58%*	*66%*	73%
Wyoming	56%	64%	78%	79%
Virginia	55%	68%	*76%*	84%
California	54%	65%	81%	87%
Colorado	54%	*62%*	*74%*	80%
Alabama	53%	63%	*71%*	75%
Mississippi	*52%*	63%	*63%*	69%
Louisiana	*50%*	64%	*66%*	75%
Washington	*50%*	*48%*	*71%*	72%
Georgia	*49%*	*61%*	*66%*	73%
Michigan	*49%*	*57%*	78%	81%
Illinois	*48%*	*59%*	80%	82%
South Carolina	*48%*	*61%*	*63%*	72%
Florida	*47%*	*60%*	*64%*	72%

Wisconsin	*47%*	*50%*	89%	89%
Ohio	*46%*	*56%*	80%	85%
District of Columbia	*43%*	*53%*	100%	90%
Nevada	*43%*	*47%*	*65%*	70%
New York	*43%*	*48%*	*73%*	75%
Texas	*42%*	*49%*	*62%*	65%
Nebraska	*40%*	*44%*	86%	85%
New Hampshire	-	-	80%	83%
North Dakota	-	-	92%	93%
USA	53%	63%	77%	81%

* Approximate: too few students to accurately estimate graduation rate.

Italics indicate below national average.

Estimated High School Graduation Rates (2010-11)

Sorted by Black Female

State	Black		White, non-Latino	
	Male	Female	Male	Female
Montana	91%	100%	80%	81%
Hawaii	63%	86%	*50%*	51%
Vermont	72%	85%	80%	81%
New Jersey	73%	78%	90%	90%
Tennessee	67%	76%	81%	83%
Arkansas	62%	75%	*75%*	80%
North Carolina	59%	74%	*73%*	82%
Arizona	77%	73%	81%	79%
Maryland	59%	72%	80%	83%
Delaware	58%	71%	*73%*	79%
South Dakota	75%	71%	83%	85%
Massachusetts	56%	70%	82%	87%
Oklahoma	63%	70%	*76%*	81%
Pennsylvania	59%	70%	86%	90%
Connecticut	59%	69%	86%	88%
Idaho	72%	69%	78%	80%
Kentucky	61%	69%	*72%*	78%
Virginia	55%	68%	*76%*	84%
West Virginia	65%	68%	*70%*	74%
Kansas	59%	67%	81%	85%
Missouri	58%	67%	81%	85%
California	54%	65%	81%	87%
Minnesota	65%	65%	93%	94%
Louisiana	*50%*	64%	*66%*	75%
Wyoming	56%	64%	78%	79%
Alabama	53%	63%	*71%*	75%
Indiana	57%	63%	77%	80%
Mississippi	*52%*	63%	*63%*	69%
Colorado	54%	*62%*	*74%*	80%
Oregon	68%	*62%*	78%	78%
Rhode Island	57%	*62%*	*75%*	79%
Alaska	69%	*61%*	77%	77%
Georgia	*49%*	*61%*	*66%*	73%
South Carolina	*48%*	*61%*	*63%*	72%
Utah	64%	*61%*	79%	79%
Florida	*47%*	*60%*	*64%*	72%
Iowa	62%	*60%*	86%	87%
Illinois	*48%*	*59%*	80%	82%
Maine	68%	*59%*	94%	100%*
New Mexico	56%	*58%*	*66%*	73%
Michigan	*49%*	*57%*	78%	81%
Ohio	*46%*	*56%*	80%	85%

District of Columbia	*43%*	*53%*	100%	90%
Wisconsin	*47%*	*50%*	89%	89%
Texas	*42%*	*49%*	*62%*	65%
New York	*43%*	*48%*	*73%*	75%
Washington	*50%*	*48%*	*71%*	72%
Nevada	*43%*	*47%*	*65%*	70%
Nebraska	*40%*	*44%*	86%	85%
New Hampshire	-	-	80%	83%
North Dakota	-	-	92%	93%
USA	53%	63%	77%	81%

* Approximate: too few students to accurately estimate graduation rate.

Italics indicate below national average.

Black Educational Attainment

Percent High School Graduate or Higher

Data on educational attainment is from the United States Census Bureau, Selected Social Characteristics in the United States (DP02) American Community Survey (ACS) three- and five-year estimates. Educational attainment is self-reported for the population 25 years and over. The High School Graduate or Higher category includes people whose highest degree was a high school diploma or its equivalent, people who attended college but did not receive a degree, and people who received an associate's, bachelor's, master's, or professional or doctorate degree. People who reported completing the 12th grade but not receiving a diploma are not included. It has been pointed out that data from this category may be deceptive, given, for example, varying proportions of people receiving GED or other alternative to high school diplomas.

Total Population and Other Groups					
Total Population	White Alone	Black Alone	Latino	Asian	American Indian
85%	87%	81%	62%	86%	77%

Educational attainment reported by Black or African-Americans is lower than that of the total U.S. population and lower than that of subgroups other than those classifying themselves as Latinos, who may be of any race, and American Indians.

Race/Ethnicity Comparative Educational Attainment

High School Diploma or Higher, Age 25 and Over

Sorted by State

State	Total Population	Asian Alone	White Alone	Black Alone	Latino	American Indian
Alabama	*81%*	*85%*	*83%*	*77%*	*56%*	*74%*
Alaska	91%	*79%*	94%	91%	77%	90%
Arizona	85%	89%	87%	88%	62%	*72%*
Arkansas	*82%*	*82%*	*84%*	*77%*	*49%*	81%
California	*81%*	86%	*84%*	87%	*57%*	*76%*
Colorado	89%	86%	91%	87%	65%	80%
Connecticut	88%	88%	91%	81%	68%	78%
Delaware	87%	91%	89%	84%	*58%*	79%
Florida	85%	86%	87%	*78%*	74%	78%
Georgia	*84%*	86%	*86%*	81%	*56%*	77%
Hawaii	90%	86%	95%	96%	87%	88%
Idaho	88%	86%	89%	83%	*53%*	80%
Illinois	86%	91%	89%	82%	*60%*	79%
Indiana	86%	89%	87%	82%	*61%*	79%
Iowa	90%	*81%*	91%	*80%*	*56%*	79%
Kansas	89%	*81%*	91%	85%	*59%*	86%
Kentucky	*81%*	88%	*81%*	81%	63%	79%
Louisiana	*81%*	*77%*	*85%*	*74%*	69%	*69%*
Maine	90%	*85%*	90%	84%	82%	81%
Maryland	88%	90%	90%	86%	62%	80%
Massachusetts	89%	*83%*	91%	82%	65%	85%
Michigan	88%	88%	90%	82%	67%	82%
Minnesota	91%	*80%*	93%	81%	*61%*	81%
Mississippi	*80%*	*76%*	*84%*	*72%*	*57%*	*67%*
Missouri	86%	86%	87%	81%	66%	84%
Montana	91%	*84%*	92%	90%	83%	80%
Nebraska	90%	*84%*	91%	84%	*52%*	79%
Nevada	*84%*	89%	*85%*	87%	*58%*	84%
New Hampshire	91%	90%	91%	86%	80%	81%
New Jersey	87%	92%	89%	83%	70%	*71%*
New Mexico	*83%*	88%	*85%*	87%	70%	*75%*
New York	*84%*	*78%*	89%	*80%*	65%	79%
North Carolina	*84%*	*84%*	*86%*	*80%*	*53%*	*67%*
North Dakota	89%	86%	90%	84%	77%	83%
Ohio	87%	89%	88%	81%	71%	81%
Oklahoma	85%	*82%*	87%	84%	*56%*	83%

Oregon	89%	86%	90%	86%	*55%*	*66%*
Pennsylvania	87%	*83%*	89%	81%	66%	83%
Rhode Island	*84%*	*79%*	*86%*	*75%*	*60%*	78%
South Carolina	*83%*	86%	*86%*	*76%*	*59%*	*73%*
South Dakota	89%	86%	90%	82%	69%	79%
Tennessee	*83%*	86%	*83%*	*80%*	*57%*	80%
Texas	*80%*	87%	*82%*	84%	*58%*	79%
Utah	91%	86%	92%	85%	64%	78%
Vermont	91%	*83%*	91%	86%	91%	*75%*
Virginia	86%	89%	88%	*80%*	68%	79%
Washington	90%	*85%*	92%	87%	*59%*	81%
West Virginia	*82%*	90%	*82%*	84%	73%	80%
Wisconsin	89%	*81%*	91%	*78%*	62%	84%
Wyoming	91%	90%	92%	89%	74%	85%
USA	85%	86%	87%	81%	62%	77%

Italics indicate below national average.

Black Educational Attainment[3]

Sorted by State

State Name	Less than High School Diploma	High School Graduate	Some College	BA or Higher
Alabama	20%	34%	*31%*	*16%*
Alaska	*11%*	*24%*	41%	24%
Arizona	*12%*	*22%*	43%	22%
Arkansas	20%	38%	*29%*	*14%*
California	*12%*	*24%*	42%	22%
Colorado	*11%*	*26%*	40%	24%
Connecticut	*15%*	36%	*30%*	19%
Delaware	*14%*	36%	*30%*	20%
Florida	20%	34%	*30%*	*16%*
Georgia	*16%*	*30%*	33%	21%
Hawaii	*6%*	*17%*	51%	27%
Idaho	‡	‡	‡	‡
Illinois	*16%*	*29%*	36%	19%
Indiana	*15%*	34%	34%	*17%*
Iowa	17%	*29%*	34%	20%
Kansas	*11%*	*29%*	42%	*11%*
Kentucky	*16%*	33%	35%	*15%*
Louisiana	24%	35%	*28%*	*13%*
Maine	‡	‡	‡	‡
Maryland	*12%*	*30%*	*32%*	26%
Massachusetts	19%	*29%*	*31%*	21%
Michigan	*16%*	32%	36%	*16%*
Minnesota	19%	*26%*	35%	20%
Mississippi	24%	31%	*30%*	*15%*
Missouri	18%	31%	35%	*17%*
Montana	‡	‡	‡	‡
Nebraska	18%	*26%*	37%	19%
Nevada	*13%*	33%	37%	*16%*
New Hampshire	‡	‡	‡	‡
New Jersey	*15%*	34%	*30%*	21%
New Mexico	*12%*	*21%*	40%	26%
New York	19%	*30%*	*30%*	21%
North Carolina	18%	32%	33%	*17%*
North Dakota	‡	‡	‡	‡
Ohio	18%	31%	36%	*16%*
Oklahoma	*11%*	35%	37%	*17%*
Oregon	*11%*	*25%*	41%	23%
Pennsylvania	*16%*	38%	*31%*	*16%*
Rhode Island	24%	*26%*	*32%*	*18%*
South Carolina	21%	35%	*29%*	*14%*
South Dakota	‡	‡	‡	‡
Tennessee	18%	34%	*32%*	*11%*

[3] Census, S0201, 2011 ACS 1- and 3-year estimates

Texas	*13%*	*30%*	36%	21%
Utah	*14%*	*25%*	38%	22%
Vermont	‡	‡	‡	‡
Virginia	17%	*30%*	*32%*	20%
Washington	*12%*	*28%*	41%	20%
West Virginia	*15%*	38%	33%	*15%*
Wisconsin	20%	33%	35%	*12%*
Wyoming	‡	‡	‡	‡
USA	17%	31%	33%	19%

‡ Population too small to calculate educational attainment percentages.

Italics indicate below national average.

Black Educational Attainment[4]

Sorted by Less than High School Diploma

The percentage of Black or African-Americans ages 25 and above reporting that they have less education than a high school diploma (or GED) varies from 6% in Hawaii to 24% in Louisiana, Mississippi and Rhode Island. Many adults in this category may have significant literacy difficulties.

State Name	Less than High School Diploma	High School Graduate	Some College	BA or Higher
Louisiana	24%	35%	*28%*	*13%*
Mississippi	24%	31%	*30%*	*15%*
Rhode Island	24%	*26%*	*32%*	*18%*
South Carolina	21%	35%	*29%*	*14%*
Alabama	20%	34%	*31%*	*16%*
Arkansas	20%	38%	*29%*	*14%*
Florida	20%	34%	*30%*	*16%*
Wisconsin	20%	33%	35%	*12%*
Massachusetts	19%	*29%*	*31%*	21%
Minnesota	19%	*26%*	35%	20%
New York	19%	*30%*	*30%*	21%
Missouri	18%	31%	35%	*17%*
Nebraska	18%	*26%*	37%	19%
North Carolina	18%	32%	33%	*17%*
Ohio	18%	31%	36%	*16%*
Tennessee	18%	34%	*32%*	*11%*
Iowa	17%	*29%*	34%	20%
Virginia	17%	*30%*	*32%*	20%
Georgia	*16%*	*30%*	33%	21%
Illinois	*16%*	*29%*	36%	19%
Kentucky	*16%*	33%	35%	*15%*
Michigan	*16%*	32%	36%	*16%*
Pennsylvania	*16%*	38%	*31%*	*16%*
Connecticut	*15%*	36%	*30%*	19%
Indiana	*15%*	34%	34%	*17%*
New Jersey	*15%*	34%	*30%*	21%
West Virginia	*15%*	38%	33%	*15%*
Delaware	*14%*	36%	*30%*	20%
Utah	*14%*	*25%*	38%	22%
Nevada	*13%*	33%	37%	*16%*
Texas	*13%*	*30%*	36%	21%
Arizona	*12%*	*22%*	43%	22%
California	*12%*	*24%*	42%	22%
Maryland	*12%*	*30%*	*32%*	26%
New Mexico	*12%*	*21%*	40%	26%
Washington	*12%*	*28%*	41%	20%
Alaska	*11%*	*24%*	41%	24%

[4] Census, S0201, 2011 ACS 1-year and 3-year estimates.

Colorado	*11%*	*26%*	40%	24%
Kansas	*11%*	*29%*	42%	*11%*
Oklahoma	*11%*	35%	37%	*17%*
Oregon	*11%*	*25%*	41%	23%
Hawaii	*6%*	*17%*	51%	27%
Idaho	‡	‡	‡	‡
Maine	‡	‡	‡	‡
Montana	‡	‡	‡	‡
New Hampshire	‡	‡	‡	‡
North Dakota	‡	‡	‡	‡
South Dakota	‡	‡	‡	‡
Vermont	‡	‡	‡	‡
Wyoming	‡	‡	‡	‡
USA	17%	31%	33%	19%

‡ Population too small to calculate educational attainment percentages.

Italics indicate below national average.

Black Educational Attainment[5]

Sorted by BA or Higher

The percentage of Black or African-Americans ages 25 and above reporting that they have a BA degree or higher varies from 11% in Tennessee and Kansas to 27% in Hawaii.

State Name	Less than High School Diploma	High School Graduate	Some College	BA or Higher
Hawaii	*6%*	*17%*	51%	27%
Maryland	*12%*	*30%*	*32%*	26%
New Mexico	*12%*	*21%*	40%	26%
Alaska	*11%*	*24%*	41%	24%
Colorado	*11%*	*26%*	40%	24%
Oregon	*11%*	*25%*	41%	23%
Arizona	*12%*	*22%*	43%	22%
California	*12%*	*24%*	42%	22%
Utah	*14%*	*25%*	38%	22%
Georgia	*16%*	*30%*	33%	21%
Massachusetts	19%	*29%*	*31%*	21%
New Jersey	*15%*	34%	*30%*	21%
New York	19%	*30%*	*30%*	21%
Texas	*13%*	*30%*	36%	21%
Delaware	*14%*	36%	*30%*	20%
Iowa	17%	*29%*	34%	20%
Minnesota	19%	*26%*	35%	20%
Virginia	17%	*30%*	*32%*	20%
Washington	*12%*	*28%*	41%	20%
Connecticut	*15%*	36%	*30%*	19%
Illinois	*16%*	*29%*	36%	19%
Nebraska	18%	*26%*	37%	19%
Rhode Island	24%	*26%*	*32%*	*18%*
Indiana	*15%*	34%	34%	*17%*
Missouri	18%	31%	35%	*17%*
North Carolina	18%	32%	33%	*17%*
Oklahoma	*11%*	35%	37%	*17%*
Alabama	20%	34%	*31%*	*16%*
Florida	20%	34%	*30%*	*16%*
Michigan	*16%*	32%	36%	*16%*
Nevada	*13%*	33%	37%	*16%*
Ohio	18%	31%	36%	*16%*
Pennsylvania	*16%*	38%	*31%*	*16%*
Kentucky	*16%*	33%	35%	*15%*
Mississippi	24%	31%	*30%*	*15%*
West Virginia	*15%*	38%	33%	*15%*
Arkansas	20%	38%	*29%*	*14%*
South Carolina	21%	35%	*29%*	*14%*

[5] Census, S0201, 2011 ACS 1- year and 3-year estimates.

Louisiana	24%	35%	*28%*	*13%*
Wisconsin	20%	33%	35%	*12%*
Kansas	*11%*	*29%*	42%	*11%*
Tennessee	18%	34%	*32%*	*11%*
Idaho	‡	‡	‡	‡
Maine	‡	‡	‡	‡
Montana	‡	‡	‡	‡
New Hampshire	‡	‡	‡	‡
North Dakota	‡	‡	‡	‡
South Dakota	‡	‡	‡	‡
Vermont	‡	‡	‡	‡
Wyoming	‡	‡	‡	‡
USA	17%	31%	33%	19%

‡ Population too small to calculate educational attainment percentages.

Italics indicate below national average.

National Assessment of Educational Progress (NAEP)

NAEP Grade 8 Reading: 2011

Nineteen percent of male Black students scored at or above Proficient in Grade 8 Reading in the state of Connecticut. Four percent of those in California did so. Sixty percent of male Black students in Mississippi and the District of Columbia, 59% of those in California and 61% of those in Arkansas scored at the Below Basic level. These compare to a national average of 20% of male White, non-Latino, students scoring at the Below Basic level and 35% scoring at the levels of Proficient or above.

Black Male Percentages at Each Level

Sorted by State

State	Below Basic	Basic	Proficient	Advanced
Alabama	57	35	8	#
Alaska	38	49	13	#
Arizona	51	36	12	#
Arkansas	61	33	6	#
California	59	37	4	#
Colorado	36	49	15	#
Connecticut	39	42	18	1
Delaware	40	47	12	#
Dist. of Columbia	60	32	8	#
Florida	51	40	9	#
Georgia	46	44	10	#
Hawaii	‡	‡	‡	‡
Idaho	‡	‡	‡	‡
Illinois	43	45	10	1
Indiana	50	41	9	#
Iowa	44	42	13	#
Kansas	52	37	12	#
Kentucky	48	41	11	#
Louisiana	54	38	8	#
Maine	‡	‡	‡	‡
Maryland	41	42	16	1
Massachusetts	35	52	13	1
Michigan	54	40	7	#
Minnesota	46	42	11	#
Mississippi	60	33	7	#
Missouri	50	42	8	#
Montana	‡	‡	‡	‡
Nebraska	37	57	7	#
Nevada	46	44	11	#
New Hampshire	‡	‡	‡	‡
New Jersey	42	46	12	#
New Mexico	‡	‡	‡	‡
New York	44	42	14	1

North Carolina	54	37	8	#
North Dakota	‡	‡	‡	‡
Ohio	52	39	9	#
Oklahoma	42	46	11	1
Oregon	‡	‡	‡	‡
Pennsylvania	50	40	10	#
Rhode Island	50	38	11	#
South Carolina	52	42	6	#
South Dakota	‡	‡	‡	‡
Tennessee	56	35	9	#
Texas	39	49	12	#
Utah	‡	‡	‡	‡
Vermont	‡	‡	‡	‡
Virginia	44	45	11	#
Washington	48	39	11	1
West Virginia	49	38	13	1
Wisconsin	56	35	9	#
Wyoming	‡	‡	‡	‡
National Public	49	41	10	#
White, non-Latino, male	20	45	32	3

Rounds to zero.

‡ Reporting standards not met.

NAEP Grade 8 Reading: 2011

Black Male Percentages at Each Level

Sorted by Percentage Below Basic

State	Below Basic	Basic	Proficient	Advanced
Massachusetts	35	52	13	1
Colorado	36	49	15	#
Nebraska	37	57	7	#
Alaska	38	49	13	#
Connecticut	39	42	18	1
Texas	39	49	12	#
Delaware	40	47	12	#
Maryland	41	42	16	1
New Jersey	42	46	12	#
Oklahoma	42	46	11	1
Illinois	43	45	10	1
Iowa	44	42	13	#
New York	44	42	14	1
Virginia	44	45	11	#
Georgia	46	44	10	#
Minnesota	46	42	11	#
Nevada	46	44	11	#
Kentucky	48	41	11	#
Washington	48	39	11	1
West Virginia	49	38	13	1
Indiana	50	41	9	#
Missouri	50	42	8	#
Pennsylvania	50	40	10	#
Rhode Island	50	38	11	#
Arizona	51	36	12	#
Florida	51	40	9	#
Kansas	52	37	12	#
Ohio	52	39	9	#
South Carolina	52	42	6	#
Louisiana	54	38	8	#
Michigan	54	40	7	#
North Carolina	54	37	8	#
Tennessee	56	35	9	#
Wisconsin	56	35	9	#
Alabama	57	35	8	#
California	59	37	4	#
Dist. of Columbia	60	32	8	#
Mississippi	60	33	7	#
Arkansas	61	33	6	#
Hawaii	‡	‡	‡	‡
Idaho	‡	‡	‡	‡
Maine	‡	‡	‡	‡

Montana	‡	‡	‡	‡
New Hampshire	‡	‡	‡	‡
New Mexico	‡	‡	‡	‡
North Dakota	‡	‡	‡	‡
Oregon	‡	‡	‡	‡
South Dakota	‡	‡	‡	‡
Utah	‡	‡	‡	‡
Vermont	‡	‡	‡	‡
Wyoming	‡	‡	‡	‡
National Public	49	41	10	#
White, non-Latino, male	20	45	32	3

Rounds to zero.

‡ Reporting standards not met.

NAEP Grade 8 Reading: 2011

Thirty percent of female Black students scored at or above Proficient in Grade 8 Reading in the state of Colorado. Ten percent of those in Mississippi did so. Forty-six percent of female Black students in District of Columbia and 47% of those in Tennessee scored at the Below Basic level. These compare to a national average of 12% of female White, non-Latino, students scoring at the Below Basic level and 47% scoring at the levels of Proficient or above.

Black Female Percentages at Each Level

Sorted by State

State	Below Basic	Basic	Proficient	Advanced
Alabama	41	46	13	#
Alaska	‡	‡	‡	‡
Arizona	33	43	24	1
Arkansas	47	40	12	#
California	35	47	16	2
Colorado	31	39	26	4
Connecticut	30	47	22	1
Delaware	28	48	23	1
Dist. of Columbia	46	38	15	1
Florida	36	46	18	1
Georgia	33	49	17	1
Hawaii	‡	‡	‡	‡
Idaho	‡	‡	‡	‡
Illinois	32	48	19	1
Indiana	31	49	18	1
Iowa	‡	‡	‡	‡
Kansas	32	49	18	1
Kentucky	35	49	16	#
Louisiana	44	43	12	#
Maine	‡	‡	‡	‡
Maryland	29	47	22	2
Massachusetts	29	42	26	3
Michigan	40	46	14	1
Minnesota	38	44	17	1
Mississippi	44	46	10	#
Missouri	39	46	15	#
Montana	‡	‡	‡	‡
Nebraska	35	43	21	1
Nevada	30	46	21	4
New Hampshire	‡	‡	‡	‡
New Jersey	26	45	28	1
New Mexico	‡	‡	‡	‡
New York	30	48	20	2
North Carolina	31	49	19	1
North Dakota	‡	‡	‡	‡
Ohio	31	50	18	1

Oklahoma	39	48	12	1
Oregon	‡	‡	‡	‡
Pennsylvania	43	41	15	#
Rhode Island	33	43	22	2
South Carolina	36	49	15	#
South Dakota	‡	‡	‡	‡
Tennessee	47	39	14	1
Texas	34	48	18	1
Utah	‡	‡	‡	‡
Vermont	‡	‡	‡	‡
Virginia	33	46	19	2
Washington	16	49	34	1
West Virginia	38	37	22	2
Wisconsin	44	43	13	#
Wyoming	‡	‡	‡	‡
National Public	35	46	17	1
White, non-Latino, female	12	41	41	6

Rounds to zero.

‡ Reporting standards not met.

NAEP Grade 8 Reading: 2011

Black Female Percentages at Each Level

Sorted by Percentage Below Basic

State	Below Basic	Basic	Proficient	Advanced
Washington	16	49	34	1
New Jersey	26	45	28	1
Delaware	28	48	23	1
Maryland	29	47	22	2
Massachusetts	29	42	26	3
Connecticut	30	47	22	1
Nevada	30	46	21	4
New York	30	48	20	2
Colorado	31	39	26	4
Indiana	31	49	18	1
North Carolina	31	49	19	1
Ohio	31	50	18	1
Illinois	32	48	19	1
Kansas	32	49	18	1
Arizona	33	43	24	1
Georgia	33	49	17	1
Rhode Island	33	43	22	2
Virginia	33	46	19	2
Texas	34	48	18	1
California	35	47	16	2
Kentucky	35	49	16	#
Nebraska	35	43	21	1
Florida	36	46	18	1
South Carolina	36	49	15	#
Minnesota	38	44	17	1
West Virginia	38	37	22	2
Missouri	39	46	15	#
Oklahoma	39	48	12	1
Michigan	40	46	14	1
Alabama	41	46	13	#
Pennsylvania	43	41	15	#
Louisiana	44	43	12	#
Mississippi	44	46	10	#
Wisconsin	44	43	13	#
Dist. of Columbia	46	38	15	1
Arkansas	47	40	12	#
Tennessee	47	39	14	1
Alaska	‡	‡	‡	‡
Hawaii	‡	‡	‡	‡
Idaho	‡	‡	‡	‡
Iowa	‡	‡	‡	‡
Maine	‡	‡	‡	‡

Montana	‡	‡	‡	‡
New Hampshire	‡	‡	‡	‡
New Mexico	‡	‡	‡	‡
North Dakota	‡	‡	‡	‡
Oregon	‡	‡	‡	‡
South Dakota	‡	‡	‡	‡
Utah	‡	‡	‡	‡
Vermont	‡	‡	‡	‡
Wyoming	‡	‡	‡	‡
National Public	35	46	17	1
White, non-Latino, female	12	41	41	6

Rounds to zero.

‡ Reporting standards not met.

NAEP Grade 8 Mathematics: 2011

Twenty-one percent of male Black students scored at or above Proficient in Grade 8 Mathematics in the state of Colorado. Six percent of those in Alabama and 7% of those in Michigan did so. Sixty-seven percent of male Black students in Alabama and 66% of those in Michigan scored at the Below Basic level. These compare to a national average of 17% of male White, non-Latino, students scoring at the Below Basic level and 64% scoring at the levels of Proficient or above.

Black Male Percentages at Each Level

Sorted by State

State	Below Basic	Basic	Proficient	Advanced
Alabama	67	27	6	#
Alaska	‡	‡	‡	‡
Arizona	40	45	14	#
Arkansas	57	33	9	1
California	62	29	9	#
Colorado	41	38	19	2
Connecticut	47	38	13	2
Delaware	47	41	12	1
Dist. of Columbia	58	29	11	2
Florida	55	36	9	#
Georgia	53	37	9	1
Hawaii	‡	‡	‡	‡
Idaho	‡	‡	‡	‡
Illinois	54	36	9	1
Indiana	47	42	10	1
Iowa	‡	‡	‡	‡
Kansas	37	43	17	3
Kentucky	52	34	12	1
Louisiana	57	34	8	#
Maine	‡	‡	‡	‡
Maryland	46	36	15	3
Massachusetts	35	38	21	5
Michigan	66	27	7	#
Minnesota	45	38	16	1
Mississippi	64	28	7	1
Missouri	62	31	7	#
Montana	‡	‡	‡	‡
Nebraska	58	34	6	2
Nevada	52	32	16	1
New Hampshire	‡	‡	‡	‡
New Jersey	40	39	18	3
New Mexico	‡	‡	‡	‡
New York	50	38	10	1
North Carolina	45	39	13	2
North Dakota	‡	‡	‡	‡
Ohio	49	38	12	1

Oklahoma	46	38	14	2
Oregon	‡	‡	‡	‡
Pennsylvania	58	32	8	1
Rhode Island	45	37	15	2
South Carolina	52	35	11	2
South Dakota	‡	‡	‡	‡
Tennessee	59	31	9	1
Texas	35	47	13	5
Utah	‡	‡	‡	‡
Vermont	‡	‡	‡	‡
Virginia	44	40	15	1
Washington	50	39	9	2
West Virginia	43	42	14	#
Wisconsin	61	30	8	1
Wyoming	‡	‡	‡	‡
National Public	52	36	11	1
White, non-Latino, Male	17	38	33	31

Rounds to zero.

‡ Reporting standards not met.

NAEP Grade 8 Mathematics: 2011

Twenty-five percent of female Black students scored at or above Proficient in Grade 8 Mathematics in the state of Colorado as did 24% in the state of Texas. Five percent of those in West Virginia and 6% of those in Rhode Island did so. Sixty-seven percent of female Black students in Michigan and 66% of those in Tennessee scored at the Below Basic level. These compare to a national average of 17% of female White, non-Latino, students scoring at the Below Basic level and 42% scoring at the levels of Proficient or above.

Black Female Percentages at Each Level

State	Below Basic	Basic	Proficient	Advanced
Alabama	60	32	7	#
Alaska	‡	‡	‡	‡
Arizona	37	41	20	2
Arkansas	56	37	7	1
California	55	31	13	2
Colorado	37	49	12	2
Connecticut	53	39	7	1
Delaware	42	43	14	1
Dist. of Columbia	54	33	11	1
Florida	53	35	11	1
Georgia	45	42	12	2
Hawaii	‡	‡	‡	‡
Idaho	‡	‡	‡	‡
Illinois	49	41	9	#
Indiana	46	43	10	1
Iowa	57	33	10	#
Kansas	45	43	11	1
Kentucky	54	35	10	2
Louisiana	50	39	10	1
Maine	‡	‡	‡	‡
Maryland	43	38	16	3
Massachusetts	34	41	22	3
Michigan	67	26	7	#
Minnesota	44	37	17	2
Mississippi	57	35	8	#
Missouri	58	34	8	#
Montana	‡	‡	‡	‡
Nebraska	58	34	8	#
Nevada	59	34	6	1
New Hampshire	‡	‡	‡	‡
New Jersey	33	46	17	3
New Mexico	‡	‡	‡	‡
New York	44	42	13	2
North Carolina	41	44	13	2
North Dakota	‡	‡	‡	‡
Ohio	51	38	10	1
Oklahoma	50	43	7	#
Oregon	‡	‡	‡	‡

Pennsylvania	53	39	8	1
Rhode Island	59	36	6	#
South Carolina	48	38	13	1
South Dakota	‡	‡	‡	‡
Tennessee	66	26	7	1
Texas	24	52	21	3
Utah	‡	‡	‡	‡
Vermont	‡	‡	‡	‡
Virginia	40	40	18	2
Washington	38	43	18	1
West Virginia	59	36	5	#
Wisconsin	52	35	11	2
Wyoming	‡	‡	‡	‡
National Public	48	39	12	1
White, non-Latino, female	17	41	33	9

Rounds to zero.

‡ Reporting standards not met.

NAEP Grade 8 Reading: 2011

Selected Districts

Eleven percent of male Black students scored at or above Proficient in Grade 8 Reading in the districts of Miami-Dade and Charlotte.[6] Three percent of those in Milwaukee did so. Seventy-three percent of male Black students in Cleveland and 70% of those in Milwaukee scored at the Below Basic level. These compare to a national average of 20% of male White, non-Latino, students scoring at the Below Basic level and 35% scoring at the levels of Proficient or above.

Black Male Percentages at Each Level

Sorted by District

Districts Assessed by NAEP	Below Basic	Basic	Proficient	Advanced
Albuquerque	‡	‡	‡	‡
Atlanta	46	45	9	#
Austin	49	42	9	#
Baltimore City	53	40	7	#
Boston	49	41	10	#
Charlotte	45	43	11	#
Chicago	51	40	8	#
Cleveland	73	24	3	#
Dallas	57	36	7	#
Detroit	63	32	5	#
District of Columbia	66	28	6	#
Fresno	‡	‡	‡	‡
Hillsborough County (FL)	49	42	9	#
Houston	45	46	9	#
Jefferson County (KY)	53	38	9	#
Los Angeles	60	31	8	1
Miami-Dade	47	41	11	#
Milwaukee	70	27	3	#
New York City	49	38	12	1
Philadelphia	55	36	9	#
San Diego	60	34	7	#
National Public	49	41	10	#
White, non-Latino, male	20	45	32	3

Rounds to zero.

‡ Reporting standards not met.

[6] New York City data under review.

NAEP Grade 8 Reading: 2011

Selected Districts

Twenty-four percent of female Black students scored at or above Proficient in Grade 8 Reading in Charlotte and 20% did so in Los Angeles.[7] Eight percent of those in Detroit and Milwaukee did so. Fifty-nine percent of female Black students in Fresno and 54% of those in Milwaukee scored at the Below Basic level. These compare to a national average of 12% of female White, non-Latino, students scoring at the Below Basic level and 47% scoring at the levels of Proficient or above.

Black Female Percentages at Each Level

Sorted by District

Districts Assessed by NAEP	Below Basic	Basic	Proficient	Advanced
Albuquerque	‡	‡	‡	‡
Atlanta	35	49	16	#
Austin	42	43	15	#
Baltimore City	47	44	9	#
Boston	40	43	16	1
Charlotte	25	51	23	1
Chicago	39	44	16	1
Cleveland	48	40	11	#
Dallas	41	48	11	#
Detroit	54	37	8	#
District of Columbia	53	34	13	1
Fresno	59	28	12	1
Hillsborough County (FL)	39	47	13	1
Houston	39	47	13	#
Jefferson County (KY)	40	44	16	#
Los Angeles	39	40	19	1
Miami-Dade	42	44	14	#
Milwaukee	54	38	8	#
New York City	33	48	17	2
Philadelphia	36	47	16	1
San Diego	38	45	16	#
National Public	35	46	17	1
White, non-Latino, female	12	41	41	6

Rounds to zero.

‡ Reporting standards not met.

[7] New York City data under review.

NAEP Grade 8 Reading: 2011

Selected Districts

Black Female Percentages at Each Level

Sorted by Percentage Below Basic

Districts Assessed by NAEP	Below Basic	Basic	Proficient	Advanced
Albuquerque	‡	‡	‡	‡
Charlotte	25	51	23	1
New York City	33	48	17	2
Atlanta	35	49	16	#
Philadelphia	36	47	16	1
San Diego	38	45	16	#
Chicago	39	44	16	1
Hillsborough County (FL)	39	47	13	1
Houston	39	47	13	#
Los Angeles	39	40	19	1
Boston	40	43	16	1
Jefferson County (KY)	40	44	16	#
Dallas	41	48	11	#
Austin	42	43	15	#
Miami-Dade	42	44	14	#
Baltimore City	47	44	9	#
Cleveland	48	40	11	#
District of Columbia	53	34	13	1
Detroit	54	37	8	#
Milwaukee	54	38	8	#
Fresno	59	28	12	1
National Public	35	46	17	1
White, non-Latino, female	12	41	41	6

Rounds to zero.

‡ Reporting standards not met.

NAEP Grade 8 Mathematics: 2011

Selected Districts

Twenty-two percent of male Black students scored at or above Proficient in Grade 8 Mathematics in Boston. Three percent of those in Detroit did so. Seventy-one percent of male Black students in Cleveland and 69% of those in Milwaukee scored at the Below Basic level. These compare to a national average of 17% of male White, non-Latino, students scoring at the Below Basic level and 64% scoring at the levels of Proficient or above.

Black Male Percentages at Each Level

Sorted by District

Districts Assessed by NAEP	Below Basic	Basic	Proficient	Advanced
Albuquerque	‡	‡	‡	‡
Atlanta	53	36	10	1
Austin	‡	‡	‡	‡
Baltimore City	56	33	9	2
Boston	40	39	18	4
Charlotte	45	41	12	2
Chicago	55	36	8	1
Cleveland	71	24	5	#
Dallas	49	42	9	#
Detroit	75	22	3	#
District of Columbia	68	23	7	1
Fresno	68	25	5	2
Hillsborough County (FL)	48	42	10	#
Houston	40	45	14	1
Jefferson County (KY)	57	30	11	1
Los Angeles	65	27	7	1
Miami-Dade	58	32	9	1
Milwaukee	69	25	5	#
New York City	55	35	9	1
Philadelphia	53	34	11	1
San Diego	63	28	9	#
National Public	52	36	11	1
White, non-Latino, Male	17	38	33	31

Rounds to zero.

‡ Reporting standards not met.

NAEP Grade 8 Mathematics: 2011

Selected Districts

Twenty-one percent of female Black students scored at or above Proficient in Grade 8 Mathematics in Boston. Three percent of those in Detroit and 5% of those in Cleveland and Milwaukee did so. Seventy-four percent of female Black students in Fresno and 71% of those in Detroit scored at the Below Basic level. These compare to a national average of 17% of female White, non-Latino, students scoring at the Below Basic level and 42% scoring at the levels of Proficient or above.

Black Female Percentages at Each Level

Sorted by District

Districts Assessed by NAEP	Below Basic	Basic	Proficient	Advanced
Albuquerque	‡	‡	‡	‡
Atlanta	48	41	10	1
Austin	‡	‡	‡	‡
Baltimore City	53	37	9	1
Boston	38	41	19	2
Charlotte	38	43	16	3
Chicago	50	40	10	#
Cleveland	67	27	5	1
Dallas	47	37	15	1
Detroit	71	25	3	#
District of Columbia	60	30	8	1
Fresno	74	19	6	#
Hillsborough County (FL)	45	45	9	1
Houston	33	49	17	1
Jefferson County (KY)	59	33	8	#
Los Angeles	63	28	8	#
Miami-Dade	58	33	8	1
Milwaukee	70	25	5	#
New York City	45	40	14	1
Philadelphia	52	36	11	2
San Diego	‡	‡	‡	‡
National Public	48	39	12	1
White, non-Latino, female	17	41	33	9

Rounds to zero.

‡ Reporting standards not met.

NAEP Grade 8 Mathematics: 2011

Selected Districts

Black Female Percentages at Each Level

Sorted by Percentage Below Basic

Districts Assessed by NAEP	Below Basic	Basic	Proficient	Advanced
Albuquerque	‡	‡	‡	‡
Austin	‡	‡	‡	‡
San Diego	‡	‡	‡	‡
Houston	33	49	17	1
Boston	38	41	19	2
Charlotte	38	43	16	3
Hillsborough County (FL)	45	45	9	1
New York City	45	40	14	1
Dallas	47	37	15	1
Atlanta	48	41	10	1
Chicago	50	40	10	#
Philadelphia	52	36	11	2
Baltimore City	53	37	9	1
Miami-Dade	58	33	8	1
Jefferson County (KY)	59	33	8	#
District of Columbia	60	30	8	1
Los Angeles	63	28	8	#
Cleveland	67	27	5	1
Milwaukee	70	25	5	#
Detroit	71	25	3	#
Fresno	74	19	6	#
National Public	48	39	12	1
White, non-Latino, female	17	41	33	9

Rounds to zero.

‡ Reporting standards not met.

Individual State Reports

This section includes the United States Department of Education's National Center for Education Statistics state data for Black, Latino and White, non-Latino, male and female students and for all districts enrolling 20,000 or more Black students. Data from the United States Department of Education's Office of Civil Rights 2009 Elementary and Secondary School Survey concerning Discipline and Advanced Placement Mathematics and National Assessment of Educational Progress 8th Grade Reading and Mathematics 2011 data, are also included.

It is assumed that the goal in each case is to close the racial and gender achievement gaps. Certain types of data are *Benchmarked* at the highest level obtained by one of the states or districts included. Each section—at the risk of repetition—is designed to be self-contained for the convenience of readers interested only in specific districts or states.

ALABAMA

Inequities in Graduation Rates

Male Black and Male White, non-Latino, students in Alabama in 2010/11 graduated at similar rates as in 2009/10, with the rate for male Black students matching the national average for that group, while the graduation rates for male White, non-Latino, students in the state continued to lag behind the national average for that group. The racial gap is narrower in Alabama than the national average, as the graduation rate for White, non-Latino, male students in the state remains behind the national average for that group.

The *Benchmark* for graduation rates of male Black students for states enrolling more than 10,000 Black male students is 77% (Arizona). The *Benchmark* for states with at least one district enrolling more than 10,000 Black male students is New Jersey (73%).

	Male Graduation Rate: 2010/11		Male Graduation Rate: 2009/10	
Jurisdiction	Black	White, non-Latino	Black	White, non-Latino
USA	53%	77%	52%	78%
Alabama	53%	*71%*	53%	*69%*

Comparison of Estimated Graduation Rates by Gender: 2010/11

The gender gap for Black students in Alabama is ten points, while that for White, non-Latino, students is four points.

	Male Graduation Rate		Female Graduation Rate	
Jurisdiction	Black	White, non-Latino	Black	White, non-Latino
USA	53%	77%	63%	78%
Alabama	53%	*71%*	63%	*75%*

National Assessment of Educational Progress (NAEP)

NAEP 8th Grade Reading results for Alabama are below those for the nation as a whole in each category.

Percentages of Male Black and Male White, Non-Latino, Students at or Above Proficient
Reading, Grade 8, 2011

	Percent at or Above Proficient		Gap
Jurisdiction	Black	White/Black	White/Black
USA	10%	35%	25%
Alabama	*8%*	*30%*	22%

NAEP 8th Grade Mathematics results for Alabama are considerably below those for the nation as a whole in each category.

Percentages of Male Black and Male White, Non-Latino, Students at or Above Proficient Mathematics, Grade 8, 2011

	Percent at or Above Proficient		Gap
Jurisdiction	Black	White, non-Latino,	White/Black
USA	12%	45%	33%
Alabama	*7%*	*30%*	24%

The *Benchmark* for male Black students in 8th Grade Reading is Connecticut, with 19% of male Black students scoring at or above Proficient. The *Benchmark* for 8th Grade Mathematics is Massachusetts, with 26% of male Black students scoring at or above Proficient.

Discipline Inequities
The U.S. Department of Education's Office for Civil Rights has not yet made out-of-school suspension data disaggregated by gender available at the state level for 2009/10. The Center for Civil Rights Remedies at The Civil Rights Project has calculated *combined* male and female percentages from the OCR samples.[8]

State	Black	White, non-Latino	Black/White Ratio
Alabama	16.3	5.6	2.9

Birmingham City Public Schools
Inequities in Graduation Rates
Male Black students in the Birmingham City public schools graduate at rates below the state and national average. There are now too few male White, non-Latino, students in the district for meaningful statistical analysis.

The *Benchmark* for graduation rates of male Black students for school districts enrolling more than 10,000 male Black students is 73% (Montgomery County, MD).

	Male Graduation Rate: 2010/11		Male Graduation Rate: 2009/10	
Jurisdiction	Black	White, non-Latino	Black	White, non-Latino
USA	53%	77%	52%	78%
Alabama	53%	*71%*	53%	*69%*
Birmingham	*40%*	*62%*	*37%*	*46%*

Discipline and Advanced Placement Inequities
Out-of-school suspension ratios are a measure of the extent to which disparate application of school discipline policies affect students from different racial and ethnic groups. Black students with disabilities were nearly twice as likely to receive out-of-school suspensions as were White, non-Latino, students. Male Black students without disabilities were two-and-a-half times as likely to receive out-of-school suspensions as were male White, non-Latino, students. Female Black students without disabilities were one and a third times as likely to receive out-of-school suspensions as were female White, non-Latino, students.

The district placed 0.19% of male Black students and no male White, non-Latino, students in Advanced Placement Mathematics.

[8] From: Losen, Daniel J. and Jonathan Gillispie. Opportunities Suspended: The Disparate Impact of Disciplinary Exclusion from School. The Center for Civil Rights Remedies at The Civil Rights Project, August 2012. *Source:* CRDC, 2009-2010 (numbers from national sample rounded to one decimal).

Mobile County Public Schools

Inequities in Graduation Rates

Male Black students in the Mobile County public schools graduate at rates below the state and national averages as do the district's male White, non-Latino, students.

The *Benchmark* for graduation rates of male Black students for school districts enrolling more than 10,000 male Black students is 73% (Montgomery County, MD).

	Male Graduation Rate: 2010/11		Male Graduation Rate: 2009/10	
Jurisdiction	Black	White, non-Latino	Black	White, non-Latino
USA	53%	77%	52%	78%
Alabama	53%	*71%*	53%	*69%*
Mobile County	*42%*	*55%*	*38%*	*49%*

Discipline and Advanced Placement Inequities

Out-of-school suspension ratios are a measure of the extent to which disparate application of school discipline policies affect students from different racial and ethnic groups. Male Black students with disabilities were more than twice as likely to receive out-of-school suspensions as were male White, non-Latino, students. Female Black students with disabilities were more than six times as likely to receive out-of-school suspensions as were female White, non-Latino, students. Male Black students without disabilities were more than twice as likely to receive out-of-school suspensions as were male White, non-Latino, students. Female Black students without disabilities were over three times as likely to receive out-of-school suspensions as were female White, non-Latino, students.

Enrollment ratios in Advanced Placement Mathematics are an indicator of the differing opportunities to learn that may be provided to students on the basis of race and ethnicity. Male Black students were enrolled in AP Mathematics at less than one quarter of the rate of White, non-Latino, students. Female Black students were enrolled in AP Mathematics at two and a half times the rate of White, non-Latino, students.[9]

Montgomery County Public Schools

Inequities in Graduation Rates

Male students in the Montgomery County public schools graduate at rates below the state and national averages.

The *Benchmark* for graduation rates of male Black students for school districts enrolling more than 10,000 male Black students is 73% (Montgomery County, MD).

	Male Graduation Rate: 2010/11		Male Graduation Rate: 2009/10	
Jurisdiction	Black	White, non-Latino	Black	White, non-Latino
USA	53%	77%	52%	78%
Alabama	53%	*71%*	53%	*69%*
Montgomery	*49%*	*74%*	*33%*	*50%*

[9] Data under review.

Discipline and Advanced Placement Inequities

Out-of-school suspension ratios are a measure of the extent to which disparate application of school discipline policies affect students from different racial and ethnic groups. Black students with disabilities were nearly twice as likely to receive out-of-school suspensions as were White, non-Latino, students. Male Black students without disabilities were four times as likely to receive out-of-school suspensions as were male White, non-Latino, students. Female Black students without disabilities were over five times as likely to receive out-of-school suspensions as were female White, non-Latino, students.

Enrollment ratios in Advanced Placement Mathematics are an indicator of the differing opportunities to learn that may be provided to students on the basis of race and ethnicity. Asian students were enrolled in AP Mathematics at twice the rate of White, non-Latino, students. Black students were enrolled in AP Mathematics at less than one-third the rate of White, non-Latino, students.

ALASKA

Inequities in Graduation Rates

Male White, non-Latino, students in Alaska in 2010/11 graduated at considerably higher rates than in 2009/10, with the rate for the very few male Black students greatly exceeding the national average for that group.

The *Benchmark* for graduation rates of male Black students for states enrolling more than 10,000 Black male students is 77% (Arizona). The *Benchmark* for states with at least one district enrolling more than 10,000 Black male students is New Jersey (73%).

	Male Graduation Rate: 2010/11		Male Graduation Rate: 2009/10	
Jurisdiction	Black	White, non-Latino	Black	White, non-Latino
USA	53%	77%	52%	78%
Alaska	69%	77%	71%	*70%*

Comparison of Estimated Graduation Rates by Gender: 2010/11

The gender gap for Black students in Alaska is reversed, while that for White, non-Latino, students is zero points.

	Male Graduation Rate		Female Graduation Rate	
Jurisdiction	Black	White, non-Latino	Black	White, non-Latino
USA	53%	77%	63%	81%
Alaska	69%	77%	*61%*	*77%*

National Assessment of Educational Progress (NAEP)

NAEP 8th Grade Reading results for Alaska are above those for the nation as a whole for the state's small numbers of male Black students and slightly below the national average for male White, non-Latino, students.

Percentages of Male Black and Male White, Non-Latino, Students at or Above Proficient
Reading, Grade 8, 2011

	Percent at or Above Proficient		Gap
Jurisdiction	Black	White, non-Latino	White/Black
USA	10%	35%	25%
Alaska	13%	*34%*	21%

NAEP 8th Grade Mathematics results for Alaska are slightly above those for the nation as a whole for the state's male White, non-Latino, students.

Percentages of Male Black and Male White, Non-Latino, Students at or Above Proficient
Mathematics, Grade 8, 2011

	Percent at or Above Proficient		Gap
Jurisdiction	Black	White, non-Latino	White/Black
USA	12%	45%	33%
Alaska	‡[10]	49%	-

[10] Indicates insufficient sample size.

The *Benchmark* for male Black students in 8th Grade Reading is Connecticut, with 19% of male Black students scoring at or above Proficient. The *Benchmark* for 8th Grade Mathematics is Massachusetts, with 26% of male Black students scoring at or above Proficient.

Discipline Inequities

The U.S. Department of Education's Office for Civil Rights has not yet made out-of-school suspension data disaggregated by gender available at the state level for 2009/10. The Center for Civil Rights Remedies at The Civil Rights Project has calculated *combined* male and female percentages from the OCR samples.[11]

State	Black	White, non-Latino	Black/White Ratio
Alaska	10.9	4.5	2.4

[11] From: Losen, Daniel J. and Jonathan Gillispie. Opportunities Suspended: The Disparate Impact of Disciplinary Exclusion from School. The Center for Civil Rights Remedies at The Civil Rights Project, August 2012. *Source:* CRDC, 2009-2010 (numbers from national sample rounded to one decimal).

ARIZONA

Inequities in Graduation Rates

Male Black students in Arizona in 2010/11 graduated at considerably lower rates than in 2009/10, while the rates for all both groups of male students exceeded the national average for those groups. No Arizona school districts enroll more than 10,000 male Black students.

The *Benchmark* for graduation rates of male Black students for states enrolling more than 10,000 Black male students is 77% (Arizona). The *Benchmark* for states with at least one district enrolling more than 10,000 Black male students is New Jersey (73%).

	Male Graduation Rate: 2010/11		Male Graduation Rate: 2009/10	
Jurisdiction	Black	White, non-Latino	Black	White, non-Latino
USA	53%	77%	52%	78%
Arizona	77%	81%	84%	82%

Comparison of Estimated Graduation Rates by Gender: 2010/11

The gender gaps in Arizona are reversed.

	Male Graduation Rate		Female Graduation Rate	
Jurisdiction	Black	White, non-Latino	Black	White, non-Latino
USA	53%	77%	63%	81%
Arizona	77%	81%	73%	79%

National Assessment of Educational Progress (NAEP)

NAEP 8th Grade Reading results for Arizona are above national averages for male Black students and at national averages for male White, non-Latino, students.

Percentages of Male Black and Male White, Non-Latino, Students at or Above Proficient
Reading, Grade 8, 2011

	Percent at or Above Proficient		Gap
Jurisdiction	Black	White, non-Latino	White/Black
USA	10%	35%	25%
Arizona	13%	35%	23%

NAEP 8th Grade Mathematics results for Arizona are slightly higher than national averages for students in each category.

Percentages of Male Black and Male White, Non-Latino, Students at or Above Proficient
Mathematics, Grade 8, 2011

	Percent at or Above Proficient		Gap
Jurisdiction	Black	White, non-Latino	White/Black
USA	12%	45%	33%
Arizona	14%	48%	*34%*

The *Benchmark* for male Black students in 8th Grade Reading is Connecticut, with 19% of male Black students scoring at or above Proficient. The *Benchmark* for 8th Grade Mathematics is Massachusetts, with 26% of male Black students scoring at or above Proficient.

Discipline Inequities

The U.S. Department of Education's Office for Civil Rights has not yet made out-of-school suspension data disaggregated by gender available at the state level for 2009/10. The Center for Civil Rights Remedies at The Civil Rights Project has calculated *combined* male and female percentages from the OCR samples.[12]

State	Black	White, non-Latino	Black/White Ratio
Arizona	12.5	4.6	2.7

[12] From: Losen, Daniel J. and Jonathan Gillispie. Opportunities Suspended: The Disparate Impact of Disciplinary Exclusion from School. The Center for Civil Rights Remedies at The Civil Rights Project, August 2012. *Source:* CRDC, 2009-2010 (numbers from national sample rounded to one decimal).

ARKANSAS

Inequities in Graduation Rates

Male students in Arkansas in 2010/11 graduated at higher rates than in 2009/10. The rate for Black students was above national averages, that for White, non-Latino, students below national averages. No Arkansas school districts enroll more than 10,000 male Black students.

The *Benchmark* for graduation rates of male Black students for states enrolling more than 10,000 Black male students is 77% (Arizona). The *Benchmark* for states with at least one district enrolling more than 10,000 Black male students is New Jersey (73%).

	Male Graduation Rate: 2010/11		Male Graduation Rate: 2009/10	
Jurisdiction	Black	White, non-Latino	Black	White, non-Latino
USA	53%	77%	52%	78%
Arkansas	62%	75%	59%	*73%*

Comparison of Estimated Graduation Rates by Gender: 2010/11

The gender gap for Black students in Arkansas is thirteen points, while that for White, non-Latino, students is five points.

	Male Graduation Rate		Female Graduation Rate	
Jurisdiction	Black	White, non-Latino	Black	White, non-Latino
USA	53%	77%	63%	81%
Arkansas	62%	*75%*	75%	*80%*

National Assessment of Educational Progress (NAEP)

NAEP 8th Grade Reading results for Arkansas are below national averages for male Black and White, non-Latino, students.

Percentages of Male Black and Male White, Non-Latino, Students at or Above Proficient
Reading, Grade 8, 2011

	Percent at or Above Proficient		Gap
Jurisdiction	Black	White, non-Latino	White/Black
USA	10%	35%	25%
Arkansas	*6%*	*29%*	23%

NAEP 8th Grade Mathematics results for Arkansas are below national averages for male Black and male White, non-Latino, students.

Percentages of Male Black and Male White, Non-Latino, Students at or Above Proficient
Mathematics, Grade 8, 2011

	Percent at or Above Proficient		Gap
Jurisdiction	Black	White, non-Latino	White/Black
USA	12%	45%	33%
Arkansas	*10%*	*38%*	28%

The *Benchmark* for male Black students in 8th Grade Reading is Connecticut, with 19% of male Black students scoring at or above Proficient. The *Benchmark* for 8th Grade Mathematics is Massachusetts, with 26% of male Black students scoring at or above Proficient.

Discipline Inequities

The U.S. Department of Education's Office for Civil Rights has not yet made out-of-school suspension data disaggregated by gender available at the state level for 2009/10. The Center for Civil Rights Remedies at The Civil Rights Project has calculated *combined* male and female percentages from the OCR samples.[13]

State	Black	White, non-Latino	Black/White Ratio
Arkansas	18.5	5.3	3.5

[13] From: Losen, Daniel J. and Jonathan Gillispie. Opportunities Suspended: The Disparate Impact of Disciplinary Exclusion from School. The Center for Civil Rights Remedies at The Civil Rights Project, August 2012. *Source:* CRDC, 2009-2010 (numbers from national sample rounded to one decimal).

CALIFORNIA

Inequities in Graduation Rates

Male students in California in 2010/11 graduated at similar rates to 2009/10 and at higher than national rates for each group. The White/Black gap slightly narrowed from 27 to 25 points.

The *Benchmark* for graduation rates of male Black students for states enrolling more than 10,000 Black male students is 77% (Arizona). The *Benchmark* for states with at least one district enrolling more than 10,000 Black male students is New Jersey (73%).

	Male Graduation Rate: 2010/11		Male Graduation Rate: 2009/10	
Jurisdiction	Black	White, non-Latino	Black	White, non-Latino
USA	53%	77%	52%	78%
California	58%	83%	56%	83%

Comparison of Estimated Graduation Rates by Gender: 2010/11

The gender gap for Black students in California is nine points, while that for White, non-Latino, students is six points.

	Male Graduation Rate		Female Graduation Rate	
Jurisdiction	Black	White, non-Latino	Black	White, non-Latino
USA	53%	77%	63%	81%
California	58%	83%	67%	89%

National Assessment of Educational Progress (NAEP)

NAEP 8th Grade Reading results for California are below national averages in each category.

Percentages of Male Black and Male White, Non-Latino, Students at or Above Proficient
Reading, Grade 8, 2011

	Percent at or Above Proficient		Gap
Jurisdiction	Black	White, non-Latino	White/Black
USA	10%	35%	25%
California	*4%*	*27%*	23%

NAEP 8th Grade Mathematics results for California are below those for the nation as a whole in each category.

Percentages of Male Black and Male White, Non-Latino, Students at or Above Proficient
Mathematics, Grade 8, 2011

	Percent at or Above Proficient		Gap
Jurisdiction	Black	White, non-Latino	White/Black
USA	12%	45%	33%
California	*9%*	*42%*	33%

The *Benchmark* for male Black students in 8th Grade Reading is Connecticut, with 19% of male Black students scoring at or above Proficient. The *Benchmark* for 8th Grade Mathematics is Massachusetts, with 26% of male Black students scoring at or above Proficient.

Discipline Inequities

The U.S. Department of Education's Office for Civil Rights has not yet made out-of-school suspension data disaggregated by gender available at the state level for 2009/10. The Center for Civil Rights Remedies at The Civil Rights Project has calculated *combined* male and female percentages from the OCR samples.[14]

State	Black	White, non-Latino	Black/White Ratio
California	17.7	5.6	3.2

Los Angeles Unified School District

Inequities in Graduation Rates

Male students in the Los Angeles public schools continue to graduate at rates below the state and national averages.

The *Benchmark* for graduation rates of male Black students for school districts enrolling more than 10,000 male Black students is 73% (Montgomery County, MD).

	Male Graduation Rate: 2010/11		Male Graduation Rate: 2009/10	
Jurisdiction	Black	White, non-Latino	Black	White, non-Latino
USA	53%	77%	52%	78%
California	58%	83%	56%	83%
Los Angeles	*45%*	*65%*	*41%*	*64%*

National Assessment of Educational Progress (NAEP)

NAEP 8th Grade Reading results for Los Angeles are below national averages for male Black students and slightly above the national average for White, non-Latino, students. The results for male Black and White, non-Latino, students are above the state averages.

Percentages of Male Black and Male White, Non-Latino, Students at or Above Proficient
Reading, Grade 8, 2011

	Percent at or Above Proficient		Gap
Jurisdiction	Black	White, non-Latino	White/Black
USA	10%	35%	25%
California	*4%*	*27%*	23%
Los Angeles	*9%*	36%	*27%*

NAEP 8th Grade Mathematics results for Los Angeles are below those for the nation and state for male Black students and above those for the nation and state for White, non-Latino, students.

[14] From: Losen, Daniel J. and Jonathan Gillispie. Opportunities Suspended: The Disparate Impact of Disciplinary Exclusion from School. The Center for Civil Rights Remedies at The Civil Rights Project, August 2012. *Source:* CRDC, 2009-2010 (numbers from national sample rounded to one decimal).

Percentages of Male Black and Male White, Non-Latino, Students at or Above Proficient
Mathematics, Grade 8, 2011

	Percent at or Above Proficient		Gap
Jurisdiction	Black	White, non-Latino	White/Black
USA	12%	45%	33%
California	*9%*	*42%*	33%
Los Angeles	*8%*	46%	*38%*

The *Benchmark* for male Black students in 8th Grade Reading is Connecticut, with 19% of male Black students scoring at or above Proficient. The *Benchmark* for 8th Grade Mathematics is Massachusetts, with 26% of male Black students scoring at or above Proficient.

Discipline and Advanced Placement Inequities
Out-of-school suspension ratios are a measure of the extent to which disparate application of school discipline policies affect students from different racial and ethnic groups. Black students with disabilities were more than four and a half times as likely to receive out-of-school suspensions as were White, non-Latino, students. Male Black students without disabilities were nearly five times as likely to receive out-of-school suspensions as were male White, non-Latino, students. Female Black students without disabilities were over nine times as likely to receive out-of-school suspensions as were female White, non-Latino, students.

Enrollment ratios in Advanced Placement Mathematics are an indicator of the differing opportunities to learn that may be provided to students on the basis of race and ethnicity. Asian students were enrolled in AP Mathematics at half again the rate of White, non-Latino, students. Black students were enrolled in AP Mathematics at less than half the rate of White, non-Latino, students.

COLORADO

Inequities in Graduation Rates

Male students in Colorado in 2010/11 graduated at similar rates as in 2009/10. No Colorado school districts enroll more than 10,000 male Black students.

The *Benchmark* for graduation rates of male Black students for states enrolling more than 10,000 Black male students is 77% (Arizona). The *Benchmark* for states with at least one district enrolling more than 10,000 Black male students is New Jersey (73%).

	Male Graduation Rate: 2010/11		Male Graduation Rate: 2009/10	
Jurisdiction	Black	White, non-Latino	Black	White, non-Latino
USA	53%	77%	52%	78%
Colorado	54%	*74%*	56%	*75%*

Comparison of Estimated Graduation Rates by Gender: 2010/11

The gender gap for Black students in Colorado is eight points, while that for White, non-Latino, students is six points.

	Male Graduation Rate		Female Graduation Rate	
Jurisdiction	Black	White, non-Latino	Black	White, non-Latino
USA	53%	77%	63%	81%
Colorado	54%	*74%*	*62%*	*80%*

National Assessment of Educational Progress (NAEP)

NAEP 8th Grade Reading results for Colorado are above those for the nation as a whole in each category.

Percentages of Male Black and Male White, Non-Latino, Students at or Above Proficient
Reading, Grade 8, 2011

	Percent at or Above Proficient		Gap
Jurisdiction	Black	White, non-Latino	White/Black
USA	10%	35%	25%
Colorado	15%	43%	*29%*

NAEP 8th Grade Mathematics results for Colorado are above national averages for male Black and White, non-Latino, students.

Percentages of Male Black and Male White, Non-Latino, Students at or Above Proficient
Mathematics, Grade 8, 2011

	Percent at or Above Proficient		Gap
Jurisdiction	Black	White, non-Latino	White/Black
USA	12%	45%	33%
Colorado	20%	55%	*35%*

The *Benchmark* for male Black students in 8th Grade Reading is Connecticut, with 19% of male Black students scoring at or above Proficient. The *Benchmark* for 8th Grade Mathematics is Massachusetts, with 26% of male Black students scoring at or above Proficient.

Discipline Inequities

The U.S. Department of Education's Office for Civil Rights has not yet made out-of-school suspension data disaggregated by gender available at the state level for 2009/10. The Center for Civil Rights Remedies at The Civil Rights Project has calculated *combined* male and female percentages from the OCR samples.[15]

State	Black	White, non-Latino	Black/White Ratio
Colorado	13.9	4.3	3.2

[15] From: Losen, Daniel J. and Jonathan Gillispie. Opportunities Suspended: The Disparate Impact of Disciplinary Exclusion from School. The Center for Civil Rights Remedies at The Civil Rights Project, August 2012. *Source:* CRDC, 2009-2010 (numbers from national sample rounded to one decimal).

CONNECTICUT

Inequities in Graduation Rates

Male students in Connecticut in 2010/11 graduated at similar rates as in 2009/10. No Connecticut school districts enroll more than 10,000 male Black students.

The *Benchmark* for graduation rates of male Black students for states enrolling more than 10,000 Black male students is 77% (Arizona). The *Benchmark* for states with at least one district enrolling more than 10,000 Black male students is New Jersey (73%).

	Male Graduation Rate: 2010/11		Male Graduation Rate: 2009/10	
Jurisdiction	Black	White, non-Latino	Black	White, non-Latino
USA	53%	77%	52%	78%
Connecticut	59%	86%	59%	85%

Comparison of Estimated Graduation Rates by Gender: 2010/11

The gender gap for Black students in Connecticut is ten points, while that for White, non-Latino, students is two points.

	Male Graduation Rate		Female Graduation Rate	
Jurisdiction	Black	White, non-Latino	Black	White, non-Latino
USA	53%	77%	63%	81%
Connecticut	59%	86%	69%	88%

National Assessment of Educational Progress (NAEP)

NAEP 8th Grade Reading results for Connecticut are above those for the nation as a whole in each category.

Percentages of Male Black and Male White, Non-Latino, Students at or Above Proficient
Reading, Grade 8, 2011

	Percent at or Above Proficient		Gap
Jurisdiction	Black	White, non-Latino	White/Black
USA	10%	35%	25%
Connecticut	19%	48%	*29%*

NAEP 8th Grade Mathematics results for Connecticut are above national averages for male Black and White, non-Latino, students.

Percentages of Male Black and Male White, Non-Latino, Students at or Above Proficient
Mathematics, Grade 8, 2011

	Percent at or Above Proficient		Gap
Jurisdiction	Black	White, non-Latino,	White/Black
USA	12%	45%	33%
Connecticut	15%	49%	*34%*

The *Benchmark* for male Black students in 8th Grade Reading is Connecticut, with 19% of male Black students scoring at or above Proficient. The *Benchmark* for 8th Grade Mathematics is Massachusetts, with 26% of male Black students scoring at or above Proficient.

Discipline Inequities

The U.S. Department of Education's Office for Civil Rights has not yet made out-of-school suspension data disaggregated by gender available at the state level for 2009/10. The Center for Civil Rights Remedies at The Civil Rights Project has calculated *combined* male and female percentages from the OCR samples.[16]

State	Black	White, non-Latino	Black/White Ratio
Connecticut	20.4	2.4	8.5

[16] From: Losen, Daniel J. and Jonathan Gillispie. Opportunities Suspended: The Disparate Impact of Disciplinary Exclusion from School. The Center for Civil Rights Remedies at The Civil Rights Project, August 2012. *Source:* CRDC, 2009-2010 (numbers from national sample rounded to one decimal).

DELAWARE

Inequities in Graduation Rates

Male students in Delaware in 2010/11 graduated at higher rates than in 2009/10. The increase for male Black students was unusually large. The rate for male White, non-Latino, students was below the national average for that group. No Delaware school districts enroll more than 10,000 male Black students.

The *Benchmark* for graduation rates of male Black students for states enrolling more than 10,000 Black male students is 77% (Arizona). The *Benchmark* for states with at least one district enrolling more than 10,000 Black male students is New Jersey (73%).

	Male Graduation Rate: 2010/11		Male Graduation Rate: 2009/10	
Jurisdiction	Black	White, non-Latino	Black	White, non-Latino
USA	53%	77%	52%	78%
Delaware	58%	*73%*	*47%*	*68%*

Comparison of Estimated Graduation Rates by Gender: 2010/11

The gender gap for Black students in Delaware is thirteen points, while that for White, non-Latino, students is six points.

	Male Graduation Rate		Female Graduation Rate	
Jurisdiction	Black	White, non-Latino	Black	White, non-Latino
USA	53%	77%	63%	81%
Delaware	58%	*73%*	71%	*79%*

National Assessment of Educational Progress (NAEP)

NAEP 8th Grade Reading results for the Delaware are above national averages for male Black students and below national averages for White, non-Latino, students.

Percentages of Male Black and Male White, Non-Latino, Students at or Above Proficient
Reading, Grade 8, 2011

	Percent at or Above Proficient		Gap
Jurisdiction	Black	White, non-Latino,	White/Black
USA	10%	35%	25%
Delaware	13%	*33%*	21%

NAEP 8th Grade Mathematics results for Delaware are at national averages for male Black students and below national averages for White, non-Latino, students.

Percentages of Male Black and Male White, Non-Latino, Students at or Above Proficient
Mathematics, Grade 8, 2011

	Percent at or Above Proficient		Gap
Jurisdiction	Black	White, non-Latino,	White/Black
USA	12%	45%	33%
Delaware	12%	*42%*	29%

The *Benchmark* for male Black students in 8th Grade Reading is Connecticut, with 19% of male Black students scoring at or above Proficient. The *Benchmark* for 8th Grade Mathematics is Massachusetts, with 26% of male Black students scoring at or above Proficient.

Discipline Inequities

The U.S. Department of Education's Office for Civil Rights has not yet made out-of-school suspension data disaggregated by gender available at the state level for 2009/10. The Center for Civil Rights Remedies at The Civil Rights Project has calculated *combined* male and female percentages from the OCR samples.[17]

State	Black	White, non-Latino	Black/White Ratio
Delaware	21.8	7.3	3.0

[17] From: Losen, Daniel J. and Jonathan Gillispie. Opportunities Suspended: The Disparate Impact of Disciplinary Exclusion from School. The Center for Civil Rights Remedies at The Civil Rights Project, August 2012. *Source:* CRDC, 2009-2010 (numbers from national sample rounded to one decimal).

DISTRICT OF COLUMBIA

Inequities in Graduation Rates

Male students in the District of Columbia in 2010/11 graduated at similar rates as in 2009/10. The rate for male Black students was below the national averages for that group.[18]

The *Benchmark* for graduation rates of male Black students for states enrolling more than 10,000 Black male students is 77% (Arizona). The *Benchmark* for states with at least one district enrolling more than 10,000 Black male students is New Jersey (73%).

	Male Graduation Rate: 2010/11		Male Graduation Rate: 2009/10	
Jurisdiction	Black	White, non-Latino	Black	White, non-Latino
USA	53%	77%	52%	78%
DC	*38%*	100%[19]	*38%*	88%

Comparison of Estimated Graduation Rates by Gender

The gender gap for Black students in the District of Columbia is ten points, while that for White, non-Latino, students is a reversed ten points.

	Male Graduation Rate		Female Graduation Rate	
Jurisdiction	Black	White, non-Latino	Black	White, non-Latino
USA	53%	77%	63%	81%
DC	*43%*	100%	*53%*	90%

National Assessment of Educational Progress (NAEP)

NAEP 8th Grade Reading results for the District of Columbia are below national averages for male Black students.

Percentages of Male Black and Male White, Non-Latino, Students at or Above Proficient
Reading, Grade 8, 2011

	Percent at or Above Proficient		Gap
Jurisdiction	Black	White, non-Latino	White/Black
USA	10%	35%	25%
DC	*8%*	‡[20]	-

NAEP 8th Grade Mathematics results for the District of Columbia are slightly above the national average for male Black students.

[18] District of Columbia student data varies considerably from year to year and could not be verified for this report.

[19] District of Columbia White, non-Latino, student data is based on very small numbers of students, resulting in anomalies in calculations.

[20] Indicates insufficient sample size.

Percentages of Male Black and Male White, Non-Latino, Students at or Above Proficient
Mathematics, Grade 8, 2011

	Percent at or Above Proficient		Gap
Jurisdiction	Black	White, non-Latino	White/Black
USA	12%	45%	33%
DC	13%	‡[21]	-

The *Benchmark* for male Black students in 8th Grade Reading is Connecticut, with 19% of male Black students scoring at or above Proficient. The *Benchmark* for 8th Grade Mathematics is Massachusetts, with 26% of male Black students scoring at or above Proficient.

Discipline and Advanced Placement Inequities

Data for students with disabilities did not meet standards. Male Black students without disabilities were seven times as likely to receive out-of-school suspensions as were male White, non-Latino, students. Female Black students without disabilities were nearly three times as likely to receive out-of-school suspensions as were female White, non-Latino, students.

Enrollment ratios in Advanced Placement Mathematics are an indicator of the differing opportunities to learn that may be provided to students on the basis of race and ethnicity. Black students were enrolled in AP Mathematics at approximately one-tenth the rate of White, non-Latino, students.

[21] Indicates insufficient sample size.

FLORIDA

Inequities in Graduation Rates

Male Black students in Florida in 2010/11 graduated at similar rates as in 2009/10 and White, non-Latino, students at higher rates. The rates for all male students were below the national averages for each group.

The *Benchmark* for graduation rates of male Black students for states enrolling more than 10,000 Black male students is 77% (Arizona). The *Benchmark* for states with at least one district enrolling more than 10,000 Black male students is New Jersey (73%).

	Male Graduation Rate: 2010/11		Male Graduation Rate: 2009/10	
Jurisdiction	Black	White, non-Latino	Black	White, non-Latino
USA	53%	77%	52%	78%
Florida	*47%*	*64%*	*47%*	*62%*

Comparison of Estimated Graduation Rates by Gender: 2010/11

The gender gap for Black students in Florida is thirteen points, while that for White, non-Latino, students is eight points.

	Male Graduation Rate		Female Graduation Rate	
Jurisdiction	Black	White, non-Latino	Black	White, non-Latino
USA	53%	77%	63%	81%
Florida	*47%*	*64%*	*60%*	*72%*

National Assessment of Educational Progress (NAEP)

NAEP 8th Grade Reading results for Florida are at the national average for male Black students and slightly below the national average for male White, non-Latino, students.

Percentages of Male Black and Male White, Non-Latino, Students at or Above Proficient
Reading, Grade 8, 2011

	Percent at or Above Proficient		Gap
Jurisdiction	Black	White, non-Latino,	White/Black
USA	10%	35%	25%
Florida	10%	*34%*	24%

NAEP 8th Grade Mathematics results for Florida's male Black and White, non-Latino, students are below national averages.

Percentages of Male Black and Male White, Non-Latino, Students at or Above Proficient
Mathematics, Grade 8, 2011

	Percent at or Above Proficient		Gap
Jurisdiction	Black	White, non-Latino	White/Black
USA	12%	45%	33%
Florida	*9%*	*38%*	29%

The *Benchmark* for male Black students in 8th Grade Reading is Connecticut, with 19% of male Black students scoring at or above Proficient. The *Benchmark* for 8th Grade Mathematics is Massachusetts, with 26% of male Black students scoring at or above Proficient.

Discipline Inequities
Omitted because of data accuracy issues.

Broward County School District
Inequities in Graduation Rates
Male Black students in the Broward County public schools graduate at rates similar to the national average and above the state average. The district's male White, non-Latino, students graduate above the state and below the national average for that group.

The *Benchmark* for graduation rates of male Black students for school districts enrolling more than 10,000 male Black students is 73% (Montgomery County, MD).

	Male Graduation Rate: 2010/11		Male Graduation Rate: 2009/10	
Jurisdiction	Black	White, non-Latino	Black	White, non-Latino
USA	53%	77%	52%	78%
Florida	*47%*	*64%*	*47%*	*62%*
Broward County	*52%*	*67%*	52%	*64%*

Discipline and Advanced Placement Inequities
Out-of-school suspension ratios are a measure of the extent to which disparate application of school discipline policies affect students from different racial and ethnic groups. Black students with disabilities were nearly half again as likely to receive out-of-school suspensions as were White, non-Latino, students. Male Black students without disabilities were two and a third times as likely to receive out-of-school suspensions as were Male White, non-Latino, students. Female Black students without disabilities were more than two and three-quarters as likely to receive out-of-school suspensions as were female White, non-Latino, students

Enrollment ratios in Advanced Placement Mathematics are an indicator of the differing opportunities to learn that may be provided to students on the basis of race and ethnicity. Male Black students were enrolled in AP Mathematics at one-quarter the rate for male White, non-Latino, students, while female Black students were enrolled in AP Mathematics at less than half the rate for female White, non-Latino, students.

Duval County Public Schools
Inequities in Graduation Rates
Male Black and Male White, non-Latino, students in the Duval County public schools graduate at rates below the state and national averages for those groups.

The *Benchmark* for graduation rates of male Black students for school districts enrolling more than 10,000 male Black students is 73% (Montgomery County, MD).

	Male Graduation Rate: 2010/11		Male Graduation Rate: 2009/10	
Jurisdiction	Black	White, non-Latino	Black	White, non-Latino
USA	53%	77%	52%	78%
Florida	*47%*	*64%*	*47%*	*62%*
Duval County	*38%*	*59%*	*36%*	*53%*

Discipline and Advanced Placement Inequities

Out-of-school suspension ratios are a measure of the extent to which disparate application of school discipline policies affect students from different racial and ethnic groups. Male Black students with disabilities were more than twice as likely to receive out-of-school suspensions as were White, non-Latino, students. Female Black students with disabilities were nearly three times as likely to receive out-of-school suspensions as were White, non-Latino, students. Male Black students without disabilities were nearly three times as likely to receive out-of-school suspensions as were male White, non-Latino, students. Female Black students without disabilities were three and a half times as likely to receive out-of-school suspensions as were female White, non-Latino, students

Enrollment ratios in Advanced Placement Mathematics are an indicator of the differing opportunities to learn that may be provided to students on the basis of race and ethnicity. Male Black students were enrolled in AP Mathematics at approximately one-quarter the rate for White, non-Latino, students. Female Black students were enrolled in AP Mathematics at less than half the rate for female White, non-Latino, students

Hillsborough County Public Schools

Inequities in Graduation Rates

Male Black students in the Hillsborough County public schools graduate at rates below the state and national averages for that group. White, non-Latino, students graduate at rates above the state and below the national average that group.

The *Benchmark* for graduation rates of male Black students for school districts enrolling more than 10,000 male Black students is 73% (Montgomery County, MD).

	Male Graduation Rate: 2010/11		Male Graduation Rate: 2009/10	
Jurisdiction	Black	White, non-Latino	Black	White, non-Latino
USA	53%	77%	52%	78%
Florida	*47%*	*64%*	*47%*	*62%*
Hillsborough County	*45%*	*67%*	*47%*	*70%*

National Assessment of Educational Progress (NAEP)

NAEP 8th Grade Reading results for Hillsborough County are slightly below the state and national averages for male Black students, and above both for male White, non-Latino, students.

Percentages of Male Black and Male White, Non-Latino, Students at or Above Proficient
Reading, Grade 8, 2011

	Percent at or Above Proficient		Gap
Jurisdiction	Black	White, non-Latino,	White/Black
USA	10%	35%	25%
Florida	10%	*34%*	24%
Hillsborough County	*9%*	39%	*29%*

NAEP 8th Grade Mathematics results for Hillsborough County's male Black students are below national but above state averages; results for male White, non-Latino, students are above state but slightly below the national averages.

Percentages of Male Black and Male White, Non-Latino, Students at or Above Proficient
Mathematics, Grade 8, 2011

	Percent at or Above Proficient		Gap
Jurisdiction	Black	White, non-Latino,	White/Black
USA	12%	45%	33%
Florida	*9%*	*38%*	29%
Hillsborough County	*10%*	*44%*	*34%*

The *Benchmark* for male Black students in 8th Grade Reading is Connecticut, with 19% of male Black students scoring at or above Proficient. The *Benchmark* for 8th Grade Mathematics is Massachusetts, with 26% of male Black students scoring at or above Proficient.

Discipline and Advanced Placement Inequities
Out-of-school suspension ratios are a measure of the extent to which disparate application of school discipline policies affect students from different racial and ethnic groups. Black students with disabilities were nearly three-quarters again as likely to receive out-of-school suspensions as were White, non-Latino, students. Male Black students without disabilities were two-and-a-quarter times as likely to receive out-of-school suspensions as were Male White, non-Latino, students. Female Black students without disabilities were more than four times as likely to receive out-of-school suspensions as were female White, non-Latino, students

Enrollment ratios in Advanced Placement Mathematics are an indicator of the differing opportunities to learn that may be provided to students on the basis of race and ethnicity. Male Black students were enrolled in AP Mathematics at one-quarter the rate for male White, non-Latino, students, while female Black students were enrolled in AP Mathematics at less than half the rate for female White, non-Latino, students.

Miami-Dade Public Schools
Inequities in Graduation Rates
Male Black and Male White, non-Latino, students in the Miami-Dade public schools graduate at rates above the state and below the national averages for those groups.

The *Benchmark* for graduation rates of male Black students for school districts enrolling more than 10,000 male Black students is 73% (Montgomery County, MD).

	Male Graduation Rate: 2010/11		Male Graduation Rate: 2009/10	
Jurisdiction	Black	White, non-Latino	Black	White, non-Latino
USA	53%	77%	52%	78%
Florida	*47%*	*64%*	*47%*	*62%*
Miami-Dade	*49%*	*69%*	*49%*	*71%*

National Assessment of Educational Progress (NAEP)
NAEP 8th Grade Reading results for Miami-Dade are above the state and national averages for male students.

Percentages of Male Black and Male White, Non-Latino, Students at or Above Proficient
Reading, Grade 8, 2011

	Percent at or Above Proficient		Gap
Jurisdiction	Black	White, non-Latino,	White/Black
USA	10%	35%	25%
Florida	10%	*34%*	24%
Miami-Dade	11%	41%	*30%*

NAEP 8th Grade Mathematics results for Miami-Dade's male Black students are below national averages; results for male White, non-Latino, students are above the national averages.

Percentages of Male Black and Male White, Non-Latino, Students at or Above Proficient
Mathematics, Grade 8, 2011

	Percent at or Above Proficient		Gap
Jurisdiction	Black	White, non-Latino,	White/Black
USA	12%	45%	33%
Florida	9%	38%	29%
Miami-Dade	10%	43%	33%

The *Benchmark* for male Black students in 8th Grade Reading is Connecticut, with 19% of male Black students scoring at or above Proficient. The *Benchmark* for 8th Grade Mathematics is Massachusetts, with 26% of male Black students scoring at or above Proficient.

Discipline and Advanced Placement Inequities
Out-of-school suspension ratios are a measure of the extent to which disparate application of school discipline policies affect students from different racial and ethnic groups. Black students with disabilities were more than half again as likely to receive out-of-school suspensions as were White, non-Latino, students. Male Black students without disabilities were more than three and a third times as likely to receive out-of-school suspensions as were Male White, non-Latino, students. Female Black students without disabilities were nearly five and a quarter times as likely to receive out-of-school suspensions as were female White, non-Latino, students

Enrollment ratios in Advanced Placement Mathematics are an indicator of the differing opportunities to learn that may be provided to students on the basis of race and ethnicity. Black students were enrolled in AP Mathematics at approximately one-quarter the rate for White, non-Latino, students.

Orange County Public Schools
Inequities in Graduation Rates
Male Black and Male White, non-Latino, students in the Orange County public schools graduate at rates above the state and below the national averages for those groups.

The *Benchmark* for graduation rates of male Black students for school districts enrolling more than 10,000 male Black students is 73% (Montgomery County, MD).

Jurisdiction	Male Graduation Rate: 2010/11		Male Graduation Rate: 2009/10	
	Black	White, non-Latino	Black	White, non-Latino
USA	53%	77%	52%	78%
Florida	47%	64%	47%	62%
Orange County	49%	66%	49%	67%

Discipline and Advanced Placement Inequities

Out-of-school suspension ratios are a measure of the extent to which disparate application of school discipline policies affect students from different racial and ethnic groups. Black students with disabilities were more than twice as likely to receive out-of-school suspensions as were White, non-Latino, students. Male Black students without disabilities were more than three and a half times as likely to receive out-of-school suspensions as were male White, non-Latino, students. Female Black students without disabilities were more than five and a third times as likely to receive out-of-school suspensions as were female White, non-Latino, students

Enrollment ratios in Advanced Placement Mathematics are an indicator of the differing opportunities to learn that may be provided to students on the basis of race and ethnicity. Male Black students were enrolled in AP Mathematics at one-fifth the rate for male White, non-Latino, students, while female Black students were enrolled in AP Mathematics at less than one-third the rate for female White, non-Latino, students.

Palm Beach County Public Schools

Inequities in Graduation Rates

Male Black and Male White, non-Latino, students in the Palm Beach County public schools graduate at rates above the state and below the national averages for those groups.

The *Benchmark* for graduation rates of male Black students for school districts enrolling more than 10,000 male Black students is 73% (Montgomery County, MD).

Jurisdiction	Male Graduation Rate: 2010/11		Male Graduation Rate: 2009/10	
	Black	White, non-Latino	Black	White, non-Latino
USA	53%	77%	52%	78%
Florida	47%	64%	47%	62%
Palm Beach County	52%	73%	55%	71%

Discipline and Advanced Placement Inequities

Out-of-school suspension ratios are a measure of the extent to which disparate application of school discipline policies affect students from different racial and ethnic groups. Black students with disabilities were more than two and a half times as likely to receive out-of-school suspensions as were White, non-Latino, students. Male Black students without disabilities were three and a quarter times as likely to receive out-of-school suspensions as were Male White, non-Latino, students. Female Black students without disabilities were more than five times as likely to receive out-of-school suspensions as were female White, non-Latino, students

Enrollment ratios in Advanced Placement Mathematics are an indicator of the differing opportunities to learn that may be provided to students on the basis of race and ethnicity. Male Black students were enrolled in AP Mathematics at less than one-fifth of the rate for male White, non-Latino, students, while female Black students were enrolled in AP Mathematics at just over one-third the rate for female White, non-Latino, students.

Pinellas County Public Schools

Inequities in Graduation Rates

Male Black students in the Pinellas County public schools graduate at rates significantly below the state and national averages for that group. Male White, non-Latino, rates have improved and are now above the state average, although remaining below the national average, for the group.

The *Benchmark* for graduation rates of male Black students for school districts enrolling more than 10,000 male Black students is 73% (Montgomery County, MD).

	Male Graduation Rate: 2010/11		Male Graduation Rate: 2009/10	
Jurisdiction	Black	White, non-Latino	Black	White, non-Latino
USA	53%	77%	52%	78%
Florida	*47%*	*64%*	*47%*	*62%*
Pinellas County	*31%*	*67%*	*34%*	*58%*

Discipline and Advanced Placement Inequities

Out-of-school suspension ratios are a measure of the extent to which disparate application of school discipline policies affect students from different racial and ethnic groups. Male Black students with disabilities were half again times as likely to receive out-of-school suspensions as were White, non-Latino, students. Female Black students with disabilities were more than two and a half times as likely to receive out-of-school suspensions as were White, non-Latino, students. Male Black students without disabilities were over twice as likely to receive out-of-school suspensions as were Male White, non-Latino, students. Female Black students without disabilities were nearly four times as likely to receive out-of-school suspensions as were female White, non-Latino, students

Enrollment ratios in Advanced Placement Mathematics are an indicator of the differing opportunities to learn that may be provided to students on the basis of race and ethnicity. Male Black students were enrolled in AP Mathematics at approximately one-tenth of the rate for male White, non-Latino, students, while female Black students were enrolled in AP Mathematics at just over one-quarter of the rate for female White, non-Latino, students.

Polk County Public Schools

Inequities in Graduation Rates

Male students in the Polk County public schools continue to graduate at rates below the state and national averages for each group.

The *Benchmark* for graduation rates of male Black students for school districts enrolling more than 10,000 male Black students is 73% (Montgomery County, MD).

	Male Graduation Rate: 2010/11		Male Graduation Rate: 2009/10	
Jurisdiction	Black	White, non-Latino	Black	White, non-Latino
USA	53%	77%	52%	78%
Florida	*47%*	*64%*	*47%*	*62%*
Polk County	*45%*	*55%*	*46%*	*57%*

Discipline and Advanced Placement Inequities

Out-of-school suspension ratios are a measure of the extent to which disparate application of school discipline policies affect students from different racial and ethnic groups. Black students with disabilities were nearly half again as likely to receive out-of-school suspensions as were White, non-Latino, students. Male Black students without disabilities were three and a quarter times as likely to receive out-of-school suspensions as were Male White, non-Latino, students.

Enrollment ratios in Advanced Placement Mathematics are an indicator of the differing opportunities to learn that may be provided to students on the basis of race and ethnicity. Black students were enrolled in AP Mathematics at just over one-quarter the rate for White, non-Latino, students.

GEORGIA

Inequities in Graduation Rates

Male students in Georgia in 2010/11 graduated at similar rates as in 2009/10. The rates for all male students were below the national averages for each group.

The *Benchmark* for graduation rates of male Black students for states enrolling more than 10,000 Black male students is 77% (Arizona). The *Benchmark* for states with at least one district enrolling more than 10,000 Black male students is New Jersey (73%).

	Male Graduation Rate: 2010/11		Male Graduation Rate: 2009/10	
Jurisdiction	Black	White, non-Latino	Black	White, non-Latino
USA	53%	77%	52%	78%
Georgia	*49%*	*66%*	*49%*	*65%*

Comparison of Estimated Graduation Rates by Gender: 2010/11

The gender gap for Black students in Georgia is twelve points, while that for White, non-Latino, students is seven points.

	Male Graduation Rate		Female Graduation Rate	
Jurisdiction	Black	White, non-Latino	Black	White, non-Latino
USA	53%	77%	63%	81%
Georgia	*49%*	*66%*	*61%*	*73%*

National Assessment of Educational Progress (NAEP)

NAEP 8th Grade Reading results for Georgia are at the national average for male Black students and below national averages for male White, non-Latino, students.

Percentages of Male Black and Male White, Non-Latino, Students at or Above Proficient
Reading, Grade 8, 2011

	Percent at or Above Proficient		Gap
Jurisdiction	Black	White, non-Latino,	White/Black
USA	10%	35%	25%
Georgia	10%	*33%*	23%

NAEP 8th Grade Mathematics results for Georgia are below national averages for male Black and White, non-Latino, students.

Percentages of Male Black and Male White, Non-Latino, Students at or Above Proficient
Mathematics, Grade 8, 2011

	Percent at or Above Proficient		Gap
Jurisdiction	Black	White, non-Latino,	White/Black
USA	12%	45%	33%
Georgia	*10%*	*41%*	31%

The *Benchmark* for male Black students in 8th Grade Reading is Connecticut, with 19% of male Black students scoring at or above Proficient. The *Benchmark* for 8th Grade Mathematics is Massachusetts, with 26% of male Black students scoring at or above Proficient.

Discipline Inequities

The U.S. Department of Education's Office for Civil Rights has not yet made out-of-school suspension data disaggregated by gender available at the state level for 2009/10. The Center for Civil Rights Remedies at The Civil Rights Project has calculated *combined* male and female percentages from the OCR samples.[22]

State	Black	White, non-Latino	Black/White Ratio
Georgia	17.1	4.9	3.5

Atlanta

Inequities in Graduation Rates

Male Black students in the Atlanta public schools graduate at rates below the state and national averages for the group. The small number of White, non-Latino, students graduate above state and below national averages with high year-to-year variability.

The *Benchmark* for graduation rates of male Black students for school districts enrolling more than 10,000 male Black students is 73% (Montgomery County, MD).

	Male Graduation Rate: 2010/11		Male Graduation Rate: 2009/10	
Jurisdiction	Black	White, non-Latino	Black	White, non-Latino
USA	53%	77%	52%	78%
Georgia	*49%*	*66%*	*49%*	*65%*
Atlanta	*42%*	87%	*42%*	*73%*

National Assessment of Educational Progress (NAEP)

NAEP 8th Grade Reading results for Atlanta are below the national average for male Black students.

Percentages of Male Black and Male White, Non-Latino, Students at or Above Proficient
Reading, Grade 8, 2011

	Percent at or Above Proficient		Gap
Jurisdiction	Black	White, non-Latino,	White/Black
USA	10%	35%	25%
Georgia	10%	*33%*	23%
Atlanta	*9%*	‡[23]	-

NAEP 8th Grade Mathematics results for Georgia are below national averages for male Black students and above national averages for male White, non-Latino, students.

[22] From: Losen, Daniel J. and Jonathan Gillispie. Opportunities Suspended: The Disparate Impact of Disciplinary Exclusion from School. The Center for Civil Rights Remedies at The Civil Rights Project, August 2012. *Source:* CRDC, 2009-2010 (numbers from national sample rounded to one decimal).

[23] Indicates insufficient sample size.

Percentages of Male Black and Male White, Non-Latino, Students at or Above Proficient Mathematics, Grade 8, 2011

	Percent at or Above Proficient		Gap
Jurisdiction	Black	White, non-Latino,	White/Black
USA	12%	45%	33%
Georgia	*10%*	*41%*	31%
Atlanta	*11%*	70%	*58%*

The *Benchmark* for male Black students in 8th Grade Reading is Connecticut, with 19% of male Black students scoring at or above Proficient. The *Benchmark* for 8th Grade Mathematics is Massachusetts, with 26% of male Black students scoring at or above Proficient.

Discipline and Advanced Placement Inequities

Out-of-school suspension ratios are a measure of the extent to which disparate application of school discipline policies affect students from different racial and ethnic groups. Black students with disabilities were nearly three times as likely to receive out-of-school suspensions as were White, non-Latino, students. Male Black students without disabilities were nearly seven and a half times as likely to receive out-of-school suspensions as were Male White, non-Latino, students. Female Black students without disabilities were over eleven and a half times as likely to receive out-of-school suspensions as were female White, non-Latino, students.

Enrollment ratios in Advanced Placement Mathematics are an indicator of the differing opportunities to learn that may be provided to students on the basis of race and ethnicity. Male Black students were enrolled in AP Mathematics at just over half the rate for male White, non-Latino, students. Female Black students were enrolled in AP Mathematics at less than one-third the rate for female White, non-Latino, students.

Chatham County

Inequities in Graduation Rates

Male students in the Chatham County public schools graduate at rates below the state and national averages for each group, fewer than half graduating.

The *Benchmark* for graduation rates of male Black students for school districts enrolling more than 10,000 male Black students is 73% (Montgomery County, MD).

	Male Graduation Rate: 2010/11		Male Graduation Rate: 2009/10	
Jurisdiction	Black	White, non-Latino	Black	White, non-Latino
USA	53%	77%	52%	78%
Georgia	*49%*	*66%*	*49%*	*65%*
Chatham County	*28%*	*49%*	*27%*	*42%*

Discipline and Advanced Placement Inequities

Out-of-school suspension ratios are a measure of the extent to which disparate application of school discipline policies affect students from different racial and ethnic groups. Black students with disabilities were nearly three times as likely to receive out-of-school suspensions as were White, non-Latino, students. Male Black students without disabilities were more than three times as likely to receive out-of-school suspensions as were Male White, non-Latino, students. Female Black students without disabilities were nearly four times as likely to receive out-of-school suspensions as were female White, non-Latino, students.

Enrollment ratios in Advanced Placement Mathematics are an indicator of the differing opportunities to learn that may be provided to students on the basis of race and ethnicity. Male Black students were enrolled in AP

Mathematics at less than half the rate for male White, non-Latino, students. Female Black students were enrolled in AP Mathematics at less than one-quarter the rate for female White, non-Latino, students.

Clayton County
Inequities in Graduation Rates
Male students in the Clayton County public schools graduate at rates below the state and national averages for each group, fewer than half graduating.

The *Benchmark* for graduation rates of male Black students for school districts enrolling more than 10,000 male Black students is 73% (Montgomery County, MD).

	Male Graduation Rate: 2010/11		Male Graduation Rate: 2009/10	
Jurisdiction	Black	White, non-Latino	Black	White, non-Latino
USA	53%	77%	52%	78%
Georgia	*49%*	*66%*	*49%*	*65%*
Clayton County	*37%*	*27%*	*35%*	*20%*

Discipline and Advanced Placement Inequities
Out-of-school suspension ratios are a measure of the extent to which disparate application of school discipline policies affect students from different racial and ethnic groups. Black students with disabilities were twice as likely to receive out-of-school suspensions as were White, non-Latino, students. Male Black students without disabilities were more than one and a half times as likely to receive out-of-school suspensions as were Male White, non-Latino, students. Female Black students without disabilities were more than two and a quarter times as likely to receive out-of-school suspensions as were female White, non-Latino, students.

Enrollment ratios in Advanced Placement Mathematics are an indicator of the differing opportunities to learn that may be provided to students on the basis of race and ethnicity. Black students were enrolled in AP Mathematics at just over half the rate for White, non-Latino, students.

Cobb County
Inequities in Graduation Rates
Male Black and Male White, non-Latino, students in the Cobb County public schools graduate at rates above the state and national averages for the group.

The *Benchmark* for graduation rates of male Black students for school districts enrolling more than 10,000 male Black students is 73% (Montgomery County, MD).

	Male Graduation Rate: 2010/11		Male Graduation Rate: 2009/10	
Jurisdiction	Black	White, non-Latino	Black	White, non-Latino
USA	53%	77%	52%	78%
Georgia	*49%*	*66%*	*49%*	*65%*
Cobb County	55%	79%	52%	*77%*

Discipline and Advanced Placement Inequities
Out-of-school suspension ratios are a measure of the extent to which disparate application of school discipline policies affect students from different racial and ethnic groups. Black students with disabilities were two and half times as likely to receive out-of-school suspensions as were White, non-Latino, students. Male Black students without disabilities were nearly four times as likely to receive out-of-school suspensions as were

Male White, non-Latino, students. Female Black students without disabilities were nearly six times as likely to receive out-of-school suspensions as were female White, non-Latino, students.

Enrollment ratios in Advanced Placement Mathematics are an indicator of the differing opportunities to learn that may be provided to students on the basis of race and ethnicity. Male Black students were enrolled in AP Mathematics at just over one-third the rate for male White, non-Latino, students. Female Black students were enrolled in AP Mathematics at just over one-quarter the rate for female White, non-Latino, students.

DeKalb County

Inequities in Graduation Rates

Male Black students in the DeKalb County public schools graduate at rates below the state national averages for the group. White, non-Latino, students graduate at rates higher than the state average and under the national average.

The *Benchmark* for graduation rates of male Black students for school districts enrolling more than 10,000 male Black students is 73% (Montgomery County, MD).

	Male Graduation Rate: 2010/11		Male Graduation Rate: 2009/10	
Jurisdiction	Black	White, non-Latino	Black	White, non-Latino
USA	53%	77%	52%	78%
Georgia	*49%*	*66%*	*49%*	*65%*
DeKalb County	*46%*	*69%*	*46%*	*72%*

Discipline and Advanced Placement Inequities

Out-of-school suspension ratios are a measure of the extent to which disparate application of school discipline policies affect students from different racial and ethnic groups. Black students with disabilities were nearly five times as likely to receive out-of-school suspensions as were White, non-Latino, students. Male Black students without disabilities were nearly six times as likely to receive out-of-school suspensions as were Male White, non-Latino, students. Female Black students without disabilities were more than seven and a half times as likely to receive out-of-school suspensions as were female White, non-Latino, students.

Enrollment ratios in Advanced Placement Mathematics are an indicator of the differing opportunities to learn that may be provided to students on the basis of race and ethnicity. Male Black students were enrolled in AP Mathematics at just over one-third the rate for male White, non-Latino, students. Female Black students were enrolled in AP Mathematics at one-fifth the rate for female White, non-Latino, students.

Fulton County

Inequities in Graduation Rates

Male Black and Male White, non-Latino, students in the Fulton County public schools graduate at rates above the state and national averages for the groups.

The *Benchmark* for graduation rates of male Black students for school districts enrolling more than 10,000 male Black students is 73% (Montgomery County, MD).

	Male Graduation Rate: 2010/11		Male Graduation Rate: 2009/10	
Jurisdiction	Black	White, non-Latino	Black	White, non-Latino
USA	53%	77%	52%	78%
Georgia	*49%*	*66%*	*49%*	*65%*
Fulton County	58%	85%	*47%*	83%

Discipline and Advanced Placement Inequities

Out-of-school suspension ratios are a measure of the extent to which disparate application of school discipline policies affect students from different racial and ethnic groups. Black students with disabilities were nearly four times as likely to receive out-of-school suspensions as were White, non-Latino, students. Male Black students without disabilities were nearly six times as likely to receive out-of-school suspensions as were Male White, non-Latino, students. Female Black students without disabilities were more nearly twelve and a half times as likely to receive out-of-school suspensions as were female White, non-Latino, students.

Enrollment ratios in Advanced Placement Mathematics are an indicator of the differing opportunities to learn that may be provided to students on the basis of race and ethnicity. Male Black students were enrolled in AP Mathematics at one-fifth the rate for male White, non-Latino, students. Female Black students were enrolled in AP Mathematics at one-tenth the rate for female White, non-Latino, students.

Gwinnett County

Inequities in Graduation Rates

Male students in the Gwinnett County public schools graduate at rates below the state national averages for each group.

The *Benchmark* for graduation rates of male Black students for school districts enrolling more than 10,000 male Black students is 73% (Montgomery County, MD).

	Male Graduation Rate: 2010/11		Male Graduation Rate: 2009/10	
Jurisdiction	Black	White, non-Latino	Black	White, non-Latino
USA	53%	77%	52%	78%
Georgia	*49%*	*66%*	*49%*	*65%*
Gwinnett County	*48%*	*64%*	*41%*	*61%*

Discipline and Advanced Placement Inequities

Out-of-school suspension ratios are a measure of the extent to which disparate application of school discipline policies affect students from different racial and ethnic groups. Male Black students with disabilities were more than twice as likely to receive out-of-school suspensions as were male White, non-Latino, students. Female Black students with disabilities were nearly three and a half times as likely to receive out-of-school suspensions as were female White, non-Latino, students. Male Black students without disabilities were three times as likely to receive out-of-school suspensions as were male White, non-Latino, students. Female Black students without disabilities were nearly three and three-quarters times as likely to receive out-of-school suspensions as were female White, non-Latino, students.

Enrollment ratios in Advanced Placement Mathematics are an indicator of the differing opportunities to learn that may be provided to students on the basis of race and ethnicity. Black students were enrolled in AP Mathematics at one-third the rate of White, non-Latino, students.

Richmond County

Inequities in Graduation Rates

Male students in the Richmond County public schools graduate at rates below the state national averages for each group, fewer than half graduating.

The *Benchmark* for graduation rates of male Black students for school districts enrolling more than 10,000 male Black students is 73% (Montgomery County, MD).

	Male Graduation Rate: 2010/11		Male Graduation Rate: 2009/10	
Jurisdiction	Black	White, non-Latino	Black	White, non-Latino
USA	53%	77%	52%	78%
Georgia	*49%*	*66%*	*49%*	*65%*
Richmond County	*33%*	*32%*	*27%*	*32%*

Discipline and Advanced Placement Inequities

Out-of-school suspension ratios are a measure of the extent to which disparate application of school discipline policies affect students from different racial and ethnic groups. Black students with disabilities were nearly a quarter again as likely to receive out-of-school suspensions as were male White, non-Latino, students. Female Black students with disabilities were nearly three and a half times as likely to receive out-of-school suspensions as were female White, non-Latino, students. Male Black students without disabilities were more than twice as likely to receive out-of-school suspensions as were male White, non-Latino, students. Female Black students without disabilities were more than three times as likely to receive out-of-school suspensions as were female White, non-Latino, students.

Enrollment ratios in Advanced Placement Mathematics are an indicator of the differing opportunities to learn that may be provided to students on the basis of race and ethnicity. Black students were enrolled in AP Mathematics at less than half the rate of White, non-Latino, students.

HAWAII

Inequities in Graduation Rates

Male Black students in Hawaii in 2010/11 graduated at higher rates than in 2009/10, higher than the group's national average. Male White, non-Latino, students graduated at rates far below the national average for that group.

The *Benchmark* for graduation rates of male Black students for states enrolling more than 10,000 Black male students is 77% (Arizona). The *Benchmark* for states with at least one district enrolling more than 10,000 Black male students is New Jersey (73%).

	Male Graduation Rate: 2010/11		Male Graduation Rate: 2009/10	
Jurisdiction	Black	White, non-Latino	Black	White, non-Latino
USA	53%	77%	52%	78%
Hawaii	63%	*50%*	60%	*39%*

Comparison of Estimated Graduation Rates by Gender: 2010/11

The gender gap for Black students in Hawaii is twenty-three points, while those for White, non-Latino, students are slightly reversed.

	Male Graduation Rate		Female Graduation Rate	
Jurisdiction	Black	White, non-Latino	Black	White, non-Latino
USA	53%	77%	63%	81%
Hawaii	63%	*50%*	86%	*51%*

National Assessment of Educational Progress (NAEP)

NAEP 8th Grade Reading results for Hawaii are below national averages for male White, non-Latino, students.

Percentages of Male Black and Male White, Non-Latino, Students at or Above Proficient
Reading, Grade 8, 2011

	Percent at or Above Proficient		Gap
Jurisdiction	Black	White, non-Latino,	White/Black
USA	10%	35%	25%
Hawaii	‡[24]	*33%*	-

NAEP 8th Grade Mathematics results for Hawaii are below the national average for male White, non-Latino, students.

	Percent at or Above Proficient		Gap
Jurisdiction	Black	White, non-Latino,	White/Black
USA	12%	45%	33%
Hawaii	‡[25]	*41%*	-

[24] Indicates insufficient sample size.

[25] Indicates insufficient sample size.

The *Benchmark* for male Black students in 8th Grade Reading is Connecticut, with 19% of male Black students scoring at or above Proficient. The *Benchmark* for 8th Grade Mathematics is Massachusetts, with 26% of male Black students scoring at or above Proficient.

Discipline Inequities

Omitted because of data accuracy issues.

IDAHO

Inequities in Graduation Rates

Male Black students in Idaho in 2010/11 graduated at higher rates than in 2009/10, remaining higher than the group's national average. Male White, non-Latino, students graduated at lower rates, but still just above the national average for that group. There are few Black students in the state.

The *Benchmark* for graduation rates of male Black students for states enrolling more than 10,000 Black male students is 77% (Arizona). The *Benchmark* for states with at least one district enrolling more than 10,000 Black male students is New Jersey (73%).

	Male Graduation Rate: 2010/11		Male Graduation Rate: 2009/10	
Jurisdiction	Black	White, non-Latino	Black	White, non-Latino
USA	53%	77%	52%	78%
Idaho	72%	78%	62%	84%

Comparison of Estimated Graduation Rates by Gender: 2010/11

The gender gap for Black students in Idaho is a reversed three points, while that for White, non-Latino, students is two points.

	Male Graduation Rate		Female Graduation Rate	
Jurisdiction	Black	White, non-Latino	Black	White, non-Latino
USA	53%	77%	63%	81%
Idaho	72%	78%	69%	*80%*

National Assessment of Educational Progress (NAEP)

NAEP 8th Grade Reading results for Idaho are below the national average for White, non-Latino, students.

Percentages of Male Black and Male White, Non-Latino, Students at or Above Proficient Reading, Grade 8, 2011

	Percent at or Above Proficient		Gap
Jurisdiction	Black	White, non-Latino,	White/Black
USA	10%	35%	25%
Idaho	‡[26]	*32%*	-

NAEP 8th Grade Mathematics results for Idaho are below national averages for male White, non-Latino, students.

Percentages of Male Black and Male White, Non-Latino, Students at or Above Proficient Mathematics, Grade 8, 2011

	Percent at or Above Proficient		Gap
Jurisdiction	Black	White, non-Latino,	White/Black
USA	12%	45%	33%
Idaho	‡[27]	42%	-

[26] Indicates insufficient sample size.

[27] Indicates insufficient sample size.

The *Benchmark* for male Black students in 8th Grade Reading is Connecticut, with 19% of male Black students scoring at or above Proficient. The *Benchmark* for 8th Grade Mathematics is Massachusetts, with 26% of male Black students scoring at or above Proficient.

Discipline Inequities

The U.S. Department of Education's Office for Civil Rights has not yet made out-of-school suspension data disaggregated by gender available at the state level for 2009/10. The Center for Civil Rights Remedies at The Civil Rights Project has calculated *combined* male and female percentages from the OCR samples.[28]

State	Black	White, non-Latino	Black/White Ratio
Idaho	4.2	3.2	1.3

[28] From: Losen, Daniel J. and Jonathan Gillispie. Opportunities Suspended: The Disparate Impact of Disciplinary Exclusion from School. The Center for Civil Rights Remedies at The Civil Rights Project, August 2012. *Source:* CRDC, 2009-2010 (numbers from national sample rounded to one decimal).

ILLINOIS

Inequities in Graduation Rates

Male Black students in Illinois in 2010/11 graduated at a lower rate than in 2009/10, lower than the group's national average. Male White, non-Latino, students also graduated at lower rates, but remained above the national average for that group.

The *Benchmark* for graduation rates of male Black students for states enrolling more than 10,000 Black male students is 77% (Arizona). The *Benchmark* for states with at least one district enrolling more than 10,000 Black male students is New Jersey (73%).

	Male Graduation Rate: 2010/11		Male Graduation Rate: 2009/10	
Jurisdiction	Black	White, non-Latino	Black	White, non-Latino
USA	53%	77%	52%	78%
Illinois	*48%*	80%	56%	91%

Comparison of Estimated Graduation Rates by Gender: 2010/11

The gender gap for Black students in Illinois is eleven points, while that for White, non-Latino, students is two points.

	Male Graduation Rate		Female Graduation Rate	
Jurisdiction	Black	White, non-Latino	Black	White, non-Latino
USA	53%	77%	63%	81%
Illinois	*48%*	80%	*59%*	82%

National Assessment of Educational Progress (NAEP)

NAEP 8th Grade Reading results for Illinois are above national averages for each category.

Percentages of Male Black and Male White, Non-Latino, Students at or Above Proficient
Reading, Grade 8, 2011

	Percent at or Above Proficient		Gap
Jurisdiction	Black	White, non-Latino	White/Black
USA	10%	35%	25%
Illinois	11%	38%	*27%*

NAEP 8th Grade Mathematics results for Illinois are below national averages for male Black students and slightly above the national average for White, non-Latino, students.

Percentages of Male Black and Male White, Non-Latino, Students at or Above Proficient
Mathematics, Grade 8, 2011

	Percent at or Above Proficient		Gap
Jurisdiction	Black	White, non-Latino	White/Black
USA	12%	45%	33%
Illinois	*10%*	46%	*36%*

The *Benchmark* for male Black students in 8th Grade Reading is Connecticut, with 19% of male Black students scoring at or above Proficient. The *Benchmark* for 8th Grade Mathematics is Massachusetts, with 26% of male Black students scoring at or above Proficient.

Discipline Inequities

The U.S. Department of Education's Office for Civil Rights has not yet made out-of-school suspension data disaggregated by gender available at the state level for 2009/10. The Center for Civil Rights Remedies at The Civil Rights Project has calculated *combined* male and female percentages from the OCR samples.[29]

State	Black	White, non-Latino	Black/White Ratio
Illinois	25.3	3.9	6.5

Chicago

Inequities in Graduation Rates

Male students in Chicago in 2010/11 graduated at lower rate than each group's state and national averages.

The *Benchmark* for graduation rates of male Black students for school districts enrolling more than 10,000 male Black students is 73% (Montgomery County, MD).

	Male Graduation Rate: 2010/11		Male Graduation Rate: 2009/10	
Jurisdiction	Black	White, non-Latino	Black	White, non-Latino
USA	53%	77%	52%	78%
Illinois	*48%*	80%	56%	91%
Chicago	*45%*	*69%*	*39%*	*66%*

National Assessment of Educational Progress (NAEP)

NAEP 8th Grade Reading results for Chicago are below state and national averages for male Black students, above national but below state averages for male White, non-Latino, students.

Percentages of Male Black and Male White, Non-Latino, Students at or Above Proficient
Reading, Grade 8, 2011

	Percent at or Above Proficient		Gap
Jurisdiction	Black	White, non-Latino	White/Black
USA	10%	35%	25%
Illinois	11%	38%	*27%*
Chicago	*9%*	36%	*27%*

NAEP 8th Grade Mathematics results for Chicago are below state and national averages for male Black students and above state and national averages for White, non-Latino, students.

[29] From: Losen, Daniel J. and Jonathan Gillispie. Opportunities Suspended: The Disparate Impact of Disciplinary Exclusion from School. The Center for Civil Rights Remedies at The Civil Rights Project, August 2012. *Source:* CRDC, 2009-2010 (numbers from national sample rounded to one decimal).

Percentages of Male Black and Male White, Non-Latino, Students at or Above Proficient Mathematics, Grade 8, 2011

	Percent at or Above Proficient		Gap
Jurisdiction	Black	White, non-Latino	White/Black
USA	12%	45%	33%
Illinois	*10%*	46%	*36%*
Chicago	*9%*	49%	*40%*

The *Benchmark* for male Black students in 8th Grade Reading is Connecticut, with 19% of male Black students scoring at or above Proficient. The *Benchmark* for 8th Grade Mathematics is Massachusetts, with 26% of male Black students scoring at or above Proficient.

Discipline and Advanced Placement Inequities

Out-of-school suspension ratios are a measure of the extent to which disparate application of school discipline policies affect students from different racial and ethnic groups. Male Black students with disabilities were more than three and a half times as likely to receive out-of-school suspensions as were male White, non-Latino, students. Female Black students with disabilities were more than four and a third times as likely to receive out-of-school suspensions as were female White, non-Latino, students. Male Black students without disabilities were five and a third times as likely to receive out-of-school suspensions as were male White, non-Latino, students. Female Black students without disabilities were nearly three and three-quarters times as likely to receive out-of-school suspensions as were female White, non-Latino, students.

Enrollment ratios in Advanced Placement Mathematics are an indicator of the differing opportunities to learn that may be provided to students on the basis of race and ethnicity. Black students were enrolled in AP Mathematics at one-third the rate of White, non-Latino, students.

INDIANA

Inequities in Graduation Rates

Male Black and Male White, non-Latino, students in Indiana in 2010/11 graduated at a higher rate than in 2009/10.

The *Benchmark* for graduation rates of male Black students for states enrolling more than 10,000 Black male students is 77% (Arizona). The *Benchmark* for states with at least one district enrolling more than 10,000 Black male students is New Jersey (73%).

	Male Graduation Rate: 2010/11		Male Graduation Rate: 2009/10	
Jurisdiction	Black	White, non-Latino	Black	White, non-Latino
USA	53%	77%	52%	78%
Indiana	57%	77%	*49%*	80%

Comparison of Estimated Graduation Rates by Gender: 2010/11

The gender gap for Black students in Indiana is six points, while that for White, non-Latino, students is three points.

	Male Graduation Rate		Female Graduation Rate	
Jurisdiction	Black	White, non-Latino	Black	White, non-Latino
USA	53%	77%	63%	81%
Indiana	57%	77%	63%	80%

National Assessment of Educational Progress (NAEP)

NAEP 8th Grade Reading results for Indiana are below national averages for male Black and White, non-Latino, students.

Percentages of Male Black and Male White, Non-Latino, Students at or Above Proficient
Reading, Grade 8, 2011

	Percent at or Above Proficient		Gap
Jurisdiction	Black	White, non-Latino	White/Black
USA	10%	35%	25%
Indiana	*9%*	*31%*	23%

NAEP 8th Grade Mathematics results for Indiana are below national averages for male Black and White, non-Latino, students.

Percentages of Male Black and Male White, Non-Latino, Students at or Above Proficient
Mathematics, Grade 8, 2011

	Percent at or Above Proficient		Gap
Jurisdiction	Black	White, non-Latino	White/Black
USA	12%	45%	33%
Indiana	*11%*	*39%*	28%

The *Benchmark* for male Black students in 8th Grade Reading is Connecticut, with 19% of male Black students scoring at or above Proficient. The *Benchmark* for 8th Grade Mathematics is Massachusetts, with 26% of male Black students scoring at or above Proficient.

Discipline Inequities

The U.S. Department of Education's Office for Civil Rights has not yet made out-of-school suspension data disaggregated by gender available at the state level for 2009/10. The Center for Civil Rights Remedies at The Civil Rights Project has calculated *combined* male and female percentages from the OCR samples.[30]

State	Black	White, non-Latino	Black/White Ratio
Indiana	19.5	5.9	3.3

[30] From: Losen, Daniel J. and Jonathan Gillispie. Opportunities Suspended: The Disparate Impact of Disciplinary Exclusion from School. The Center for Civil Rights Remedies at The Civil Rights Project, August 2012. *Source:* CRDC, 2009-2010 (numbers from national sample rounded to one decimal).

IOWA

Inequities in Graduation Rates

The few male Black students in Iowa in 2010/11 graduated at a much higher rate than in 2009/10, higher than the group's national average. Male White, non-Latino, students graduated at slightly lower rates than in the previous year.

The *Benchmark* for graduation rates of male Black students for states enrolling more than 10,000 Black male students is 77% (Arizona). The *Benchmark* for states with at least one district enrolling more than 10,000 Black male students is New Jersey (73%).

	Male Graduation Rate: 2010/11		Male Graduation Rate: 2009/10	
Jurisdiction	Black	White, non-Latino	Black	White, non-Latino
USA	53%	77%	52%	78%
Iowa	62%	86%	*41%*	90%

Comparison of Estimated Graduation Rates by Gender: 2010/11

The gender gap for Black students in Iowa is reversed by two points, while that for White, non-Latino, students is one point.

	Male Graduation Rate		Female Graduation Rate	
Jurisdiction	Black	White, non-Latino	Black	White, non-Latino
USA	53%	77%	63%	81%
Iowa	62%	86%	*60%*	87%

National Assessment of Educational Progress (NAEP)

NAEP 8th Grade Reading results for Iowa are above the national average for male Black students and below national averages for male White, non-Latino, students.

Percentages of Male Black and Male White, Non-Latino, Students at or Above Proficient
Reading, Grade 8, 2011

	Percent at or Above Proficient		Gap
Jurisdiction	Black	White, non-Latino	White/Black
USA	10%	35%	25%
Iowa	13%	*30%*	17%

NAEP 8th Grade Mathematics results for Iowa are below national averages for male White, non-Latino, students.

Percentages of Male Black and Male White, Non-Latino, Students at or Above Proficient
Mathematics, Grade 8, 2011

	Percent at or Above Proficient		Gap
Jurisdiction	Black	White, non-Latino	White/Black
USA	12%	45%	33%
Iowa	‡[31]	*38%*	-

[31] Indicates insufficient sample size.

The *Benchmark* for male Black students in 8th Grade Reading is Connecticut, with 19% of male Black students scoring at or above Proficient. The *Benchmark* for 8th Grade Mathematics is Massachusetts, with 26% of male Black students scoring at or above Proficient.

Discipline Inequities

The U.S. Department of Education's Office for Civil Rights has not yet made out-of-school suspension data disaggregated by gender available at the state level for 2009/10. The Center for Civil Rights Remedies at The Civil Rights Project has calculated *combined* male and female percentages from the OCR samples.[32]

State	Black	White, non-Latino	Black/White Ratio
Iowa	13.9	3	4.6

[32] From: Losen, Daniel J. and Jonathan Gillispie. Opportunities Suspended: The Disparate Impact of Disciplinary Exclusion from School. The Center for Civil Rights Remedies at The Civil Rights Project, August 2012. *Source:* CRDC, 2009-2010 (numbers from national sample rounded to one decimal).

KANSAS

Inequities in Graduation Rates

The few male Black students in Kansas in 2010/11 graduated at a higher rate than in 2009/10, exceeding the group's national average.

The *Benchmark* for graduation rates of male Black students for states enrolling more than 10,000 Black male students is 77% (Arizona). The *Benchmark* for states with at least one district enrolling more than 10,000 Black male students is New Jersey (73%).

	Male Graduation Rate: 2010/11		Male Graduation Rate: 2009/10	
Jurisdiction	Black	White, non-Latino	Black	White, non-Latino
USA	53%	77%	52%	78%
Kansas	59%	81%	*47%*	81%

Comparison of Estimated Graduation Rates by Gender: 2010/11

The gender gap for Black students in Kansas is eight points, while that for White, non-Latino, students is four points.

	Male Graduation Rate		Female Graduation Rate	
Jurisdiction	Black	White, non-Latino	Black	White, non-Latino
USA	53%	77%	63%	81%
Kansas	59%	81%	67%	85%

National Assessment of Educational Progress (NAEP)

NAEP 8th Grade Reading results for Kansas are above national averages for male Black and White, non-Latino, students.

Percentages of Male Black and Male White, Non-Latino, Students at or Above Proficient
Reading, Grade 8, 2011

	Percent at or Above Proficient		Gap
Jurisdiction	Black	White, non-Latino	White/Black
USA	10%	35%	25%
Kansas	12%	36%	24%

NAEP 8th Grade Mathematics results for Kansas are above those for the nation as a whole in each category.

Percentages of Male Black and Male White, Non-Latino, Students at or Above Proficient
Mathematics, Grade 8, 2011

	Percent at or Above Proficient		Gap
Jurisdiction	Black	White, non-Latino	White/Black
USA	12%	45%	33%
Kansas	20%	48%	28%

The *Benchmark* for male Black students in 8th Grade Reading is Connecticut, with 19% of male Black students scoring at or above Proficient. The *Benchmark* for 8th Grade Mathematics is Massachusetts, with 26% of male Black students scoring at or above Proficient.

Discipline Inequities

The U.S. Department of Education's Office for Civil Rights has not yet made out-of-school suspension data disaggregated by gender available at the state level for 2009/10. The Center for Civil Rights Remedies at The Civil Rights Project has calculated *combined* male and female percentages from the OCR samples.[33]

State	Black	White, non-Latino	Black/White Ratio
Kansas	16.8	4	4.2

[33] From: Losen, Daniel J. and Jonathan Gillispie. Opportunities Suspended: The Disparate Impact of Disciplinary Exclusion from School. The Center for Civil Rights Remedies at The Civil Rights Project, August 2012. *Source:* CRDC, 2009-2010 (numbers from national sample rounded to one decimal).

KENTUCKY

Inequities in Graduation Rates

Male Black students in Kentucky in 2010/11 graduated at a slightly lower rate than in 2009/10, but still over the group's national average. Male White, non-Latino, students graduated at slightly higher rates, but still quite a bit below the national average for that group.

The *Benchmark* for graduation rates of male Black students for states enrolling more than 10,000 Black male students is 77% (Arizona). The *Benchmark* for states with at least one district enrolling more than 10,000 Black male students is New Jersey (73%).

	Male Graduation Rate: 2010/11		Male Graduation Rate: 2009/10	
Jurisdiction	Black	White, non-Latino	Black	White, non-Latino
USA	53%	77%	52%	78%
Kentucky	61%	*72%*	65%	*71%*

Comparison of Estimated Graduation Rates by Gender: 2010/11

The gender gap for Black students in Kentucky is eight points, while that for White, non-Latino, students is six points.

	Male Graduation Rate		Female Graduation Rate	
Jurisdiction	Black	White, non-Latino	Black	White, non-Latino
USA	53%	77%	63%	81%
Kentucky	61%	*72%*	69%	*78%*

National Assessment of Educational Progress (NAEP)

NAEP 8th Grade Reading results for Kentucky are slightly above the national average for male Black students and slightly below the national average for male White, non-Latino, students.

Percentages of Male Black and Male White, Non-Latino, Students at or Above Proficient
Reading, Grade 8, 2011

	Percent at or Above Proficient		Gap
Jurisdiction	Black	White, non-Latino	White/Black
USA	10%	35%	25%
Kentucky	11%	*34%*	23%

NAEP 8th Grade Mathematics results for Kentucky are above the national average for male Black students and below the national averages for male White, non-Latino, students.

Percentages of Male Black and Male White, Non-Latino, Students at or Above Proficient
Mathematics, Grade 8, 2011

	Percent at or Above Proficient		Gap
Jurisdiction	Black	White, non-Latino	White/Black
USA	12%	45%	33%
Kentucky	14%	*35%*	21%

The *Benchmark* for male Black students in 8th Grade Reading is Connecticut, with 19% of male Black students scoring at or above Proficient. The *Benchmark* for 8th Grade Mathematics is Massachusetts, with 26% of male Black students scoring at or above Proficient.

Discipline Inequities

The U.S. Department of Education's Office for Civil Rights has not yet made out-of-school suspension data disaggregated by gender available at the state level for 2009/10. The Center for Civil Rights Remedies at The Civil Rights Project has calculated *combined* male and female percentages from the OCR samples.[34]

State	Black	White, non-Latino	Black/White Ratio
Kentucky	13.9	4.6	3.0

Jefferson County

Inequities in Graduation Rates

Male Black and Male White, non-Latino, students in Jefferson County in 2010/11 graduated at lower rates than state and national averages.

The *Benchmark* for graduation rates of male Black students for school districts enrolling more than 10,000 male Black students is 73% (Montgomery County, MD).

	Male Graduation Rate: 2010/11		Male Graduation Rate: 2009/10	
Jurisdiction	Black	White, non-Latino	Black	White, non-Latino
USA	53%	77%	52%	78%
Kentucky	61%	*72%*	65%	*71%*
Jefferson County	*50%*	*69%*	*49%*	*53%*

National Assessment of Educational Progress (NAEP)

NAEP 8th Grade Reading results for Jefferson County (Louisville) are below the state and national averages for male Black and White, non-Latino, students.

Percentages of Male Black and Male White, Non-Latino, Students at or Above Proficient
Reading, Grade 8, 2011

	Percent at or Above Proficient		Gap
Jurisdiction	Black	White, non-Latino	White/Black
USA	10%	35%	25%
Kentucky	11%	*34%*	23%
Jefferson County	*9%*	*33%*	24%

NAEP 8th Grade Mathematics results for Jefferson County are below state but above national averages for male Black students and below state and national averages for male, White, non-Latino, students.

[34] From: Losen, Daniel J. and Jonathan Gillispie. Opportunities Suspended: The Disparate Impact of Disciplinary Exclusion from School. The Center for Civil Rights Remedies at The Civil Rights Project, August 2012. *Source:* CRDC, 2009-2010 (numbers from national sample rounded to one decimal).

Percentages of Male Black and Male White, Non-Latino, Students at or Above Proficient Mathematics, Grade 8, 2011

	Percent at or Above Proficient		Gap
Jurisdiction	Black	White, non-Latino	White/Black
USA	12%	45%	33%
Kentucky	14%	*35%*	21%
Jefferson County	13%	*32%*	19%

The *Benchmark* for male Black students in 8th Grade Reading is Connecticut, with 19% of male Black students scoring at or above Proficient. The *Benchmark* for 8th Grade Mathematics is Massachusetts, with 26% of male Black students scoring at or above Proficient.

Discipline and Advanced Placement Inequities

Out-of-school suspension ratios are a measure of the extent to which disparate application of school discipline policies affect students from different racial and ethnic groups. Male Black students with disabilities were more than twice as likely to receive out-of-school suspensions as were male White, non-Latino, students. Female Black students with disabilities were more than three and a half times as likely to receive out-of-school suspensions as were female White, non-Latino, students. Black students without disabilities were two and a third times as likely to receive out-of-school suspensions as were White, non-Latino, students.

Enrollment ratios in Advanced Placement Mathematics are an indicator of the differing opportunities to learn that may be provided to students on the basis of race and ethnicity. Male Black students were enrolled in AP Mathematics at one-quarter the rate of male White, non-Latino, students. Female Black students were enrolled in AP Mathematics at just over one-third the rate of female White, non-Latino, students.

LOUISIANA

Inequities in Graduation Rates

Male Black students in Louisiana in 2010/11 graduated at a slightly higher rate than in 2009/10, but still below the group's national average. Male White, non-Latino, students graduated at higher rates, but still quite a bit below the national average for that group.

The *Benchmark* for graduation rates of male Black students for states enrolling more than 10,000 Black male students is 77% (Arizona). The *Benchmark* for states with at least one district enrolling more than 10,000 Black male students is New Jersey (73%).

	Male Graduation Rate: 2010/11		Male Graduation Rate: 2009/10	
Jurisdiction	Black	White, non-Latino	Black	White, non-Latino
USA	53%	77%	52%	78%
Louisiana	*50%*	*66%*	*49%*	*63%*

Comparison of Estimated Graduation Rates by Gender: 2010/11

The gender gap for Black students in Louisiana is fourteen points, while that for White, non-Latino, students is nine points.

	Male Graduation Rate		Female Graduation Rate	
Jurisdiction	Black	White, non-Latino	Black	White, non-Latino
USA	53%	77%	63%	81%
Louisiana	*50%*	*66%*	64%	*75%*

National Assessment of Educational Progress (NAEP)

NAEP 8th Grade Reading results for Louisiana are below national averages for male Black and White, non-Latino, students.

Percentages of Male Black and Male White, Non-Latino, Students at or Above Proficient
Reading, Grade 8, 2011

	Percent at or Above Proficient		Gap
Jurisdiction	Black	White, non-Latino	White/Black
USA	10%	35%	25%
Louisiana	*8%*	*26%*	18%

NAEP 8th Grade Mathematics results for Louisiana significantly below national averages for male Black and White, non-Latino, students.

Percentages of Male Black and Male White, Non-Latino, Students at or Above Proficient
Mathematics, Grade 8, 2011

	Percent at or Above Proficient		Gap
Jurisdiction	Black	White, non-Latino	White/Black
USA	12%	45%	33%
Louisiana	*9%*	*31%*	22%

The *Benchmark* for male Black students in 8th Grade Reading is Connecticut, with 19% of male Black students scoring at or above Proficient. The *Benchmark* for 8th Grade Mathematics is Massachusetts, with 26% of male Black students scoring at or above Proficient.

Discipline Inequities

The U.S. Department of Education's Office for Civil Rights has not yet made out-of-school suspension data disaggregated by gender available at the state level for 2009/10. The Center for Civil Rights Remedies at The Civil Rights Project has calculated *combined* male and female percentages from the OCR samples.[35]

State	Black	White, non-Latino	Black/White Ratio
Louisiana	15.3	7	2.2

Caddo Parish

Inequities in Graduation Rates

Male Black students in Caddo Parish in 2010/11 graduated at a slightly higher rate than in 2009/10, but below the national average. The graduation rate for White, non-Latino, male students was approximately unchanged and below state and national averages.

The *Benchmark* for graduation rates of male Black students for school districts enrolling more than 10,000 male Black students is 73% (Montgomery County, MD).

	Male Graduation Rate: 2010/11		Male Graduation Rate: 2009/10	
Jurisdiction	Black	White, non-Latino	Black	White, non-Latino
USA	53%	77%	52%	78%
Louisiana	*50%*	*66%*	*49%*	*63%*
Caddo Parish	*41%*	*57%*	*39%*	*58%*

Discipline and Advanced Placement Inequities

Out-of-school suspension ratios are a measure of the extent to which disparate application of school discipline policies affect students from different racial and ethnic groups. Male Black students with disabilities were half again as likely to receive out-of-school suspensions as were male White, non-Latino, students. Female Black students with disabilities were nearly twice as likely to receive out-of-school suspensions as were female White, non-Latino, students. Male Black students without disabilities were two and a quarter times as likely to receive out-of-school suspensions as were male White, non-Latino, students. Female Black students without disabilities were nearly three times as likely to receive out-of-school suspensions as were female White, non-Latino, students.

Enrollment ratios in Advanced Placement Mathematics are an indicator of the differing opportunities to learn that may be provided to students on the basis of race and ethnicity. Male Black students were enrolled in AP Mathematics at one-tenth the rate of male White, non-Latino, students. Female Black students were enrolled in AP Mathematics at just over one-tenth the rate of female White, non-Latino, students.

---

[35] From: Losen, Daniel J. and Jonathan Gillispie. Opportunities Suspended: The Disparate Impact of Disciplinary Exclusion from School. The Center for Civil Rights Remedies at The Civil Rights Project, August 2012. *Source:* CRDC, 2009-2010 (numbers from national sample rounded to one decimal).

East Baton Rouge Parish

Inequities in Graduation Rates

Male Black and Male White, non-Latino, students in East Baton Rouge Parish in 2010/11 graduated at higher rates than in 2009/10. The extraordinary change in the graduation rate of White, non-Latino, male students is an effect of variation in a small group population.

The *Benchmark* for graduation rates of male Black students for school districts enrolling more than 10,000 male Black students is 73% (Montgomery County, MD).

	Male Graduation Rate: 2010/11		Male Graduation Rate: 2009/10	
Jurisdiction	Black	White, non-Latino	Black	White, non-Latino
USA	53%	77%	52%	78%
Louisiana	*50%*	*66%*	*49%*	*63%*
East Baton Rouge Parish	*45%*	87%	*42%*	*44%*

Discipline and Advanced Placement Inequities

Out-of-school suspension ratios are a measure of the extent to which disparate application of school discipline policies affect students from different racial and ethnic groups. Male Black students without disabilities were more than two and a half times as likely to receive out-of-school suspensions as were male White, non-Latino, students. Female Black students without disabilities were five and a quarter times as likely to receive out-of-school suspensions as were female White, non-Latino, students.

Enrollment ratios in Advanced Placement Mathematics are an indicator of the differing opportunities to learn that may be provided to students on the basis of race and ethnicity. Male Black students were enrolled in AP Mathematics at just over one-tenth the rate of male White, non-Latino, students. Female Black students were enrolled in AP Mathematics at approximately one-sixth the rate of female White, non-Latino, students.

Jefferson Parish

Inequities in Graduation Rates

Male Black and Male White, non-Latino, students in Jefferson Parish in 2010/11 graduated at a higher rate than in 2009/10.

The *Benchmark* for graduation rates of male Black students for school districts enrolling more than 10,000 male Black students is 73% (Montgomery County, MD).

	Male Graduation Rate: 2010/11		Male Graduation Rate: 2009/10	
Jurisdiction	Black	White, non-Latino	Black	White, non-Latino
USA	53%	77%	52%	78%
Louisiana	*50%*	*66%*	*49%*	*63%*
Jefferson Parish	56%	*63%*	*50%*	*56%*

Discipline and Advanced Placement Inequities

Out-of-school suspension ratios are a measure of the extent to which disparate application of school discipline policies affect students from different racial and ethnic groups. Male Black students with disabilities were more than twice as likely to receive out-of-school suspensions as were male White, non-Latino, students. Female Black students with disabilities were more than three times as likely to receive out-of-school suspensions as were female White, non-Latino, students. Male Black students without disabilities were more than two and a half times as likely to receive out-of-school suspensions as were White, non-Latino, students.

Female Black students without disabilities were more than three and a half times as likely to receive out-of-school suspensions as were White, non-Latino, students.

Enrollment ratios in Advanced Placement Mathematics are an indicator of the differing opportunities to learn that may be provided to students on the basis of race and ethnicity. Male Black students were enrolled in AP Mathematics at less than half the rate of male White, non-Latino, students.

MAINE

Inequities in Graduation Rates

The very few male Black students in Maine in 2010/11 graduated at a lower rate than in 2009/10, but still above the group's national average. Male White, non-Latino, students graduated at higher rates, far above the national average for that group.

The *Benchmark* for graduation rates of male Black students for states enrolling more than 10,000 Black male students is 77% (Arizona). The *Benchmark* for states with at least one district enrolling more than 10,000 Black male students is New Jersey (73%).

	Male Graduation Rate: 2010/11		Male Graduation Rate: 2009/10	
Jurisdiction	Black	White, non-Latino	Black	White, non-Latino
USA	53%	77%	52%	78%
Maine	68%	94%	84%	80%

Comparison of Estimated Graduation Rates by Gender: 2010/11

The gender gap for Black students in Maine is inverted by nine points, while that for White, non-Latino, students is six points.

	Male Graduation Rate		Female Graduation Rate	
Jurisdiction	Black	White, non-Latino	Black	White, non-Latino
USA	53%	77%	63%	81%
Maine	68%	94%	*59%*	100%

National Assessment of Educational Progress (NAEP)

NAEP 8th Grade Reading results for Maine are slightly below the national average for male White, non-Latino, students.

Percentages of Male Black and Male White, Non-Latino, Students at or Above Proficient
Reading, Grade 8, 2011

	Percent at or Above Proficient		Gap
Jurisdiction	Black	White, non-Latino	White/Black
USA	10%	35%	25%
Maine	‡[36]	*34%*	-

NAEP 8th Grade Mathematics results for Maine are below the national average for male White, non-Latino, students.

Percentages of Male Black and Male White, Non-Latino, Students at or Above Proficient
Mathematics, Grade 8, 2011

	Percent at or Above Proficient		Gap
Jurisdiction	Black	White, non-Latino	White/Black
USA	12%	45%	33%
Maine	‡[37]	*39%*	-

---

[36] Indicates insufficient sample size.

[37] Indicates insufficient sample size.

The *Benchmark* for male Black students in 8th Grade Reading is Connecticut, with 19% of male Black students scoring at or above Proficient. The *Benchmark* for 8th Grade Mathematics is Massachusetts, with 26% of male Black students scoring at or above Proficient.

Discipline Inequities

The U.S. Department of Education's Office for Civil Rights has not yet made out-of-school suspension data disaggregated by gender available at the state level for 2009/10. The Center for Civil Rights Remedies at The Civil Rights Project has calculated *combined* male and female percentages from the OCR samples.[38]

State	Black	White, non-Latino	Black/White Ratio
Maine	8.7	4.6	1.9

[38] From: Losen, Daniel J. and Jonathan Gillispie. Opportunities Suspended: The Disparate Impact of Disciplinary Exclusion from School. The Center for Civil Rights Remedies at The Civil Rights Project, August 2012. *Source:* CRDC, 2009-2010 (numbers from national sample rounded to one decimal).

MARYLAND

Inequities in Graduation Rates

Male Black students in Maryland in 2010/11 graduated at higher rates than in 2009/10, again above the group's national average. Male White, non-Latino, students graduated at slightly lower rates than in the previous year.

The *Benchmark* for graduation rates of male Black students for states enrolling more than 10,000 Black male students is 77% (Arizona). The *Benchmark* for states with at least one district enrolling more than 10,000 Black male students is New Jersey (73%).

	Male Graduation Rate: 2010/11		Male Graduation Rate: 2009/10	
Jurisdiction	Black	White, non-Latino	Black	White, non-Latino
USA	53%	77%	52%	78%
Maryland	59%	80%	57%	81%

Comparison of Estimated Graduation Rates by Gender: 2010/11

The gender gap for Black students in Maryland is thirteen points, while that for White, non-Latino, students is three points.

	Male Graduation Rate		Female Graduation Rate	
Jurisdiction	Black	White, non-Latino	Black	White, non-Latino
USA	53%	77%	63%	81%
Maryland	59%	80%	72%	83%

National Assessment of Educational Progress (NAEP)

NAEP 8th Grade Reading results for Maryland are considerably above national averages for male Black and White, non-Latino, students.

Percentages of Male Black and Male White, Non-Latino, Students at or Above Proficient
Reading, Grade 8, 2011

	Percent at or Above Proficient		Gap
Jurisdiction	Black	White, non-Latino	White/Black
USA	10%	35%	25%
Maryland	17%	45%	*28%*

NAEP 8th Grade Mathematics results for Maryland are considerably above those for the nation as a whole in each category.

Percentages of Male Black and Male White, Non-Latino, Students at or Above Proficient
Mathematics, Grade 8, 2011

	Percent at or Above Proficient		Gap
Jurisdiction	Black	White, non-Latino	White/Black
USA	12%	45%	33%
Maryland	17%	59%	*41%*

The *Benchmark* for male Black students in 8th Grade Reading is Connecticut, with 19% of male Black students scoring at or above Proficient. The *Benchmark* for 8th Grade Mathematics is Massachusetts, with 26% of male Black students scoring at or above Proficient.

Discipline Inequities

The U.S. Department of Education's Office for Civil Rights has not yet made out-of-school suspension data disaggregated by gender available at the state level for 2009/10. The Center for Civil Rights Remedies at The Civil Rights Project has calculated *combined* male and female percentages from the OCR samples.[39]

State	Black	White, non-Latino	Black/White Ratio
Maryland	11	4.9	2.2

Baltimore City

Inequities in Graduation Rates

Male students in Baltimore in 2010/11 graduated at higher rates than in 2009/10, but below the state and national averages for each group.

The *Benchmark* for graduation rates of male Black students for school districts enrolling more than 10,000 male Black students is 73% (Montgomery County, MD).

	Male Graduation Rate: 2010/11		Male Graduation Rate: 2009/10	
Jurisdiction	Black	White, non-Latino	Black	White, non-Latino
USA	53%	77%	52%	78%
Maryland	59%	80%	57%	81%
Baltimore City	*45%*	*46%*	*40%*	*43%*

National Assessment of Educational Progress (NAEP)

NAEP 8th Grade Reading results for Baltimore are below state and national averages for male Black students.

Percentages of Male Black and Male White, Non-Latino, Students at or Above Proficient
Reading, Grade 8, 2011

	Percent at or Above Proficient		Gap
Jurisdiction	Black	White, non-Latino	White/Black
USA	10%	35%	25%
Maryland	17%	45%	28%
Baltimore City	*7%*	‡[40]	-

NAEP 8th Grade Mathematics results for Baltimore are below state and national averages for male Black students.

[39] From: Losen, Daniel J. and Jonathan Gillispie. Opportunities Suspended: The Disparate Impact of Disciplinary Exclusion from School. The Center for Civil Rights Remedies at The Civil Rights Project, August 2012. *Source:* CRDC, 2009-2010 (numbers from national sample rounded to one decimal). Maryland had a large district removed from the sample so its estimates should be reviewed with extra caution.

[40] Indicates insufficient sample size.

Percentages of Male Black and Male White, Non-Latino, Students at or Above Proficient Mathematics, Grade 8, 2011

	Percent at or Above Proficient		Gap
Jurisdiction	Black	White, non-Latino	White/Black
USA	12%	45%	33%
Maryland	17%	59%	*41%*
Baltimore City	*11%*	‡[41]	-

The *Benchmark* for male Black students in 8th Grade Reading is Connecticut, with 19% of male Black students scoring at or above Proficient. The *Benchmark* for 8th Grade Mathematics is Massachusetts, with 26% of male Black students scoring at or above Proficient.

Discipline and Advanced Placement Inequities

Out-of-school suspension ratios are a measure of the extent to which disparate application of school discipline policies affect students from different racial and ethnic groups. Male Black students with disabilities were nearly twice as likely to receive out-of-school suspensions than were White, non-Latino, students. Female Black students with disabilities were more than eight times as likely to receive out-of-school suspensions than were White, non-Latino, students. Male Black students without disabilities were two and a third times as likely to receive out-of-school suspensions as were male White, non-Latino, students. Female Black students without disabilities were nearly four times as likely to receive out-of-school suspensions as were female White, non-Latino, students.

Enrollment ratios in Advanced Placement Mathematics are an indicator of the differing opportunities to learn that may be provided to students on the basis of race and ethnicity. Black students were enrolled in AP Mathematics at approximately one-third the rate of White, non-Latino, students.

Baltimore County

Inequities in Graduation Rates

Male students in Baltimore County continue to graduate at higher rates than the national averages for each group.

The *Benchmark* for graduation rates of male Black students for school districts enrolling more than 10,000 male Black students is 73% (Montgomery County, MD).

	Male Graduation Rate: 2010/11		Male Graduation Rate: 2009/10	
Jurisdiction	Black	White, non-Latino	Black	White, non-Latino
USA	53%	77%	52%	78%
Maryland	59%	80%	57%	81%
Baltimore County	68%	78%	67%	79%

Discipline and Advanced Placement Inequities

Out-of-school suspension ratios are a measure of the extent to which disparate application of school discipline policies affect students from different racial and ethnic groups. Black students with disabilities were nearly twice as likely to receive out-of-school suspensions than were White, non-Latino, students. Male Black students without disabilities were two and a third times as likely to receive out-of-school suspensions as were male White, non-Latino, students. Female Black students without disabilities were nearly three times as likely to receive out-of-school suspensions as were female White, non-Latino, students.

[41] Indicates insufficient sample size.

Enrollment ratios in Advanced Placement Mathematics are an indicator of the differing opportunities to learn that may be provided to students on the basis of race and ethnicity. Black students were enrolled in AP Mathematics at half or less than the rate of White, non-Latino, students.

Montgomery County

Inequities in Graduation Rates

Male students in Montgomery County continued to graduate at higher rates than the state and national averages for each group.

The *Benchmark* for graduation rates of male Black students for school districts enrolling more than 10,000 male Black students is 73% (Montgomery County, MD).

	Male Graduation Rate: 2010/11		Male Graduation Rate: 2009/10	
Jurisdiction	Black	White, non-Latino	Black	White, non-Latino
USA	53%	77%	52%	78%
Maryland	59%	80%	57%	81%
Montgomery County	73%	87%	74%	91%

Discipline and Advanced Placement Inequities

Out-of-school suspension ratios are a measure of the extent to which disparate application of school discipline policies affect students from different racial and ethnic groups. Male Black students with disabilities were three and a half times as likely to receive out-of-school suspensions than were male White, non-Latino, students. Female Black students with disabilities were nearly eight and a half times as likely to receive out-of-school suspensions as were female White, non-Latino, students. Male Black students without disabilities were four and a half times as likely to receive out-of-school suspensions as were male White, non-Latino, students. Female Black students without disabilities were nearly seven times as likely to receive out-of-school suspensions as were female White, non-Latino, students.

Enrollment ratios in Advanced Placement Mathematics are an indicator of the differing opportunities to learn that may be provided to students on the basis of race and ethnicity. Black students were enrolled in AP Mathematics at one-third or less than the rate of White, non-Latino, students.

Prince George's County

Inequities in Graduation Rates

Male Black students in Prince George's County continue to graduate at higher rates than the national average for the group, but below the state average. White, non-Latino, students graduated at rates below both the state and national averages.

The *Benchmark* for graduation rates of male Black students for school districts enrolling more than 10,000 male Black students is 73% (Montgomery County, MD).

	Male Graduation Rate: 2010/11		Male Graduation Rate: 2009/10	
Jurisdiction	Black	White, non-Latino	Black	White, non-Latino
USA	53%	77%	52%	78%
Maryland	59%	80%	57%	81%
Prince George's	58%	*64%*	55%	*60%*

Discipline and Advanced Placement Inequities

Out-of-school suspension ratios are a measure of the extent to which disparate application of school discipline policies affect students from different racial and ethnic groups. Male Black students with disabilities were two and a half times as likely to receive out-of-school suspensions than were male White, non-Latino, students. Female Black students with disabilities were nearly six times as likely to receive out-of-school suspensions as were female White, non-Latino, students. Male Black students without disabilities were three and a half times as likely to receive out-of-school suspensions as were male White, non-Latino, students. Female Black students without disabilities were nearly three times as likely to receive out-of-school suspensions as were female White, non-Latino, students.

Enrollment ratios in Advanced Placement Mathematics are an indicator of the differing opportunities to learn that may be provided to students on the basis of race and ethnicity. Black students were enrolled in AP Mathematics at one-quarter or less than the rate of White, non-Latino, students.

MASSACHUSETTS

Inequities in Graduation Rates

Male students in Massachusetts in 2010/11 graduated at lower rates than in 2009/10, but male Black and White, non-Latino, rates were again above each group's national average.

The *Benchmark* for graduation rates of male Black students for states enrolling more than 10,000 Black male students is 77% (Arizona). The *Benchmark* for states with at least one district enrolling more than 10,000 Black male students is New Jersey (73%).

	Male Graduation Rate: 2010/11		Male Graduation Rate: 2009/10	
Jurisdiction	Black	White, non-Latino	Black	White, non-Latino
USA	53%	77%	52%	78%
Massachusetts	56%	82%	60%	83%

Comparison of Estimated Graduation Rates by Gender: 2010/11

The gender gap for Black students in Massachusetts is fourteen points, while that for White, non-Latino, students is five points.

	Male Graduation Rate		Female Graduation Rate	
Jurisdiction	Black	White, non-Latino	Black	White, non-Latino
USA	53%	77%	63%	81%
Massachusetts	56%	82%	70%	87%

National Assessment of Educational Progress (NAEP)

NAEP 8th Grade Reading results for Massachusetts male Black and White, non-Latino, students are considerably above national averages.

Percentages of Male Black and Male White, Non-Latino, Students at or Above Proficient
Reading, Grade 8, 2011

	Percent at or Above Proficient		Gap
Jurisdiction	Black	White, non-Latino	White/Black
USA	10%	35%	25%
Massachusetts	13%	48%	*35%*

NAEP 8th Grade Mathematics results for Massachusetts are considerably above those for the nation as a whole for male Black and White, non-Latino, students.

Percentages of Male Black and Male White, Non-Latino, Students at or Above Proficient
Mathematics, Grade 8, 2011

	Percent at or Above Proficient		Gap
Jurisdiction	Black	White, non-Latino	White/Black
USA	12%	45%	33%
Massachusetts	26%	58%	32%

The *Benchmark* for male Black students in 8th Grade Reading is Connecticut, with 19% of male Black students scoring at or above Proficient. The *Benchmark* for 8th Grade Mathematics is Massachusetts, with 26% of male Black students scoring at or above Proficient.

Discipline Inequities

The U.S. Department of Education's Office for Civil Rights has not yet made out-of-school suspension data disaggregated by gender available at the state level for 2009/10. The Center for Civil Rights Remedies at The Civil Rights Project has calculated *combined* male and female percentages from the OCR samples.[42]

State	Black	White, non-Latino	Black/White Ratio
Massachusetts	11.5	4.3	2.7

Boston

Inequities in Graduation Rates

Male students in Boston in 2010/11 graduated at lower rates than in 2009/10, below each group's state and national average.

The *Benchmark* for graduation rates of male Black students for school districts enrolling more than 10,000 male Black students is 73% (Montgomery County, MD).

	Male Graduation Rate: 2010/11		Male Graduation Rate: 2009/10	
Jurisdiction	Black	White, non-Latino	Black	White, non-Latino
USA	53%	77%	52%	78%
Massachusetts	56%	82%	60%	83%
Boston	*49%*	*65%*	*50%*	*68%*

National Assessment of Educational Progress (NAEP)

NAEP 8th Grade Reading results for Boston male Black and White, non-Latino, students are at national but below state averages; those for male White, non-Latino, students are above national but below state averages.

Percentages of Male Black and Male White, Non-Latino, Students at or Above Proficient
Reading, Grade 8, 2011

	Percent at or Above Proficient		Gap
Jurisdiction	Black	White, non-Latino	White/Black
USA	10%	35%	25%
Massachusetts	13%	48%	*35%*
Boston	10%	45%	*35%*

NAEP 8th Grade Mathematics results for Boston are above those for the nation as a whole for male Black and White, non-Latino, students; they are below state rates for male Black students and male White, non-Latino, students.

42 From: Losen, Daniel J. and Jonathan Gillispie. Opportunities Suspended: The Disparate Impact of Disciplinary Exclusion from School. The Center for Civil Rights Remedies at The Civil Rights Project, August 2012. *Source:* CRDC, 2009-2010 (numbers from national sample rounded to one decimal).

Percentages of Male Black and Male White, Non-Latino, Students at or Above Proficient
Mathematics, Grade 8, 2011

	Percent at or Above Proficient		Gap
Jurisdiction	Black	White, non-Latino	White/Black
USA	12%	45%	33%
Massachusetts	26%	58%	32%
Boston	22%	56%	*35%*

The *Benchmark* for male Black students in 8th Grade Reading is Connecticut, with 19% of male Black students scoring at or above Proficient. The *Benchmark* for 8th Grade Mathematics is Massachusetts, with 26% of male Black students scoring at or above Proficient.

Discipline and Advanced Placement Inequities

Out-of-school suspension ratios are a measure of the extent to which disparate application of school discipline policies affect students from different racial and ethnic groups. Male Black students with disabilities were more than twice as likely to receive out-of-school suspensions than were male White, non-Latino, students. Female Black students with disabilities were also more than twice as likely to receive out-of-school suspensions as were female White, non-Latino, students. Male Black students without disabilities were nearly half again as likely to receive out-of-school suspensions as were male White, non-Latino, students. Female Black students without disabilities were nearly two and a quarter times as likely to receive out-of-school suspensions as were female White, non-Latino, students.

Enrollment ratios in Advanced Placement Mathematics are an indicator of the differing opportunities to learn that may be provided to students on the basis of race and ethnicity. Black students were enrolled in AP Mathematics at between and three-quarters of the rate of White, non-Latino, students.

MICHIGAN

Inequities in Graduation Rates

Male students in Michigan in 2010/11 graduated at higher rates than in 2009/10, White, non-Latino, students graduating at rates slightly above that group's national average.

The *Benchmark* for graduation rates of male Black students for states enrolling more than 10,000 Black male students is 77% (Arizona). The *Benchmark* for states with at least one district enrolling more than 10,000 Black male students is New Jersey (73%).

	Male Graduation Rate: 2010/11		Male Graduation Rate: 2009/10	
Jurisdiction	Black	White, non-Latino	Black	White, non-Latino
USA	53%	77%	52%	78%
Michigan	*49%*	78%	*37%*	*74%*

Comparison of Estimated Graduation Rates by Gender: 2010/11

The gender gap for Black students in Michigan is eight points, while that for White, non-Latino, students is three points.

	Male Graduation Rate		Female Graduation Rate	
Jurisdiction	Black	White, non-Latino	Black	White, non-Latino
USA	53%	77%	63%	81%
Michigan	*49%*	78%	*57%*	81%

National Assessment of Educational Progress (NAEP)

NAEP 8th Grade Reading results for Michigan are below national averages for male Black and White, non-Latino, students.

Percentages of Male Black and Male White, Non-Latino, Students at or Above Proficient
Reading, Grade 8, 2011

	Percent at or Above Proficient		Gap
Jurisdiction	Black	White, non-Latino	White/Black
USA	10%	35%	25%
Michigan	*7%*	*29%*	23%

NAEP 8th Grade Mathematics results for Michigan are below national averages for Black and White, non-Latino, students.

Percentages of Male Black and Male White, Non-Latino, Students at or Above Proficient
Mathematics, Grade 8, 2011

	Percent at or Above Proficient		Gap
Jurisdiction	Black	White, non-Latino	White/Black
USA	12%	45%	33%
Michigan	*7%*	*37%*	30%

The *Benchmark* for male Black students in 8th Grade Reading is Connecticut, with 19% of male Black students scoring at or above Proficient. The *Benchmark* for 8th Grade Mathematics is Massachusetts, with 26% of male Black students scoring at or above Proficient.

Discipline Inequities

The U.S. Department of Education's Office for Civil Rights has not yet made out-of-school suspension data disaggregated by gender available at the state level for 2009/10. The Center for Civil Rights Remedies at The Civil Rights Project has calculated *combined* male and female percentages from the OCR samples.[43]

State	Black	White, non-Latino	Black/White Ratio
Michigan	22.1	6.2	3.6

Detroit

Inequities in Graduation Rates

Male students in Detroit in 2010/11 were reported as graduating at remarkably higher rates than in 2009/10, remaining, however, far below each group's state and national averages.

The *Benchmark* for graduation rates of male Black students for school districts enrolling more than 10,000 male Black students is 73% (Montgomery County, MD).

	Male Graduation Rate: 2010/11		Male Graduation Rate: 2009/10	
Jurisdiction	Black	White, non-Latino	Black	White, non-Latino
USA	53%	77%	52%	78%
Michigan	*49%*	78%	*37%*	*74%*
Detroit	*35%*	*38%*	*20%*	*7%*

National Assessment of Educational Progress (NAEP)

NAEP 8th Grade Reading results for Detroit are below state and national averages for male Black students.

Percentages of Male Black and Male White, Non-Latino, Students at or Above Proficient
Reading, Grade 8, 2011

	Percent at or Above Proficient		Gap
Jurisdiction	Black	White, non-Latino	White/Black
USA	10%	35%	25%
Michigan	*7%*	*29%*	23%
Detroit	*5%*	‡[44]	-

NAEP 8th Grade Mathematics results for Detroit are below state and national averages for Black students.

[43] From: Losen, Daniel J. and Jonathan Gillispie. Opportunities Suspended: The Disparate Impact of Disciplinary Exclusion from School. The Center for Civil Rights Remedies at The Civil Rights Project, August 2012. *Source:* CRDC, 2009-2010 (numbers from national sample rounded to one decimal).

[44] Indicates insufficient sample size.

Percentages of Male Black and Male White, Non-Latino, Students at or Above Proficient Mathematics, Grade 8, 2011

	Percent at or Above Proficient		Gap
Jurisdiction	Black	White, non-Latino	White/Black
USA	12%	45%	33%
Michigan	*7%*	*37%*	30%
Detroit	*3%*	‡[45]	-

The *Benchmark* for male Black students in 8th Grade Reading is Connecticut, with 19% of male Black students scoring at or above Proficient. The *Benchmark* for 8th Grade Mathematics is Massachusetts, with 26% of male Black students scoring at or above Proficient.

Discipline and Advanced Placement Inequities

Out-of-school suspension ratios are a measure of the extent to which disparate application of school discipline policies affect students from different racial and ethnic groups. Male Black students with disabilities were twice as likely to receive out-of-school suspensions as were male White, non-Latino, students. Female Black students with disabilities were five times as likely to receive out-of-school suspensions as were female White, non-Latino, students. Male Black students without disabilities were more than two and a half times as likely to receive out-of-school suspensions as were White, non-Latino, students. Female Black students without disabilities were nearly three times as likely to receive out-of-school suspensions as were White, non-Latino, students.

Enrollment ratios in Advanced Placement Mathematics are an indicator of the differing opportunities to learn that may be provided to students on the basis of race and ethnicity. Male Black students were enrolled in AP Mathematics at one-fifth the rate of male White, non-Latino, students. Female Black students were enrolled in AP Mathematics at less than half the rate of female White, non-Latino, students.

[45] Indicates insufficient sample size.

MINNESOTA

Inequities in Graduation Rates
Male students in Minnesota in 2010/11 graduated at similar rates as in 2009/10.

The *Benchmark* for graduation rates of male Black students for states enrolling more than 10,000 Black male students is 77% (Arizona). The *Benchmark* for states with at least one district enrolling more than 10,000 Black male students is New Jersey (73%).

	Male Graduation Rate: 2010/11		Male Graduation Rate: 2009/10	
Jurisdiction	Black	White, non-Latino	Black	White, non-Latino
USA	53%	77%	52%	78%
Minnesota	65%	93%	65%	89%

Comparison of Estimated Graduation Rates by Gender: 2010/11
The gender gaps for students in Minnesota are minimal.

	Male Graduation Rate		Female Graduation Rate	
Jurisdiction	Black	White, non-Latino	Black	White, non-Latino
USA	53%	77%	63%	81%
Minnesota	65%	93%	65%	94%

National Assessment of Educational Progress (NAEP)
NAEP 8th Grade Reading results for Minnesota are above national averages in each category.

Percentages of Male Black and Male White, Non-Latino, Students at or Above Proficient
Reading, Grade 8, 2011

	Percent at or Above Proficient		Gap
Jurisdiction	Black	White, non-Latino	White/Black
USA	10%	35%	25%
Minnesota	12%	38%	*27%*

NAEP 8th Grade Mathematics results for Minnesota are above those for the nation as a whole in each category.

Percentages of Male Black and Male White, Non-Latino, Students at or Above Proficient
Mathematics, Grade 8, 2011

	Percent at or Above Proficient		Gap
Jurisdiction	Black	White, non-Latino	White/Black
USA	12%	45%	33%
Minnesota	17%	54%	*37%*

The *Benchmark* for male Black students in 8th Grade Reading is Connecticut, with 19% of male Black students scoring at or above Proficient. The *Benchmark* for 8th Grade Mathematics is Massachusetts, with 26% of male Black students scoring at or above Proficient.

Discipline Inequities

The U.S. Department of Education's Office for Civil Rights has not yet made out-of-school suspension data disaggregated by gender available at the state level for 2009/10. The Center for Civil Rights Remedies at The Civil Rights Project has calculated *combined* male and female percentages from the OCR samples.[46]

State	Black	White, non-Latino	Black/White Ratio
Minnesota	17.6	2.3	7.7

[46] From: Losen, Daniel J. and Jonathan Gillispie. Opportunities Suspended: The Disparate Impact of Disciplinary Exclusion from School. The Center for Civil Rights Remedies at The Civil Rights Project, August 2012. *Source:* CRDC, 2009-2010 (numbers from national sample rounded to one decimal).

MISSISSIPPI

Inequities in Graduation Rates

Male students in Mississippi in 2010/11 graduated at similar rates as in 2009/10, below each group's national average.

The *Benchmark* for graduation rates of male Black students for states enrolling more than 10,000 Black male students is 77% (Arizona). The *Benchmark* for states with at least one district enrolling more than 10,000 Black male students is New Jersey (73%).

	Male Graduation Rate: 2010/11		Male Graduation Rate: 2009/10	
Jurisdiction	Black	White, non-Latino	Black	White, non-Latino
USA	53%	77%	52%	78%
Mississippi	*52%*	*63%*	*51%*	*62%*

Comparison of Estimated Graduation Rates by Gender: 2010/11

The gender gap for Black students in Mississippi is eleven points, while that for White, non-Latino, students is six points.

	Male Graduation Rate		Female Graduation Rate	
Jurisdiction	Black	White, non-Latino	Black	White, non-Latino
USA	53%	77%	63%	81%
Mississippi	*52%*	*63%*	63%	*69%*

National Assessment of Educational Progress (NAEP)

NAEP 8th Grade Reading results for Mississippi are below those for the nation as a whole for male Black and White, non-Latino, students.

Percentages of Male Black and Male White, Non-Latino, Students at or Above Proficient
Reading, Grade 8, 2011

	Percent at or Above Proficient		Gap
Jurisdiction	Black	White, non-Latino	White/Black
USA	10%	35%	25%
Mississippi	*7%*	*27%*	19%

NAEP 8th Grade Mathematics results for Mississippi are below those for the nation as a whole for male Black and White, non-Latino, students.

Percentages of Male Black and Male White, Non-Latino, Students at or Above Proficient
Mathematics, Grade 8, 2011

	Percent at or Above Proficient		Gap
Jurisdiction	Black	White, non-Latino	White/Black
USA	12%	45%	33%
Mississippi	*8%*	*28%*	20%

The *Benchmark* for male Black students in 8th Grade Reading is Connecticut, with 19% of male Black students scoring at or above Proficient. The *Benchmark* for 8th Grade Mathematics is Massachusetts, with 26% of male Black students scoring at or above Proficient.

Discipline Inequities
The U.S. Department of Education's Office for Civil Rights has not yet made out-of-school suspension data disaggregated by gender available at the state level for 2009/10. The Center for Civil Rights Remedies at The Civil Rights Project has calculated *combined* male and female percentages from the OCR samples.[47]

State	Black	White, non-Latino	Black/White Ratio
Mississippi	17.6	6.4	2.8

Jackson City
Inequities in Graduation Rates
Male students in Jackson in 2010/11 graduated at higher rates than in 2009/10, but remained considerably below each group's national average. Male White, non-Latino, students graduated at higher rates in 2010/11 than in 2009/10, but remained considerably below the national average for that group. The year-on-year change for male Black students is notable.

The *Benchmark* for graduation rates of male Black students for states enrolling more than 10,000 Black male students is 77% (Arizona). The *Benchmark* for states with at least one district enrolling more than 10,000 Black male students is New Jersey (73%).

	Male Graduation Rate: 2010/11		Male Graduation Rate: 2009/10	
Jurisdiction	Black	White, non-Latino	Black	White, non-Latino
USA	53%	77%	52%	78%
Mississippi	*52%*	*63%*	*51%*	*62%*
Jackson	*43%*	*53%*	*28%*	*42%*

Discipline and Advanced Placement Inequities
Out-of-school suspension ratios are a measure of the extent to which disparate application of school discipline policies affect students from different racial and ethnic groups. Female Black students without disabilities were more than twice as likely to receive out-of-school suspensions as were White, non-Latino, students.

Enrollment ratios in Advanced Placement Mathematics are an indicator of the differing opportunities to learn that may be provided to students on the basis of race and ethnicity. Male Black students were enrolled in AP Mathematics at one-fifth the rate of male White, non-Latino, students. Female Black students were enrolled in AP Mathematics at less than half the rate of female White, non-Latino, students.

[47] From: Losen, Daniel J. and Jonathan Gillispie. Opportunities Suspended: The Disparate Impact of Disciplinary Exclusion from School. The Center for Civil Rights Remedies at The Civil Rights Project, August 2012. *Source:* CRDC, 2009-2010 (numbers from national sample rounded to one decimal).

MISSOURI

Inequities in Graduation Rates

Male Black students in Missouri in 2010/11 graduated at slightly higher rates in 2009/10, above the group's national average. Male White, non-Latino, students graduated at the same rates in 2010/11 as in 2009/10, also above the national average for that group.

The *Benchmark* for graduation rates of male Black students for states enrolling more than 10,000 Black male students is 77% (Arizona). The *Benchmark* for states with at least one district enrolling more than 10,000 Black male students is New Jersey (73%).

	Male Graduation Rate: 2010/11		Male Graduation Rate: 2009/10	
Jurisdiction	Black	White, non-Latino	Black	White, non-Latino
USA	53%	77%	52%	78%
Missouri	58%	81%	56%	81%

Comparison of Estimated Graduation Rates by Gender: 2010/11

The gender gap for Black students in Missouri is nine points, while that for White, non-Latino, students is four points.

	Male Graduation Rate		Female Graduation Rate	
Jurisdiction	Black	White, non-Latino	Black	White, non-Latino
USA	53%	77%	63%	81%
Missouri	58%	81%	67%	85%

National Assessment of Educational Progress (NAEP)

NAEP 8th Grade Reading results for Missouri are below national averages for male Black and White, non-Latino, students.

Percentages of Male Black and Male White, Non-Latino, Students at or Above Proficient
Reading, Grade 8, 2011

	Percent at or Above Proficient		Gap
Jurisdiction	Black	White, non-Latino	White/Black
USA	10%	35%	25%
Missouri	*8%*	*33%*	25%

NAEP 8th Grade Mathematics results for Missouri are below national averages for male Black and White, non-Latino, students.

Percentages of Male Black and Male White, Non-Latino, Students at or Above Proficient
Mathematics, Grade 8, 2011

	Percent at or Above Proficient		Gap
Jurisdiction	Black	White, non-Latino	White/Black
USA	12%	45%	33%
Missouri	*7%*	*38%*	31%

The *Benchmark* for male Black students for 8th Grade Reading is Connecticut, with 19% of male Black students scoring at or above Proficient. The *Benchmark* for 8th Grade Mathematics is Massachusetts, with 26% of male Black students scoring at or above Proficient.

Discipline Inequities

The U.S. Department of Education's Office for Civil Rights has not yet made out-of-school suspension data disaggregated by gender available at the state level for 2009/10. The Center for Civil Rights Remedies at The Civil Rights Project has calculated *combined* male and female percentages from the OCR samples.[48]

State	Black	White, non-Latino	Black/White Ratio
Missouri	22.8	4.4	5.2

St. Louis

Inequities in Graduation Rates

Male Black and White, non-Latino, students in St. Louis in 2010/11 graduated at higher rates than in 2009/10, but each group remained below state and national averages.

The *Benchmark* for graduation rates of male Black students for school districts enrolling more than 10,000 male Black students is 73% (Montgomery County, MD).

	Male Graduation Rate: 2010/11		Male Graduation Rate: 2009/10	
Jurisdiction	Black	White, non-Latino	Black	White, non-Latino
USA	53%	77%	52%	78%
Missouri	58%	81%	56%	81%
St. Louis	*37%*	*45%*	*33%*	*41%*

Discipline and Advanced Placement Inequities

Out-of-school suspension ratios are a measure of the extent to which disparate application of school discipline policies affect students from different racial and ethnic groups. Male Black students with disabilities were more than twice as likely to receive out-of-school suspensions as were male White, non-Latino, students. Female Black students with disabilities were more than three times as likely to receive out-of-school suspensions as were female White, non-Latino, students. Male Black students without disabilities were more than three times as likely to receive out-of-school suspensions as were White, non-Latino, students. Female Black students without disabilities were nearly five times as likely to receive out-of-school suspensions as were White, non-Latino, students.

Enrollment ratios in Advanced Placement Mathematics are an indicator of the differing opportunities to learn that may be provided to students on the basis of race and ethnicity. Black students were enrolled in AP Mathematics at approximately half the rate of White, non-Latino, students.

---

48 From: Losen, Daniel J. and Jonathan Gillispie. Opportunities Suspended: The Disparate Impact of Disciplinary Exclusion from School. The Center for Civil Rights Remedies at The Civil Rights Project, August 2012. *Source:* CRDC, 2009-2010 (numbers from national sample rounded to one decimal).

MONTANA

Inequities in Graduation Rates

The very few male Black students in Montana in 2010/11 graduated at higher rates than in 2009/10, far above each group's national average. Male White, non-Latino, students graduated at slightly lower rates in 2010/11 than in 2009/10, but were also above the national average for that group.

The *Benchmark* for graduation rates of male Black students for states enrolling more than 10,000 Black male students is 77% (Arizona). The *Benchmark* for states with at least one district enrolling more than 10,000 Black male students is New Jersey (73%).

	Male Graduation Rate: 2010/11		Male Graduation Rate: 2009/10	
Jurisdiction	Black	White, non-Latino	Black	White, non-Latino
USA	53%	77%	52%	78%
Montana	91%	80%	63%	82%

Comparison of Estimated Graduation Rates by Gender: 2010/11

The gender gap for Black students in Montana is nine points, while that for White, non-Latino, students is one point.

	Male Graduation Rate		Female Graduation Rate	
Jurisdiction	Black	White, non-Latino	Black	White, non-Latino
USA	53%	77%	63%	81%
Montana	91%	80%	100%	81%

National Assessment of Educational Progress (NAEP)

NAEP 8th Grade Reading results for Montana are above the national average for male White, non-Latino, students.

Percentages of Male Black and Male White, Non-Latino, Students at or Above Proficient
Reading, Grade 8, 2011

	Percent at or Above Proficient		Gap
Jurisdiction	Black	White, non-Latino	White/Black
USA	10%	35%	25%
Montana	‡	38%	-

NAEP 8th Grade Mathematics results for Montana are above the national average for male White, non-Latino, students.

Percentages of Male Black and Male White, Non-Latino, Students at or Above Proficient
Mathematics, Grade 8, 2011

	Percent at or Above Proficient		Gap
Jurisdiction	Black	White, non-Latino	White/Black
USA	12%	45%	33%
Montana	‡	50%	-

The *Benchmark* for male Black students for 8th Grade Reading is Connecticut, with 19% of male Black students scoring at or above Proficient. The *Benchmark* for 8th Grade Mathematics is Massachusetts, with 26% of male Black students scoring at or above Proficient.

Discipline Inequities

The U.S. Department of Education's Office for Civil Rights has not yet made out-of-school suspension data disaggregated by gender available at the state level for 2009/10. The Center for Civil Rights Remedies at The Civil Rights Project has calculated *combined* male and female percentages from the OCR samples.[49]

State	Black	White, non-Latino	Black/White Ratio
Montana	3.4	3.8	0.9

[49] From: Losen, Daniel J. and Jonathan Gillispie. Opportunities Suspended: The Disparate Impact of Disciplinary Exclusion from School. The Center for Civil Rights Remedies at The Civil Rights Project, August 2012. *Source:* CRDC, 2009-2010 (numbers from national sample rounded to one decimal).

NEBRASKA

Inequities in Graduation Rates

The few male Black students in Nebraska in 2010/11 graduated at a lower rate than in 2009/10, below the group's national average. Male White, non-Latino, students graduated at the same rate in 2010/11 as in 2009/10, above the national average for that group.

The *Benchmark* for graduation rates of male Black students for states enrolling more than 10,000 Black male students is 77% (Arizona). The *Benchmark* for states with at least one district enrolling more than 10,000 Black male students is New Jersey (73%).

	Male Graduation Rate: 2010/11		Male Graduation Rate: 2009/10	
Jurisdiction	Black	White, non-Latino	Black	White, non-Latino
USA	53%	77%	52%	78%
Nebraska	*40%*	86%	*44%*	86%

Comparison of Estimated Graduation Rates by Gender: 2010/11

The gender gap for Black students in Nebraska is four points, while that for White, non-Latino, students is a reversed single point.

	Male Graduation Rate		Female Graduation Rate	
Jurisdiction	Black	White, non-Latino	Black	White, non-Latino
USA	53%	77%	63%	81%
Nebraska	*40%*	86%	*44%*	85%

National Assessment of Educational Progress (NAEP)

NAEP 8th Grade Reading results for Nebraska are below national averages for male Black and White, non-Latino, students.

Percentages of Male Black and Male White, Non-Latino, Students at or Above Proficient
Reading, Grade 8, 2011

	Percent at or Above Proficient		Gap
Jurisdiction	Black	White, non-Latino	White/Black
USA	10%	35%	25%
Nebraska	*7%*	*34%*	*27%*

NAEP 8th Grade Mathematics results for Nebraska are below those for the nation as a whole in each category.

Percentages of Male Black and Male White, Non-Latino, Students at or Above Proficient
Mathematics, Grade 8, 2011

	Percent at or Above Proficient		Gap
Jurisdiction	Black	White, non-Latino	White/Black
USA	12%	45%	33%
Nebraska	*8%*	*41%*	*34%*

The *Benchmark* for male Black students for 8th Grade Reading is Connecticut, with 19% of male Black students scoring at or above Proficient. The *Benchmark* for 8th Grade Mathematics is Massachusetts, with 26% of male Black students scoring at or above Proficient.

Discipline Inequities
The U.S. Department of Education's Office for Civil Rights has not yet made out-of-school suspension data disaggregated by gender available at the state level for 2009/10. The Center for Civil Rights Remedies at The Civil Rights Project has calculated *combined* male and female percentages from the OCR samples.[50]

State	Black	White, non-Latino	Black/White Ratio
Nebraska	17.6	3.6	4.9

[50] From: Losen, Daniel J. and Jonathan Gillispie. Opportunities Suspended: The Disparate Impact of Disciplinary Exclusion from School. The Center for Civil Rights Remedies at The Civil Rights Project, August 2012. *Source:* CRDC, 2009-2010 (numbers from national sample rounded to one decimal).

NEVADA

Inequities in Graduation Rates

Male Black students in Nevada in 2010/11 graduated at a lower rate than in 2009/10, below the group's national average. Male White, non-Latino, students graduated at higher rates in 2010/11 than in 2009/10, but still below the national average for that group.

The *Benchmark* for graduation rates of male Black students for states enrolling more than 10,000 Black male students is 77% (Arizona). The *Benchmark* for states with at least one district enrolling more than 10,000 Black male students is New Jersey (73%).

	Male Graduation Rate: 2010/11		Male Graduation Rate: 2009/10	
Jurisdiction	Black	White, non-Latino	Black	White, non-Latino
USA	53%	77%	52%	78%
Nevada	*43%*	*65%*	52%	*61%*

Comparison of Estimated Graduation Rates by Gender: 2010/11

The gender gap for Black students in Nevada is four points, while that for White, non-Latino, students is five points.

	Male Graduation Rate		Female Graduation Rate	
Jurisdiction	Black	White, non-Latino	Black	White, non-Latino
USA	53%	77%	63%	81%
Nevada	*43%*	*65%*	*47%*	*70%*

National Assessment of Educational Progress (NAEP)

NAEP 8th Grade Reading results for Nevada are above the national average for male Black students and below the national averages for male White, non-Latino, students.

Percentages of Male Black and Male White, Non-Latino, Students at or Above Proficient
Reading, Grade 8, 2011

	Percent at or Above Proficient		Gap
Jurisdiction	Black	White, non-Latino	White/Black
USA	10%	35%	25%
Nevada	11%	*29%*	18%

NAEP 8th Grade Mathematics results for Nevada are above the national average for male Black students and below the national averages for male White, non-Latino, students.

Percentages of Male Black and Male White, Non-Latino, Students at or Above Proficient
Mathematics, Grade 8, 2011

	Percent at or Above Proficient		Gap
Jurisdiction	Black	White, non-Latino	White/Black
USA	12%	45%	33%
Nevada	16%	*44%*	27%

The *Benchmark* for male Black students for 8th Grade Reading is Connecticut, with 19% of male Black students scoring at or above Proficient. The *Benchmark* for 8th Grade Mathematics is Massachusetts, with 26% of male Black students scoring at or above Proficient.

Discipline Inequities

The U.S. Department of Education's Office for Civil Rights has not yet made out-of-school suspension data disaggregated by gender available at the state level for 2009/10. The Center for Civil Rights Remedies at The Civil Rights Project has calculated *combined* male and female percentages from the OCR samples.[51]

State	Black	White, non-Latino	Black/White Ratio
Nevada	22.6	8.2	2.8

Clark County

Inequities in Graduation Rates

Male Black and White, non-Latino, students in Clark County in 2010/11 graduated at higher rates than estimates for 2009/10, but below each group's national average.

The *Benchmark* for graduation rates of male Black students for school districts enrolling more than 10,000 male Black students is 73% (Montgomery County, MD).

	Male Graduation Rate: 2010/11		Male Graduation Rate: 2009/10	
Jurisdiction	Black	White, non-Latino	Black	White, non-Latino
USA	53%	77%	52%	78%
Nevada	*43%*	*65%*	52%	*61%*
Clark County	*43%*	*59%*	*22%*	*37%*

Discipline and Advanced Placement Inequities

Out-of-school suspension ratios are a measure of the extent to which disparate application of school discipline policies affect students from different racial and ethnic groups. Male Black students with disabilities were nearly three times as likely to receive out-of-school suspensions as were male White, non-Latino, students. Female Black students with disabilities were more than three times as likely to receive out-of-school suspensions as were female White, non-Latino, students. Male Black students without disabilities were more than three times as likely to receive out-of-school suspensions as were White, non-Latino, students. Female Black students without disabilities were nearly five times as likely to receive out-of-school suspensions as were White, non-Latino, students.

Enrollment ratios in Advanced Placement Mathematics are an indicator of the differing opportunities to learn that may be provided to students on the basis of race and ethnicity. Black students were enrolled in AP Mathematics at less than half the rate of White, non-Latino, students.

[51] From: Losen, Daniel J. and Jonathan Gillispie. Opportunities Suspended: The Disparate Impact of Disciplinary Exclusion from School. The Center for Civil Rights Remedies at The Civil Rights Project, August 2012. *Source:* CRDC, 2009-2010 (numbers from national sample rounded to one decimal).

NEW HAMPSHIRE

Inequities in Graduation Rates

Graduation rates for the very few Black students in New Hampshire could not be meaningfully estimated. Male White, non-Latino, students graduated at the same rate in 2010/11 as in 2009/10.

The *Benchmark* for graduation rates of male Black students for states enrolling more than 10,000 Black male students is 77% (Arizona). The *Benchmark* for states with at least one district enrolling more than 10,000 Black male students is New Jersey (73%).

	Male Graduation Rate: 2010/11		Male Graduation Rate: 2009/10	
Jurisdiction	Black	White, non-Latino	Black	White, non-Latino
USA	53%	77%	52%	78%
New Hampshire	-	80%	60%	80%

Comparison of Estimated Graduation Rates by Gender: 2010/11

The gender gap for White, non-Latino, students is 3 points.

	Male Graduation Rate		Female Graduation Rate	
Jurisdiction	Black	White, non-Latino	Black	White, non-Latino
USA	53%	77%	63%	81%
New Hampshire	-	80%	-	83%

National Assessment of Educational Progress (NAEP)

NAEP 8th Grade Reading results for New Hampshire are at the national average for male White, non-Latino, students.

Percentages of Male Black and Male White, Non-Latino, Students at or Above Proficient
Reading, Grade 8, 2011

	Percent at or Above Proficient		Gap
Jurisdiction	Black	White, non-Latino	White/Black
USA	10%	35%	25%
New Hampshire	‡[52]	35%	-

NAEP 8th Grade Mathematics results for New Hampshire are slightly below the national average for male White, non-Latino, students.

Percentages of Male Black and Male White, Non-Latino, Students at or Above Proficient
Mathematics, Grade 8, 2011

	Percent at or Above Proficient		Gap
Jurisdiction	Black	White, non-Latino	White/Black
USA	12%	45%	33%
New Hampshire	‡	*44%*	-

[52] Indicates insufficient sample size.

The *Benchmark* for male Black students for 8th Grade Reading is Connecticut, with 19% of male Black students scoring at or above Proficient. The *Benchmark* for 8th Grade Mathematics is Massachusetts, with 26% of male Black students scoring at or above Proficient.

Discipline Inequities

The U.S. Department of Education's Office for Civil Rights has not yet made out-of-school suspension data disaggregated by gender available at the state level for 2009/10. The Center for Civil Rights Remedies at The Civil Rights Project has calculated *combined* male and female percentages from the OCR samples.[53]

State	Black	White, non-Latino	Black/White Ratio
New Hampshire	11.4	6.1	1.9

[53] From: Losen, Daniel J. and Jonathan Gillispie. Opportunities Suspended: The Disparate Impact of Disciplinary Exclusion from School. The Center for Civil Rights Remedies at The Civil Rights Project, August 2012. *Source:* CRDC, 2009-2010 (numbers from national sample rounded to one decimal).

NEW JERSEY

Inequities in Graduation Rates

Male Black students in New Jersey in 2010/11 graduated at a higher rate than in 2009/10, above the group's national average. Male White, non-Latino, students graduated at the same rate in 2010/11 as in 2009/10, much above the national average for that group. Estimated graduation rates for the state are based on data published by its State Education Department.

The *Benchmark* for graduation rates of male Black students for states enrolling more than 10,000 Black male students is 77% (Arizona). The *Benchmark* for states with at least one district enrolling more than 10,000 Black male students is New Jersey (73%).

	Male Graduation Rate: 2010/11		Male Graduation Rate: 2009/10	
Jurisdiction	Black	White, non-Latino	Black	White, non-Latino
USA	53%	77%	52%	78%
New Jersey	73%	90%	63%	90%

Comparison of Estimated Graduation Rates by Gender: 2010/11

The gender gap for Black students in New Jersey is five points, while that for White, non-Latino, students is zero points.

	Male Graduation Rate		Female Graduation Rate	
Jurisdiction	Black	White, non-Latino	Black	White, non-Latino
USA	53%	77%	63%	81%
New Jersey	73%	90%	78%	90%

National Assessment of Educational Progress (NAEP)

NAEP 8th Grade Reading results for New Jersey are above national averages for male Black and White, non-Latino, students.

Percentages of Male Black and Male White, Non-Latino, Students at or Above Proficient
Reading, Grade 8, 2011

	Percent at or Above Proficient		Gap
Jurisdiction	Black	White, non-Latino	White/Black
USA	10%	35%	25%
New Jersey	12%	49%	*37%*

NAEP 8th Grade Mathematics results for New Jersey are above those for the nation as a whole in each category.

Percentages of Male Black and Male White, Non-Latino, Students at or Above Proficient
Mathematics, Grade 8, 2011

	Percent at or Above Proficient		Gap
Jurisdiction	Black	White, non-Latino	White/Black
USA	12%	45%	33%
New Jersey	22%	61%	*39%*

The *Benchmark* for male Black students for 8th Grade Reading is Connecticut, with 19% of male Black students scoring at or above Proficient. The *Benchmark* for 8th Grade Mathematics is Massachusetts, with 26% of male Black students scoring at or above Proficient.

Discipline Inequities
The U.S. Department of Education's Office for Civil Rights has not yet made out-of-school suspension data disaggregated by gender available at the state level for 2009/10. The Center for Civil Rights Remedies at The Civil Rights Project has calculated *combined* male and female percentages from the OCR samples.[54]

State	Black	White, non-Latino	Black/White Ratio
New Jersey	12	3.3	3.6

Newark
Inequities in Graduation Rates
Male Black students in Newark in 2010/11 graduated at a slightly higher rate than in 2009/10, above the group's state and national averages. Male White, non-Latino, students graduated at a lower rate in 2010/11 than in 2009/10, below the state and national averages for that group. Estimated graduation rates for the district are based on data published by its State Education Department. As questions have been raised about this data Newark has not been identified as a benchmark district.

The *Benchmark* for graduation rates of male Black students for school districts enrolling more than 10,000 male Black students is 73% (Montgomery County, MD).

	Male Graduation Rate: 2010/11		Male Graduation Rate: 2009/10	
Jurisdiction	Black	White, non-Latino	Black	White, non-Latino
USA	53%	77%	52%	78%
New Jersey	73%	90%	63%	90%
Newark	76%	*65%*	74%	*67%*

Discipline and Advanced Placement Inequities
Out-of-school suspension ratios are a measure of the extent to which disparate application of school discipline policies affect students from different racial and ethnic groups. Male Black students with disabilities were over half again as likely to receive out-of-school suspensions as were male White, non-Latino, students. Male Black students without disabilities were nearly nine times as likely to receive out-of-school suspensions as were White, non-Latino, students.

Enrollment ratios in Advanced Placement Mathematics are an indicator of the differing opportunities to learn that may be provided to students on the basis of race and ethnicity. Male Black students were enrolled in AP Mathematics at less than half the rate of male White, non-Latino, students. Female Black students were enrolled in AP Mathematics at just a quarter the rate of female White, non-Latino, students.

[54] From: Losen, Daniel J. and Jonathan Gillispie. Opportunities Suspended: The Disparate Impact of Disciplinary Exclusion from School. The Center for Civil Rights Remedies at The Civil Rights Project, August 2012. *Source:* CRDC, 2009-2010 (numbers from national sample rounded to one decimal).

NEW MEXICO

Inequities in Graduation Rates

Male Black students in New Mexico in 2010/11 graduated at a higher rate than in 2009/10, above the group's national average. Male White, non-Latino, students graduated at a higher rate in 2010/11 as in 2009/10, but still below the national average for that group.

The *Benchmark* for graduation rates of male Black students for states enrolling more than 10,000 Black male students is 77% (Arizona). The *Benchmark* for states with at least one district enrolling more than 10,000 Black male students is New Jersey (73%).

	Male Graduation Rate: 2010/11		Male Graduation Rate: 2009/10	
Jurisdiction	Black	White, non-Latino	Black	White, non-Latino
USA	53%	77%	52%	78%
New Mexico	56%	*66%*	*49%*	*62%*

Comparison of Estimated Graduation Rates by Gender: 2010/11

The gender gap for Black students in New Mexico is two points, while that for White, non-Latino, students is seven points.

	Male Graduation Rate		Female Graduation Rate	
Jurisdiction	Black	White, non-Latino	Black	White, non-Latino
USA	53%	77%	63%	81%
New Mexico	56%	*66%*	*58%*	*73%*

National Assessment of Educational Progress (NAEP)

NAEP 8th Grade Reading results for New Mexico are below national averages for male White, non-Latino, students.

Percentages of Male Black and Male White, Non-Latino, Students at or Above Proficient
Reading, Grade 8, 2011

	Percent at or Above Proficient		Gap
Jurisdiction	Black	White, non-Latino	White/Black
USA	10%	35%	25%
New Mexico	‡[55]	*30%*	-

NAEP 8th Grade Mathematics results for New Mexico are below national averages for White, non-Latino, students.

Percentages of Male Black and Male White, Non-Latino, Students at or Above Proficient
Mathematics, Grade 8, 2011

	Percent at or Above Proficient		Gap
Jurisdiction	Black	White, non-Latino	White/Black
USA	12%	45%	33%
New Mexico	‡	*41%*	-

[55] Indicates insufficient sample size.

The *Benchmark* for male Black students for 8th Grade Reading is Connecticut, with 19% of male Black students scoring at or above Proficient. The *Benchmark* for 8th Grade Mathematics is Massachusetts, with 26% of male Black students scoring at or above Proficient.

Discipline Inequities
The U.S. Department of Education's Office for Civil Rights has not yet made out-of-school suspension data disaggregated by gender available at the state level for 2009/10. The Center for Civil Rights Remedies at The Civil Rights Project has calculated *combined* male and female percentages from the OCR samples.[56]

State	Black	White, non-Latino	Black/White Ratio
New Mexico	6.1	4.4	1.4

[56] From: Losen, Daniel J. and Jonathan Gillispie. Opportunities Suspended: The Disparate Impact of Disciplinary Exclusion from School. The Center for Civil Rights Remedies at The Civil Rights Project, August 2012. *Source:* CRDC, 2009-2010 (numbers from national sample rounded to one decimal).

NEW YORK

Inequities in Graduation Rates
Male Black students in New York in 2010/11 graduated at a higher rate than in 2009/10, below the group's national average. Male White, non-Latino, students graduated at a lower rate in 2010/11 than in 2009/10, below the national average for that group. *These data are under review.* [57]

The *Benchmark* for graduation rates of male Black students for states enrolling more than 10,000 Black male students is 77% (Arizona). The *Benchmark* for states with at least one district enrolling more than 10,000 Black male students is New Jersey (73%).

	Male Graduation Rate: 2010/11		Male Graduation Rate: 2009/10	
Jurisdiction	Black	White, non-Latino	Black	White, non-Latino
USA	53%	77%	52%	78%
New York	*43%*	*73%*	*37%*	78%

Comparison of Estimated Graduation Rates by Gender: 2010/11
The gender gap for Black students in New York is five points, while that for White, non-Latino, students is two points.

	Male Graduation Rate		Female Graduation Rate	
Jurisdiction	Black	White, non-Latino	Black	White, non-Latino
USA	53%	77%	63%	81%
New York	*43%*	*73%*	*48%*	*75%*

National Assessment of Educational Progress (NAEP)
NAEP 8th Grade Reading results for New York are above those for the nation as a whole in each category.

Percentages of Male Black and Male White, Non-Latino, Students at or Above Proficient
Reading, Grade 8, 2011

	Percent at or Above Proficient		Gap
Jurisdiction	Black	White, non-Latino	White/Black
USA	10%	35%	25%
New York	15%	39%	24%

NAEP 8th Grade Mathematics results for New York are below those for the nation as a whole in each category.

[57] New York State enrollment and diploma data has been reported to the National Center for Education Statistics irregularly and is not considered as reliable as data from other states. The data presented here are best estimates, given the data available. They do not include "local diplomas," a non-college preparatory certificate that is in the process of abolition.

Percentages of Male Black and Male White, Non-Latino, Students at or Above Proficient
Mathematics, Grade 8, 2011

	Percent at or Above Proficient		Gap
Jurisdiction	Black	White, non-Latino	White/Black
USA	12%	45%	33%
New York	*11%*	*40%*	29%

The *Benchmark* for male Black students for 8th Grade Reading is Connecticut, with 19% of male Black students scoring at or above Proficient. The *Benchmark* for 8th Grade Mathematics is Massachusetts, with 26% of male Black students scoring at or above Proficient.

Discipline Inequities
Omitted because of data accuracy issues.

New York City
Inequities in Graduation Rates
Male Black students in New York City in 2010/11 graduated at a higher rate than in 2009/10, still far below the group's state and national averages. Male White, non-Latino, students graduated at a slightly lower rate in 2010/11 than in 2009/10, also below state and national averages. *These data are under review.* [58]

The *Benchmark* for graduation rates of male Black students for school districts enrolling more than 10,000 male Black students is 73% (Montgomery County, MD).

	Male Graduation Rate: 2010/11		Male Graduation Rate: 2009/10	
Jurisdiction	Black	White, non-Latino	Black	White, non-Latino
USA	53%	77%	52%	78%
New York	*43%*	*73%*	*37%*	78%
New York City	*38%*	*66%*	*28%*	*57%*

National Assessment of Educational Progress (NAEP)
NAEP 8th Grade Reading results for New York City for male Black students are above those for the nation, but below those for the state; results for male White, non-Latino, students are below those for both the state and nation.

Percentages of Male Black and Male White, Non-Latino, Students at or Above Proficient
Reading, Grade 8, 2011

	Percent at or Above Proficient		Gap
Jurisdiction	Black	White, non-Latino	White/Black
USA	10%	35%	25%
New York	15%	39%	24%
New York City	13%	*32%*	19%

[58] New York State enrollment and diploma data has been reported to the National Center for Education Statistics irregularly and is not considered as reliable as data from other states. The data presented here are best estimates, given the data available. They do not include "local diplomas," a non-college preparatory certificate that is in the process of abolition.

NAEP 8th Grade Mathematics results for New York City are below those for the state and nation for male Black students and above those for the state and nation for male White, non-Latino, students.

Percentages of Male Black and Male White, Non-Latino, Students at or Above Proficient
Mathematics, Grade 8, 2011

	Percent at or Above Proficient		Gap
Jurisdiction	Black	White, non-Latino	White/Black
USA	12%	45%	33%
New York	*11%*	*40%*	29%
New York City	*10%*	47%	*37%*

The *Benchmark* for male Black students for 8th Grade Reading is Connecticut, with 19% of male Black students scoring at or above Proficient. The *Benchmark* for 8th Grade Mathematics is Massachusetts, with 26% of male Black students scoring at or above Proficient.

Discipline and Advanced Placement Inequities

Out-of-school suspension ratios are a measure of the extent to which disparate application of school discipline policies affect students from different racial and ethnic groups. Male Black students with disabilities were nearly five times as likely to receive out-of-school suspensions than were male White, non-Latino, students. Female Black students with disabilities were more than seven and a quarter times as likely to receive out-of-school suspensions as were female White, non-Latino, students. Male Black students without disabilities were more than two and a third times as likely to receive out-of-school suspensions as were male White, non-Latino, students. Female Black students without disabilities were nearly than three and a quarter times as likely to receive out-of-school suspensions as were female White, non-Latino, students.

Enrollment ratios in Advanced Placement Mathematics are an indicator of the differing opportunities to learn that may be provided to students on the basis of race and ethnicity. Male Black students were enrolled in AP Mathematics at less than one-fifth of the rate of male White, non-Latino, students. Female Black students were enrolled in AP Mathematics at approximately between one-fifth and one-quarter of the rate of female White, non-Latino, students.

Rochester

Inequities in Graduation Rates

Male Black students in Rochester in 2009/10 graduated at a much lower rate than in 2007/8, far below the group's state and national averages. Male White, non-Latino, students graduated at a lower rate in 2010/11 than in 2009/10, also far below the state and national averages for that group. *These data are under review.* [59]

The *Benchmark* for graduation rates of male Black students for school districts enrolling more than 10,000 male Black students is 73% (Montgomery County, MD).

[59] New York State enrollment and diploma data has been reported to the National Center for Education Statistics irregularly and is not considered as reliable as data from other states. The data presented here are best estimates, given the data available. They do not include "local diplomas," a non-college preparatory certificate that is in the process of abolition.

	Male Graduation Rate: 2010/11		Male Graduation Rate: 2009/10	
Jurisdiction	Black	White, non-Latino	Black	White, non-Latino
USA	53%	77%	52%	78%
New York	*43%*	*73%*	*37%*	78%
Rochester	*16%*	*43%*	*9%*	*31%*

Discipline and Advanced Placement Inequities

Out-of-school suspension ratios are a measure of the extent to which disparate application of school discipline policies affect students from different racial and ethnic groups. The District did not report out-of-school suspension data.

Enrollment ratios in Advanced Placement Mathematics are an indicator of the differing opportunities to learn that may be provided to students on the basis of race and ethnicity. Black students were enrolled in AP Mathematics at approximately one quarter the rate of White, non-Latino, students.

NORTH CAROLINA

Inequities in Graduation Rates

Male Black students in North Carolina in 2010/11 graduated at a higher rate than in 2009/10, surpassing the group's national average. Male White, non-Latino, students also graduated at a higher rate in 2010/11 than in 2009/10, but did not reach the national average for that group.

The *Benchmark* for graduation rates of male Black students for states enrolling more than 10,000 Black male students is 77% (Arizona). The *Benchmark* for states with at least one district enrolling more than 10,000 Black male students is New Jersey (73%).

	Male Graduation Rate: 2010/11		Male Graduation Rate: 2009/10	
Jurisdiction	Black	White, non-Latino	Black	White, non-Latino
USA	53%	77%	52%	78%
North Carolina	59%	*73%*	58%	*71%*

Comparison of Estimated Graduation Rates by Gender: 2010/11

The gender gap for Black students in North Carolina is fifteen points, while that for White, non-Latino, students is nine points.

	Male Graduation Rate		Female Graduation Rate	
Jurisdiction	Black	White, non-Latino	Black	White, non-Latino
USA	53%	77%	63%	81%
North Carolina	59%	*73%*	74%	82%

National Assessment of Educational Progress (NAEP)

NAEP 8th Grade Reading results for North Carolina are below the national averages for male Black and White, non-Latino, students.

Percentages of Male Black and Male White, Non-Latino, Students at or Above Proficient
Reading, Grade 8, 2011

	Percent at or Above Proficient		Gap
Jurisdiction	Black	White, non-Latino	White/Black
USA	10%	35%	25%
North Carolina	*9%*	*33%*	25%

NAEP 8th Grade Mathematics results for North Carolina are above those for the nation as a whole for male Black and White, non-Latino, students.

Percentages of Male Black and Male White, Non-Latino, Students at or Above Proficient
Mathematics, Grade 8, 2011

	Percent at or Above Proficient		Gap
Jurisdiction	Black	White, non-Latino	White/Black
USA	12%	45%	33%
North Carolina	15%	49%	*34%*

The *Benchmark* for male Black students for 8th Grade Reading is Connecticut, with 19% of male Black students scoring at or above Proficient. The *Benchmark* for 8th Grade Mathematics is Massachusetts, with 26% of male Black students scoring at or above Proficient.

Discipline Inequities
The U.S. Department of Education's Office for Civil Rights has not yet made out-of-school suspension data disaggregated by gender available at the state level for 2009/10. The Center for Civil Rights Remedies at The Civil Rights Project has calculated *combined* male and female percentages from the OCR samples.[60]

State	Black	White, non-Latino	Black/White Ratio
North Carolina	16.3	6.1	2.7

Charlotte-Mecklenburg
Inequities in Graduation Rates
Male Black students in Charlotte in 2010/11 graduated at a lower rate than in 2009/10, below the group's state and national averages. Male White, non-Latino, students graduated at a higher rate in 2010/11 than in 2009/10, above the state and national averages for that group.

The *Benchmark* for graduation rates of male Black students for school districts enrolling more than 10,000 male Black students is 73% (Montgomery County, MD).

	Male Graduation Rate: 2010/11		Male Graduation Rate: 2009/10	
Jurisdiction	Black	White, non-Latino	Black	White, non-Latino
USA	53%	77%	52%	78%
North Carolina	59%	*73%*	58%	*71%*
Charlotte	*38%*	79%	*44%*	*72%*

National Assessment of Educational Progress (NAEP)
NAEP 8th Grade Reading results for Charlotte are above state and national averages for male students.

Percentages of Male Black and Male White, Non-Latino, Students at or Above Proficient
Reading, Grade 8, 2011

	Percent at or Above Proficient		Gap
Jurisdiction	Black	White, non-Latino	White/Black
USA	10%	35%	25%
North Carolina	*9%*	*33%*	25%
Charlotte	12%	50%	*38%*

NAEP 8th Grade Mathematics results for Charlotte are above those for the nation as a whole for male students and above those for the state for male White, non-Latino, students.

[60] From: Losen, Daniel J. and Jonathan Gillispie. Opportunities Suspended: The Disparate Impact of Disciplinary Exclusion from School. The Center for Civil Rights Remedies at The Civil Rights Project, August 2012. *Source:* CRDC, 2009-2010 (numbers from national sample rounded to one decimal).

Percentages of Male Black and Male White, Non-Latino, Students at or Above Proficient Mathematics, Grade 8, 2011

	Percent at or Above Proficient		Gap
Jurisdiction	Black	White, non-Latino	White/Black
USA	12%	45%	33%
North Carolina	15%	49%	*34%*
Charlotte	14%	69%	*55%*

The *Benchmark* for male Black students for 8th Grade Reading is Connecticut, with 19% of male Black students scoring at or above Proficient. The *Benchmark* for 8th Grade Mathematics is Massachusetts, with 26% of male Black students scoring at or above Proficient.

Discipline and Advanced Placement Inequities

Out-of-school suspension ratios are a measure of the extent to which disparate application of school discipline policies affect students from different racial and ethnic groups. Male Black students with disabilities were two and a half times as likely to receive out-of-school suspensions than were male White, non-Latino, students. Female Black students with disabilities were more than three and a half times as likely to receive out-of-school suspensions as were female White, non-Latino, students. Male Black students without disabilities were more than three and a half times as likely to receive out-of-school suspensions as were male White, non-Latino, students. Female Black students without disabilities were four and three-quarters times as likely to receive out-of-school suspensions as were female White, non-Latino, students.

Enrollment ratios in Advanced Placement Mathematics are an indicator of the differing opportunities to learn that may be provided to students on the basis of race and ethnicity. Male Black students were enrolled in AP Mathematics at less than one-fifth of the rate of male White, non-Latino, students. Female Black students were enrolled in AP Mathematics at one-quarter of the rate of female White, non-Latino, students.

Cumberland County

Inequities in Graduation Rates

Male Black students in Cumberland County in 2010/11 graduated at a lower rate than in 2009/10, below the group's state and national averages. Male White, non-Latino, students also graduated at a lower rate in 2010/11 than in 2009/10, below the state and national averages for that group.

The *Benchmark* for graduation rates of male Black students for school districts enrolling more than 10,000 male Black students is 73% (Montgomery County, MD).

	Male Graduation Rate: 2010/11		Male Graduation Rate: 2009/10	
Jurisdiction	Black	White, non-Latino	Black	White, non-Latino
USA	53%	77%	52%	78%
North Carolina	59%	*73%*	58%	*71%*
Cumberland	*46%*	*64%*	68%	*69%*

Discipline and Advanced Placement Inequities

Out-of-school suspension ratios are a measure of the extent to which disparate application of school discipline policies affect students from different racial and ethnic groups. Male Black students with disabilities were nearly twice as likely to receive out-of-school suspensions than were male White, non-Latino, students. Female Black students with disabilities were nearly three times as likely to receive out-of-school suspensions as were female White, non-Latino, students. Male Black students without disabilities were twice as likely to receive out-of-school suspensions as were male White, non-Latino, students. Female Black students without disabilities were nearly three times as likely to receive out-of-school suspensions as were female White, non-Latino, students.

Enrollment ratios in Advanced Placement Mathematics are an indicator of the differing opportunities to learn that may be provided to students on the basis of race and ethnicity. Male Black students were enrolled in AP Mathematics at approximately one-third the rate of male White, non-Latino, students. Female Black students were enrolled in AP Mathematics at approximately one-quarter of the rate of female White, non-Latino, students.

Guilford County

Inequities in Graduation Rates

Male Black students in Guilford County in 2010/11 graduated at a lower rate than in 2009/10, below the group's state and national averages. Male White, non-Latino, students graduated at a higher rate in 2010/11 than in 2009/10, above the state and national averages for that group.

The *Benchmark* for graduation rates of male Black students for school districts enrolling more than 10,000 male Black students is 73% (Montgomery County, MD).

	Male Graduation Rate: 2010/11		Male Graduation Rate: 2009/10	
Jurisdiction	Black	White, non-Latino	Black	White, non-Latino
USA	53%	77%	52%	78%
North Carolina	59%	*73%*	58%	*71%*
Guilford County	*48%*	83%	67%	80%

Discipline and Advanced Placement Inequities

Out-of-school suspension ratios are a measure of the extent to which disparate application of school discipline policies affect students from different racial and ethnic groups. Male Black students with disabilities were nearly twice as likely to receive out-of-school suspensions than were male White, non-Latino, students. Female Black students with disabilities were nearly four times as likely to receive out-of-school suspensions as were female White, non-Latino, students. Male Black students without disabilities were nearly three times as likely to receive out-of-school suspensions as were male White, non-Latino, students. Female Black students without disabilities were more than four times as likely to receive out-of-school suspensions as were female White, non-Latino, students.

Enrollment ratios in Advanced Placement Mathematics are an indicator of the differing opportunities to learn that may be provided to students on the basis of race and ethnicity. Black students were enrolled in AP Mathematics at approximately one-quarter the rate of White, non-Latino, students.

Wake County

Inequities in Graduation Rates

Male Black students in Wake County in 2010/11 graduated at a lower rate than in 2009/10. Male White, non-Latino, students graduated at a lower rate in 2010/11 than in 2009/10, remaining above the state and national averages for that group.

The *Benchmark* for graduation rates of male Black students for school districts enrolling more than 10,000 male Black students is 73% (Montgomery County, MD).

	Male Graduation Rate: 2010/11		Male Graduation Rate: 2009/10	
Jurisdiction	Black	White, non-Latino	Black	White, non-Latino
USA	53%	77%	52%	78%
North Carolina	59%	*73%*	58%	*71%*
Wake County	*50%*	80%	59%	85%

Discipline and Advanced Placement Inequities

Out-of-school suspension ratios are a measure of the extent to which disparate application of school discipline policies affect students from different racial and ethnic groups. Male Black students with disabilities were five and three quarters times as likely to receive out-of-school suspensions than were male White, non-Latino, students. Female Black students with disabilities were more than eight times as likely to receive out-of-school suspensions as were female White, non-Latino, students. Male Black students without disabilities were more than four and a quarter times as likely to receive out-of-school suspensions as were male White, non-Latino, students. Female Black students without disabilities were more than six and a half times as likely to receive out-of-school suspensions as were female White, non-Latino, students.

Enrollment ratios in Advanced Placement Mathematics are an indicator of the differing opportunities to learn that may be provided to students on the basis of race and ethnicity. Black students were enrolled in AP Mathematics at less than one-fifth of the rate of White, non-Latino, students.

NORTH DAKOTA

Inequities in Graduation Rates

There were too few Black students in North Dakota for meaningful analysis. Male White, non-Latino, students graduated at a slightly higher rate in 2010/11 than in 2009/10.

The *Benchmark* for graduation rates of male Black students for states enrolling more than 10,000 Black male students is 77% (Arizona). The *Benchmark* for states with at least one district enrolling more than 10,000 Black male students is New Jersey (73%).

	Male Graduation Rate: 2010/11		Male Graduation Rate: 2009/10	
Jurisdiction	Black	White, non-Latino	Black	White, non-Latino
USA	53%	77%	52%	78%
North Dakota	-	92%	-	91%

Comparison of Estimated Graduation Rates by Gender: 2010/11

The gender gap for White, non-Latino, students is one point.

	Male Graduation Rate		Female Graduation Rate	
Jurisdiction	Black	White, non-Latino	Black	White, non-Latino
USA	53%	77%	63%	81%
North Dakota	-	92%	-	93%

National Assessment of Educational Progress (NAEP)

NAEP 8th Grade Reading results for North Dakota are below the national average for White, non-Latino, students.

Percentages of Male Black and Male White, Non-Latino, Students at or Above Proficient
Reading, Grade 8, 2011

	Percent at or Above Proficient		Gap
Jurisdiction	Black	White, non-Latino	White/Black
USA	10%	35%	25%
North Dakota	‡[61]	*30%*	-

NAEP 8th Grade Mathematics results for North Dakota are above the national average for White, non-Latino, students.

Percentages of Male Black and Male White, Non-Latino, Students at or Above Proficient
Mathematics, Grade 8, 2011

	Percent at or Above Proficient		Gap
Jurisdiction	Black	White, non-Latino	White/Black
USA	12%	45%	33%
North Dakota	‡[62]	49%	-

[61] Indicates insufficient sample size.

[62] Indicates insufficient sample size.

The *Benchmark* for male Black students for 8th Grade Reading is Connecticut, with 19% of male Black students scoring at or above Proficient. The *Benchmark* for 8th Grade Mathematics is Massachusetts, with 26% of male Black students scoring at or above Proficient.

Discipline Inequities

The U.S. Department of Education's Office for Civil Rights has not yet made out-of-school suspension data disaggregated by gender available at the state level for 2009/10. The Center for Civil Rights Remedies at The Civil Rights Project has calculated *combined* male and female percentages from the OCR samples.[63]

State	Black	White, non-Latino	Black/White Ratio
North Dakota	3.6	1.6	2.3

[63] From: Losen, Daniel J. and Jonathan Gillispie. Opportunities Suspended: The Disparate Impact of Disciplinary Exclusion from School. The Center for Civil Rights Remedies at The Civil Rights Project, August 2012. *Source:* CRDC, 2009-2010 (numbers from national sample rounded to one decimal).

OHIO

Inequities in Graduation Rates

Male Black students in Ohio graduated at a higher rate in 2010/11 than in 2009/10, but below the national average for the group. Male White, non-Latino, students graduated at the same rate in 2010/11 as in 2009/10.

The *Benchmark* for graduation rates of male Black students for states enrolling more than 10,000 Black male students is 77% (Arizona). The *Benchmark* for states with at least one district enrolling more than 10,000 Black male students is New Jersey (73%).

	Male Graduation Rate: 2010/11		Male Graduation Rate: 2009/10	
Jurisdiction	Black	White, non-Latino	Black	White, non-Latino
USA	53%	77%	52%	78%
Ohio	*46%*	80%	*45%*	80%

Comparison of Estimated Graduation Rates by Gender: 2010/11

The gender gap for Black students in Ohio is ten points, while that for White, non-Latino, students is five points.

	Male Graduation Rate		Female Graduation Rate	
Jurisdiction	Black	White, non-Latino	Black	White, non-Latino
USA	53%	77%	63%	81%
Ohio	*46%*	80%	*56%*	85%

National Assessment of Educational Progress (NAEP)

NAEP 8th Grade Reading results for Ohio are below those for the nation as a whole for Black male students and above the national average for White, non-Latino, students.

Percentages of Male Black and Male White, Non-Latino, Students at or Above Proficient
Reading, Grade 8, 2011

	Percent at or Above Proficient		Gap
Jurisdiction	Black	White, non-Latino	White/ Black
USA	10%	35%	25%
Ohio	*9%*	38%	*30%*

NAEP 8th Grade Mathematics results for Ohio are above those for the nation as a whole in each category.

Percentages of Male Black and Male White, Non-Latino, Students at or Above Proficient
Mathematics, Grade 8, 2011

	Percent at or Above Proficient		Gap
Jurisdiction	Black	White, non-Latino	White/Black
USA	12%	45%	33%
Ohio	13%	47%	*34%*

The *Benchmark* for male Black students for 8th Grade Reading is Connecticut, with 19% of male Black students scoring at or above Proficient. The *Benchmark* for 8th Grade Mathematics is Massachusetts, with 26% of male Black students scoring at or above Proficient.

Discipline Inequities
The U.S. Department of Education's Office for Civil Rights has not yet made out-of-school suspension data disaggregated by gender available at the state level for 2009/10. The Center for Civil Rights Remedies at The Civil Rights Project has calculated *combined* male and female percentages from the OCR samples.[64]

State	Black	White, non-Latino	Black/White Ratio
Ohio	18.6	4.6	4.0

Cincinnati
Inequities in Graduation Rates
Male Black students in Cincinnati graduated at a slightly higher rate than in 2009/10, but still below state and national averages. Male White, non-Latino, students graduated at a higher rate in 2010/11 than in 2009/10, also below state and national averages for that group.

The *Benchmark* for graduation rates of male Black students for school districts enrolling more than 10,000 male Black students is 73% (Montgomery County, MD).

	Male Graduation Rate: 2010/11		Male Graduation Rate: 2009/10	
Jurisdiction	Black	White, non-Latino	Black	White, non-Latino
USA	53%	77%	52%	78%
Ohio	*46%*	80%	*45%*	80%
Cincinnati	*34%*	*53%*	*33%*	*49%*

Discipline and Advanced Placement Inequities
Out-of-school suspension ratios are a measure of the extent to which disparate application of school discipline policies affect students from different racial and ethnic groups. Male Black students with disabilities were three times as likely to receive out-of-school suspensions than were male White, non-Latino, students. Male Black students without disabilities were more than five times as likely to receive out-of-school suspensions as were male White, non-Latino, students. Female Black students without disabilities were more than eight and a half times as likely to receive out-of-school suspensions as were female White, non-Latino, students.

Enrollment ratios in Advanced Placement Mathematics are an indicator of the differing opportunities to learn that may be provided to students on the basis of race and ethnicity. Black students were enrolled in AP Mathematics at less than one-fifth of the rate of White, non-Latino, students.

Cleveland
Inequities in Graduation Rates
Male Black students in Cleveland graduated at a higher rate from 2009/10, but remained below state and national averages. Male White, non-Latino, students graduated at a lower rate in 2010/11 than in 2009/10; the rate was also below state and national averages for that group.

The *Benchmark* for graduation rates of male Black students for school districts enrolling more than 10,000 male Black students is 73% (Montgomery County, MD).

[64] From: Losen, Daniel J. and Jonathan Gillispie. Opportunities Suspended: The Disparate Impact of Disciplinary Exclusion from School. The Center for Civil Rights Remedies at The Civil Rights Project, August 2012. *Source:* CRDC, 2009-2010 (numbers from national sample rounded to one decimal).

Jurisdiction	Male Graduation Rate: 2010/11		Male Graduation Rate: 2009/10	
	Black	White, non-Latino	Black	White, non-Latino
USA	53%	77%	52%	78%
Ohio	*46%*	80%	*45%*	80%
Cleveland	*33%*	*28%*	*28%*	*37%*

National Assessment of Educational Progress (NAEP)
NAEP 8th Grade Reading results for Cleveland are below those both for the state and for the nation as a whole for male students.

Percentages of Male Black and Male White, Non-Latino, Students at or Above Proficient
Reading, Grade 8, 2011

	Percent at or Above Proficient		Gap
Jurisdiction	Black	White, non-Latino	White/Black
USA	10%	35%	25%
Ohio	*9%*	38%	*30%*
Cleveland	*3%*	*17%*	14%

NAEP 8th Grade Mathematics results for Cleveland are below those for the state and for nation as a whole for male students.

Percentages of Male Black and Male White, Non-Latino, Students at or Above Proficient
Mathematics, Grade 8, 2011

	Percent at or Above Proficient		Gap
Jurisdiction	Black	White, non-Latino	White/Black
USA	12%	45%	33%
Ohio	13%	47%	*34%*
Cleveland	*6%*	*29%*	23%

The *Benchmark* for male Black students for 8th Grade Reading is Connecticut, with 19% of male Black students scoring at or above Proficient. The *Benchmark* for 8th Grade Mathematics is Massachusetts, with 26% of male Black students scoring at or above Proficient.

Discipline and Advanced Placement Inequities
Out-of-school suspension ratios are a measure of the extent to which disparate application of school discipline policies affect students from different racial and ethnic groups. Male Black students with disabilities were more than twice as likely to receive out-of-school suspensions than were male White, non-Latino, students. Female Black students with disabilities were nearly three times as likely to receive out-of-school suspensions than were male White, non-Latino, students. Male Black students without disabilities were more than twice as likely to receive out-of-school suspensions as were male White, non-Latino, students. Female Black students without disabilities were nearly three times as likely to receive out-of-school suspensions as were female White, non-Latino, students.

Enrollment ratios in Advanced Placement Mathematics are an indicator of the differing opportunities to learn that may be provided to students on the basis of race and ethnicity. Black students were enrolled in AP Mathematics at between three-quarters and half of the rate of White, non-Latino, students.

Columbus

Inequities in Graduation Rates

Male Black students in Columbus graduated at the same rate in 2010/11 as in 2009/10, remaining below state and national averages. Male White, non-Latino, students graduated at a higher rate in 2010/11 than in 2009/10, but substantially below state and national averages for that group.

The *Benchmark* for graduation rates of male Black students for school districts enrolling more than 10,000 male Black students is 73% (Montgomery County, MD).

	Male Graduation Rate: 2010/11		Male Graduation Rate: 2009/10	
Jurisdiction	Black	White, non-Latino	Black	White, non-Latino
USA	53%	77%	52%	78%
Ohio	*46%*	80%	*45%*	80%
Columbus	*41%*	*46%*	*41%*	*43%*

Discipline and Advanced Placement Inequities

Out-of-school suspension ratios are a measure of the extent to which disparate application of school discipline policies affect students from different racial and ethnic groups. Male Black students with disabilities were more than half again as likely to receive out-of-school suspensions than were male White, non-Latino, students. Female Black students with disabilities were more than twice as likely to receive out-of-school suspensions than were male White, non-Latino, students. Black students without disabilities were twice as likely to receive out-of-school suspensions as were White, non-Latino, students.

Enrollment ratios in Advanced Placement Mathematics are an indicator of the differing opportunities to learn that may be provided to students on the basis of race and ethnicity. Black students were enrolled in AP Mathematics at less than half the rate of White, non-Latino, students.

OKLAHOMA

Inequities in Graduation Rates

Male Black students in Oklahoma graduated at a slightly lower rate than in 2009/10, but above the national average for the group. Male White, non-Latino, students graduated at the same rate in 2010/11 as in 2009/10, reaching a rate slightly lower than the national average for that group.

The *Benchmark* for graduation rates of male Black students for states enrolling more than 10,000 Black male students is 77% (Arizona). The *Benchmark* for states with at least one district enrolling more than 10,000 Black male students is New Jersey (73%).

	Male Graduation Rate: 2010/11		Male Graduation Rate: 2009/10	
Jurisdiction	Black	White, non-Latino	Black	White, non-Latino
USA	53%	77%	52%	78%
Oklahoma	63%	*76%*	64%	*76%*

Comparison of Estimated Graduation Rates by Gender: 2010/11

The gender gap for Black students in Oklahoma is seven points, while that for White, non-Latino, students is five points.

	Male Graduation Rate		Female Graduation Rate	
Jurisdiction	Black	White, non-Latino	Black	White, non-Latino
USA	53%	77%	63%	81%
Oklahoma	63%	*76%*	70%	81%

National Assessment of Educational Progress (NAEP)

NAEP 8th Grade Reading results for Oklahoma are slightly above the national average for male Black students. White, non-Latino, students results were substantially below the national average for that group.

Percentages of Male Black and Male White, Non-Latino, Students at or Above Proficient
Reading, Grade 8, 2011

	Percent at or Above Proficient		Gap
Jurisdiction	Black	White, non-Latino	White/Black
USA	10%	35%	25%
Oklahoma	11%	*25%*	13%

NAEP 8th Grade Mathematics results for Oklahoma are above the national average for male Black students and below the national averages for male White, non-Latino, students.

Percentages of Male Black and Male White, Non-Latino, Students at or Above Proficient
Mathematics, Grade 8, 2011

	Percent at or Above Proficient		Gap
Jurisdiction	Black	White, non-Latino	White/Black
USA	12%	45%	33%
Oklahoma	15%	*34%*	19%

The *Benchmark* for male Black students for 8th Grade Reading is Connecticut, with 19% of male Black students scoring at or above Proficient. The *Benchmark* for 8th Grade Mathematics is Massachusetts, with 26% of male Black students scoring at or above Proficient.

Discipline Inequities

The U.S. Department of Education's Office for Civil Rights has not yet made out-of-school suspension data disaggregated by gender available at the state level for 2009/10. The Center for Civil Rights Remedies at The Civil Rights Project has calculated *combined* male and female percentages from the OCR samples.[65]

State	Black	White, non-Latino	Black/White Ratio
Oklahoma	18.3	5.8	3.2

[65] From: Losen, Daniel J. and Jonathan Gillispie. Opportunities Suspended: The Disparate Impact of Disciplinary Exclusion from School. The Center for Civil Rights Remedies at The Civil Rights Project, August 2012. *Source:* CRDC, 2009-2010 (numbers from national sample rounded to one decimal).

OREGON

Inequities in Graduation Rates

The few male Black students in Oregon graduated at a lower rate than in 2009/10, still above the national average for the group. Male White, non-Latino, students graduated at a slightly higher rate in 2010/11 than in 2009/10, reaching a rate slightly higher than the national average for that group..

The *Benchmark* for graduation rates of male Black students for states enrolling more than 10,000 Black male students is 77% (Arizona). The *Benchmark* for states with at least one district enrolling more than 10,000 Black male students is New Jersey (73%).

	Male Graduation Rate: 2010/11		Male Graduation Rate: 2009/10	
Jurisdiction	Black	White, non-Latino	Black	White, non-Latino
USA	53%	77%	52%	78%
Oregon	68%	78%	72%	*77%*

Comparison of Estimated Graduation Rates by Gender: 2010/11

The gender gap for Black students in Oregon is a reversed six points, while that for White, non-Latino, students is zero. This is most unusual.

	Male Graduation Rate		Female Graduation Rate	
Jurisdiction	Black	White, non-Latino	Black	White, non-Latino
USA	53%	77%	63%	81%
Oregon	68%	78%	*62%*	*78%*

National Assessment of Educational Progress (NAEP)

NAEP 8th Grade Reading results for Oregon are below those for the nation as a whole for White, non-Latino, students.

Percentages of Male Black and Male White, Non-Latino, Students at or Above Proficient
Reading, Grade 8, 2011

	Percent at or Above Proficient		Gap
Jurisdiction	Black	White, non-Latino	White/Black
USA	10%	35%	25%
Oregon	‡[66]	*33%*	-

NAEP 8th Grade Mathematics results for Oregon are below those for the nation as a whole for White, non-Latino, students.

Percentages of Male Black and Male White, Non-Latino, Students at or Above Proficient
Mathematics, Grade 8, 2011

	Percent at or Above Proficient		Gap
Jurisdiction	Black	White, non-Latino	White/Black
USA	12%	45%	33%
Oregon	‡	*40%*	-

[66] Indicates insufficient sample size.

The *Benchmark* for male Black students for 8th Grade Reading is Connecticut, with 19% of male Black students scoring at or above Proficient. The *Benchmark* for 8th Grade Mathematics is Massachusetts, with 26% of male Black students scoring at or above Proficient.

Discipline Inequities

The U.S. Department of Education's Office for Civil Rights has not yet made out-of-school suspension data disaggregated by gender available at the state level for 2009/10. The Center for Civil Rights Remedies at The Civil Rights Project has calculated *combined* male and female percentages from the OCR samples.[67]

State	Black	White, non-Latino	Black/White Ratio
Oregon	12.5	4.9	2.6

[67] From: Losen, Daniel J. and Jonathan Gillispie. Opportunities Suspended: The Disparate Impact of Disciplinary Exclusion from School. The Center for Civil Rights Remedies at The Civil Rights Project, August 2012. *Source:* CRDC, 2009-2010 (numbers from national sample rounded to one decimal).

PENNSYLVANIA

Inequities in Graduation Rates

Male Black students in Pennsylvania graduated at a higher rate than in 2009/10, above the national average for the group. Male White, non-Latino, students graduated at a much higher rate in 2010/11 than the 2009/10 estimate, reaching a rate higher than the national average for that group.

The *Benchmark* for graduation rates of male Black students for states enrolling more than 10,000 Black male students is 77% (Arizona). The *Benchmark* for states with at least one district enrolling more than 10,000 Black male students is New Jersey (73%).

	Male Graduation Rate: 2010/11		Male Graduation Rate: 2009/10	
Jurisdiction	Black	White, non-Latino	Black	White, non-Latino
USA	53%	77%	52%	78%
Pennsylvania	59%	86%	57%	*65%*

Comparison of Estimated Graduation Rates by Gender: 2010/11

The gender gap for Black students in Pennsylvania is eleven points, while that for White, non-Latino, students is four points.

	Male Graduation Rate		Female Graduation Rate	
Jurisdiction	Black	White, non-Latino	Black	White, non-Latino
USA	53%	77%	63%	81%
Pennsylvania	59%	86%	70%	90%

National Assessment of Educational Progress (NAEP)

NAEP 8th Grade Reading results for Pennsylvania are at the national average for male Black students and above the national average for male White, non-Latino, students.

Percentages of Male Black and Male White, Non-Latino, Students at or Above Proficient
Reading, Grade 8, 2011

	Percent at or Above Proficient		Gap
Jurisdiction	Black	White, non-Latino	White/Black
USA	10%	35%	25%
Pennsylvania	10%	39%	*29%*

NAEP 8th Grade Mathematics results for Pennsylvania are below the national average for male Black students and above the national averages for male White, non-Latino, students.

Percentages of Male Black and Male White, Non-Latino, Students at or Above Proficient
Mathematics, Grade 8, 2011

	Percent at or Above Proficient		Gap
Jurisdiction	Black	White, non-Latino	White/Black
USA	12%	45%	33%
Pennsylvania	*10%*	49%	*39%*

The *Benchmark* for male Black students for 8th Grade Reading is Connecticut, with 19% of male Black students scoring at or above Proficient. The *Benchmark* for 8th Grade Mathematics is Massachusetts, with 26% of male Black students scoring at or above Proficient.

Discipline Inequities

The U.S. Department of Education's Office for Civil Rights has not yet made out-of-school suspension data disaggregated by gender available at the state level for 2009/10. The Center for Civil Rights Remedies at The Civil Rights Project has calculated *combined* male and female percentages from the OCR samples.[68]

State	Black	White, non-Latino	Black/White Ratio
Pennsylvania	16.7	3.6	4.6

Philadelphia

Inequities in Graduation Rates

Male Black students in Philadelphia graduated at a slightly higher rate than the 2009/10 estimate, far below the state and national averages for the group. Male White, non-Latino, students also graduated at higher rates than in 2009/10, but also far lower than the state and national averages for that group. There was a remarkably small amount of attrition reported between grades 11 and 12.

The *Benchmark* for graduation rates of male Black students for school districts enrolling more than 10,000 male Black students is 73% (Montgomery County, MD).

	Male Graduation Rate: 2010/11		Male Graduation Rate: 2009/10	
Jurisdiction	Black	White, non-Latino	Black	White, non-Latino
USA	53%	77%	52%	78%
Pennsylvania	59%	86%	57%	*65%*
Philadelphia	*25%*	*41%*	*24%*	*39%*

National Assessment of Educational Progress (NAEP)

NAEP 8th Grade Reading results for Philadelphia are below state and national averages for male students in both groups.

Percentages of Male Black and Male White, Non-Latino, Students at or Above Proficient
Reading, Grade 8, 2011

	Percent at or Above Proficient		Gap
Jurisdiction	Black	White, non-Latino	White/Black
USA	10%	35%	25%
Pennsylvania	10%	39%	29%
Philadelphia	*9%*	*27%*	18%

NAEP 8th Grade Mathematics results for Philadelphia are below state and national averages for White, non-Latino, students and above state and national averages for male Black students.

[68] From: Losen, Daniel J. and Jonathan Gillispie. Opportunities Suspended: The Disparate Impact of Disciplinary Exclusion from School. The Center for Civil Rights Remedies at The Civil Rights Project, August 2012. *Source:* CRDC, 2009-2010 (numbers from national sample rounded to one decimal).

Percentages of Male Black and Male White, Non-Latino, Students at or Above Proficient
Mathematics, Grade 8, 2011

	Percent at or Above Proficient		Gap
Jurisdiction	Black	White, non-Latino	White/Black
USA	12%	45%	33%
Pennsylvania	*10%*	49%	*39%*
Philadelphia	13%	*33%*	21%

The *Benchmark* for male Black students for 8th Grade Reading is Connecticut, with 19% of male Black students scoring at or above Proficient. The *Benchmark* for 8th Grade Mathematics is Massachusetts, with 26% of male Black students scoring at or above Proficient.

Discipline and Advanced Placement Inequities

Out-of-school suspension ratios are a measure of the extent to which disparate application of school discipline policies affect students from different racial and ethnic groups. Black students with disabilities were more than twice as likely to receive out-of-school suspensions than were male White, non-Latino, students. Male Black students without disabilities were two and a third times as likely to receive out-of-school suspensions as were male White, non-Latino, students. Female Black students without disabilities were three times as likely to receive out-of-school suspensions as were female White, non-Latino, students.

Enrollment ratios in Advanced Placement Mathematics are an indicator of the differing opportunities to learn that may be provided to students on the basis of race and ethnicity. Black students were enrolled in AP Mathematics at approximately half the rate of White, non-Latino, students.

RHODE ISLAND

Inequities in Graduation Rates

Male Black students in Rhode Island graduated at a lower rate in 2010/11 than in 2009/10, but still above the national average for the group. Male White, non-Latino, students graduated at the same rates in 2010/11 as in 2009/10, rates somewhat lower than the national averages for that groups.

The *Benchmark* for graduation rates of male Black students for states enrolling more than 10,000 Black male students is 77% (Arizona). The *Benchmark* for states with at least one district enrolling more than 10,000 Black male students is New Jersey (73%).

	Male Graduation Rate: 2010/11		Male Graduation Rate: 2009/10	
Jurisdiction	Black	White, non-Latino	Black	White, non-Latino
USA	53%	77%	52%	78%
Rhode Island	57%	*75%*	64%	*75%*

Comparison of Estimated Graduation Rates by Gender: 2010/11

The gender gap for Black students in Rhode Island is five points, while that for White, non-Latino, students is four points.

	Male Graduation Rate		Female Graduation Rate	
Jurisdiction	Black	White, non-Latino	Black	White, non-Latino
USA	53%	77%	63%	81%
Rhode Island	57%	*75%*	*62%*	*79%*

National Assessment of Educational Progress (NAEP)

NAEP 8th Grade Reading results for Rhode Island are above the national average for male Black students and at the national average for male White, non-Latino, students.

Percentages of Male Black and Male White, Non-Latino, Students at or Above Proficient
Reading, Grade 8, 2011

	Percent at or Above Proficient		Gap
Jurisdiction	Black	White, non-Latino	White/Black
USA	10%	35%	25%
Rhode Island	12%	35%	23%

NAEP 8th Grade Mathematics results for Rhode Island are above the national average for male Black students and below the national average for male White, non-Latino, students.

Percentages of Male Black and Male White, Non-Latino, Students at or Above Proficient
Mathematics, Grade 8, 2011

	Percent at or Above Proficient		Gap
Jurisdiction	Black	White, non-Latino	White/Black
USA	12%	45%	33%
Rhode Island	17%	43%	25%

The *Benchmark* for male Black students for 8th Grade Reading is Connecticut, with 19% of male Black students scoring at or above Proficient. The *Benchmark* for 8th Grade Mathematics is Massachusetts, with 26% of male Black students scoring at or above Proficient.

Discipline Inequities

The U.S. Department of Education's Office for Civil Rights has not yet made out-of-school suspension data disaggregated by gender available at the state level for 2009/10. The Center for Civil Rights Remedies at The Civil Rights Project has calculated *combined* male and female percentages from the OCR samples.[69]

State	Black	White, non-Latino	Black/White Ratio
Rhode Island	15.6	7	2.2

[69] From: Losen, Daniel J. and Jonathan Gillispie. Opportunities Suspended: The Disparate Impact of Disciplinary Exclusion from School. The Center for Civil Rights Remedies at The Civil Rights Project, August 2012. *Source:* CRDC, 2009-2010 (numbers from national sample rounded to one decimal).

SOUTH CAROLINA

Inequities in Graduation Rates

Male Black students in South Carolina graduated at a higher rate than in 2009/10, but still below the national average for the group. Male White, non-Latino, students also graduated at a higher rate in 2010/11 than in 2009/10, but at a rate that remained much lower than the national average for that group.

The *Benchmark* for graduation rates of male Black students for states enrolling more than 10,000 Black male students is 77% (Arizona). The *Benchmark* for states with at least one district enrolling more than 10,000 Black male students is New Jersey (73%).

	Male Graduation Rate: 2010/11		Male Graduation Rate: 2009/10	
Jurisdiction	Black	White, non-Latino	Black	White, non-Latino
USA	53%	77%	52%	78%
South Carolina	*48%*	*63%*	*46%*	*62%*

Comparison of Estimated Graduation Rates by Gender: 2010/11

The gender gap for Black students in South Carolina is thirteen points, while that for White, non-Latino, students is nine points.

	Male Graduation Rate		Female Graduation Rate	
Jurisdiction	Black	White, non-Latino	Black	White, non-Latino
USA	53%	77%	63%	81%
South Carolina	*48%*	*63%*	*61%*	*72%*

National Assessment of Educational Progress (NAEP)

NAEP 8th Grade Reading results for South Carolina are below those for the nation as a whole for male Black and White, non-Latino, students.

Percentages of Male Black and Male White, Non-Latino, Students at or Above Proficient
Reading, Grade 8, 2011

	Percent at or Above Proficient		Gap
Jurisdiction	Black	White, non-Latino	White/Black
USA	10%	35%	25%
South Carolina	*6%*	*31%*	25%

NAEP 8th Grade Mathematics results for South Carolina are above national averages for male Black and below the national average for male White, non-Latino, students.

Percentages of Male Black and Male White, Non-Latino, Students at or Above Proficient
Mathematics, Grade 8, 2011

	Percent at or Above Proficient		Gap
Jurisdiction	Black	White, non-Latino	White/Black
USA	12%	45%	33%
South Carolina	13%	*42%*	29%

The *Benchmark* for male Black students for 8th Grade Reading is Connecticut, with 19% of male Black students scoring at or above Proficient. The *Benchmark* for 8th Grade Mathematics is Massachusetts, with 26% of male Black students scoring at or above Proficient.

Discipline Inequities

The U.S. Department of Education's Office for Civil Rights has not yet made out-of-school suspension data disaggregated by gender available at the state level for 2009/10. The Center for Civil Rights Remedies at The Civil Rights Project has calculated *combined* male and female percentages from the OCR samples.[70]

State	Black	White, non-Latino	Black/White Ratio
South Carolina	21	7.9	2.7

Charleston

Inequities in Graduation Rates

Male Black students in Charleston graduated at a much higher rate than in 2009/10, but still below the state and national averages for the group. Male White, non-Latino, students graduated at a lower rate in 2010/11 than in 2009/10, a rate between the state and national averages for that group.

The *Benchmark* for graduation rates of male Black students for school districts enrolling more than 10,000 male Black students is 73% (Montgomery County, MD).

	Male Graduation Rate: 2010/11		Male Graduation Rate: 2009/10	
Jurisdiction	Black	White, non-Latino	Black	White, non-Latino
USA	53%	77%	52%	78%
South Carolina	*48%*	*63%*	*46%*	*62%*
Charleston	*45%*	*72%*	*36%*	*67%*

Discipline and Advanced Placement Inequities

Out-of-school suspension ratios are a measure of the extent to which disparate application of school discipline policies affect students from different racial and ethnic groups. Male Black students with disabilities were nearly three times as likely to receive out-of-school suspensions than were male White, non-Latino, students. Male Black students without disabilities were four times as likely to receive out-of-school suspensions as were male White, non-Latino, students. Female Black students without disabilities were nearly seven times as likely to receive out-of-school suspensions as were female White, non-Latino, students.

Enrollment ratios in Advanced Placement Mathematics are an indicator of the differing opportunities to learn that may be provided to students on the basis of race and ethnicity. Male Black students were enrolled in AP Mathematics at less than one-fifth the rate of male White, non-Latino, students. Female Black students were enrolled in AP Mathematics at less than one-third the rate of female White, non-Latino, students.

---

[70] From: Losen, Daniel J. and Jonathan Gillispie. Opportunities Suspended: The Disparate Impact of Disciplinary Exclusion from School. The Center for Civil Rights Remedies at The Civil Rights Project, August 2012. *Source:* CRDC, 2009-2010 (numbers from national sample rounded to one decimal).

SOUTH DAKOTA

Inequities in Graduation Rates

The few male Black students in South Dakota graduated at a higher rate than in 2009/10, above the national average for the group. Male White, non-Latino, students also graduated at a higher rate in 20010/11 than in 2009/10.

The *Benchmark* for graduation rates of male Black students for states enrolling more than 10,000 Black male students is 77% (Arizona). The *Benchmark* for states with at least one district enrolling more than 10,000 Black male students is New Jersey (73%).

	Male Graduation Rate: 2010/11		Male Graduation Rate: 2009/10	
Jurisdiction	Black	White, non-Latino	Black	White, non-Latino
USA	53%	77%	52%	78%
South Dakota	75%	83%	65%	81%

Comparison of Estimated Graduation Rates by Gender: 2010/11

The gender gap for Black students in South Dakota is a reversed four points, while that for White, non-Latino, students is two points.

	Male Graduation Rate		Female Graduation Rate	
Jurisdiction	Black	White, non-Latino	Black	White, non-Latino
USA	53%	77%	63%	81%
South Dakota	75%	83%	71%	85%

National Assessment of Educational Progress (NAEP)

NAEP 8th Grade Reading results for South Dakota are below those for the nation as a whole for White, non-Latino, students.

Percentages of Male Black and Male White, Non-Latino, Students at or Above Proficient
Reading, Grade 8, 2011

	Percent at or Above Proficient		Gap
Jurisdiction	Black	White, non-Latino	White/Black
USA	10%	35%	25%
South Dakota	‡[71]	*33%*	-

NAEP 8th Grade Mathematics results for South Dakota are above those for the nation as a whole for White, non-Latino, students.

Percentages of Male Black and Male White, Non-Latino, Students at or Above Proficient
Mathematics, Grade 8, 2011

	Percent at or Above Proficient		Gap
Jurisdiction	Black	White, non-Latino	White/Black
USA	12%	45%	33%
South Dakota	‡[72]	48%	-

[71] Indicates insufficient sample size.

[72] Indicates insufficient sample size.

The *Benchmark* for male Black students for 8th Grade Reading is Connecticut, with 19% of male Black students scoring at or above Proficient. The *Benchmark* for 8th Grade Mathematics is Massachusetts, with 26% of male Black students scoring at or above Proficient.

Discipline Inequities

The U.S. Department of Education's Office for Civil Rights has not yet made out-of-school suspension data disaggregated by gender available at the state level for 2009/10. The Center for Civil Rights Remedies at The Civil Rights Project has calculated *combined* male and female percentages from the OCR samples.[73]

State	Black	White, non-Latino	Black/White Ratio
South Dakota	7.1	2.2	3.2

[73] From: Losen, Daniel J. and Jonathan Gillispie. Opportunities Suspended: The Disparate Impact of Disciplinary Exclusion from School. The Center for Civil Rights Remedies at The Civil Rights Project, August 2012. *Source:* CRDC, 2009-2010 (numbers from national sample rounded to one decimal).

TENNESSEE

Inequities in Graduation Rates

Male Black students in Tennessee graduated at a higher rate than in 2009/10, above the national average for the group. Male White, non-Latino, students also graduated at a higher rate in 2010/11 than in 2009/10, a rate higher than the national average for that group.

The *Benchmark* for graduation rates of male Black students for states enrolling more than 10,000 Black male students is 77% (Arizona). The *Benchmark* for states with at least one district enrolling more than 10,000 Black male students is New Jersey (73%).

	Male Graduation Rate: 2010/11		Male Graduation Rate: 2009/10	
Jurisdiction	Black	White, non-Latino	Black	White, non-Latino
USA	53%	77%	52%	78%
Tennessee	67%	81%	62%	*76%*

Comparison of Estimated Graduation Rates by Gender: 2010/11

The gender gap for Black students in Tennessee is nine points, while that for White, non-Latino, students is two points.

	Male Graduation Rate		Female Graduation Rate	
Jurisdiction	Black	White, non-Latino	Black	White, non-Latino
USA	53%	77%	63%	81%
Tennessee	67%	81%	76%	83%

National Assessment of Educational Progress (NAEP)

NAEP 8th Grade Reading results for Tennessee are below national averages for male Black and White, non-Latino, students.

Percentages of Male Black and Male White, Non-Latino, Students at or Above Proficient
Reading, Grade 8, 2011

	Percent at or Above Proficient		Gap
Jurisdiction	Black	White, non-Latino	White/Black
USA	10%	35%	25%
Tennessee	*9%*	*26%*	17%

NAEP 8th Grade Mathematics results for Tennessee are below those for the nation as a whole in each category.

Percentages of Male Black and Male White, Non-Latino, Students at or Above Proficient
Mathematics, Grade 8, 2011

	Percent at or Above Proficient		Gap
Jurisdiction	Black	White, non-Latino	White/Black
USA	12%	45%	33%
Tennessee	*10%*	*31%*	21%

The *Benchmark* for male Black students for 8th Grade Reading is Connecticut, with 19% of male Black students scoring at or above Proficient. The *Benchmark* for 8th Grade Mathematics is Massachusetts, with 26% of male Black students scoring at or above Proficient.

Discipline Inequities

The U.S. Department of Education's Office for Civil Rights has not yet made out-of-school suspension data disaggregated by gender available at the state level for 2009/10. The Center for Civil Rights Remedies at The Civil Rights Project has calculated *combined* male and female percentages from the OCR samples.[74]

State	Black	White, non-Latino	Black/White Ratio
Tennessee	21.1	4.7	4.5

Memphis

Inequities in Graduation Rates

Male Black students in Memphis graduated at a slightly higher rate than in 2009/10, below the state and national averages for the group. Male White, non-Latino, students graduated at a slightly lower rate in 2010/11 than in 2009/10, a rate lower than the state and national averages for that group.

The *Benchmark* for graduation rates of male Black students for school districts enrolling more than 10,000 male Black students is 73% (Montgomery County, MD).

	Male Graduation Rate: 2010/11		Male Graduation Rate: 2009/10	
Jurisdiction	Black	White, non-Latino	Black	White, non-Latino
USA	53%	77%	52%	78%
Tennessee	67%	81%	62%	*76%*
Memphis	*45%*	*66%*	*43%*	*67%*

Discipline and Advanced Placement Inequities

Out-of-school suspension ratios are a measure of the extent to which disparate application of school discipline policies affect students from different racial and ethnic groups. Male Black students with disabilities were nearly half again as likely to receive out-of-school suspensions than were male White, non-Latino, students. Female Black students with disabilities were more than two and a half times as likely to receive out-of-school suspensions than were female White, non-Latino, students. Male Black students without disabilities were more than twice as likely to receive out-of-school suspensions as were male White, non-Latino, students. Female Black students without disabilities were nearly four times as likely to receive out-of-school suspensions as were female White, non-Latino, students.

Enrollment ratios in Advanced Placement Mathematics are an indicator of the differing opportunities to learn that may be provided to students on the basis of race and ethnicity. Male Black students were enrolled in AP Mathematics at less than one-fifth the rate of male White, non-Latino, students. Female Black students were enrolled in AP Mathematics at less than one-third the rate of female White, non-Latino, students.

---

[74] From: Losen, Daniel J. and Jonathan Gillispie. Opportunities Suspended: The Disparate Impact of Disciplinary Exclusion from School. The Center for Civil Rights Remedies at The Civil Rights Project, August 2012. *Source:* CRDC, 2009-2010 (numbers from national sample rounded to one decimal).

Nashville-Davidson

Inequities in Graduation Rates

Male Black students in Nashville graduated at a lower rate than in 2009/10, below the state and national averages for the group. Male White, non-Latino, students graduated at a lower rate than in 2009/10, a rate much lower than the state and national averages for that group.

The *Benchmark* for graduation rates of male Black students for school districts enrolling more than 10,000 male Black students is 73% (Montgomery County, MD).

	Male Graduation Rate: 2010/11		Male Graduation Rate: 2009/10	
Jurisdiction	Black	White, non-Latino	Black	White, non-Latino
USA	53%	77%	52%	78%
Tennessee	67%	81%	62%	*76%*
Nashville	*36%*	*47%*	*47%*	*56%*

Discipline and Advanced Placement Inequities

Out-of-school suspension ratios are a measure of the extent to which disparate application of school discipline policies affect students from different racial and ethnic groups. Male Black students with disabilities were nearly half again as likely to receive out-of-school suspensions than were male White, non-Latino, students. Female Black students with disabilities were nearly four times as likely to receive out-of-school suspensions than were female White, non-Latino, students. Male Black students without disabilities were more than twice as likely to receive out-of-school suspensions as were male White, non-Latino, students. Female Black students without disabilities were nearly three times as likely to receive out-of-school suspensions as were female White, non-Latino, students.

Enrollment ratios in Advanced Placement Mathematics are an indicator of the differing opportunities to learn that may be provided to students on the basis of race and ethnicity. Black students were enrolled in AP Mathematics at one-third of the rate of White, non-Latino, students.

TEXAS

Inequities in Graduation Rates

Male Black students in Texas graduated at a slightly higher rate than in 2009/10, just above the national average for the group. Male White, non-Latino, students also graduated at a slightly higher rate in 2010/11 than in 2009/10, but at a rate just lower than the national average for that group.

The *Benchmark* for graduation rates of male Black students for states enrolling more than 10,000 Black male students is 77% (Arizona). The *Benchmark* for states with at least one district enrolling more than 10,000 Black male students is New Jersey (73%).

	Male Graduation Rate: 2010/11		Male Graduation Rate: 2009/10	
Jurisdiction	Black	White, non-Latino	Black	White, non-Latino
USA	53%	77%	52%	78%
Texas	54%	*76%*	53%	*75%*

Comparison of Estimated Graduation Rates by Gender: 2010/11

The gender gap for Black students in Texas is nine points, while that for White, non-Latino, students is three points.

	Male Graduation Rate		Female Graduation Rate	
Jurisdiction	Black	White, non-Latino	Black	White, non-Latino
USA	53%	77%	63%	81%
Texas	54%	76%	63%	*79%*

National Assessment of Educational Progress (NAEP)

NAEP 8th Grade Reading results for Texas are above those for the nation as a whole for male Black and White, non-Latino, students.

Percentages of Male Black and Male White, Non-Latino, Students at or Above Proficient
Reading, Grade 8, 2011

	Percent at or Above Proficient		Gap
Jurisdiction	Black	White, non-Latino	White/Black
USA	10%	35%	25%
Texas	12%	41%	*29%*

NAEP 8th Grade Mathematics results for Texas are above those for the nation as a whole in each category.

Percentages of Male Black and Male White, Non-Latino, Students at or Above Proficient
Mathematics, Grade 8, 2011

	Percent at or Above Proficient		Gap
Jurisdiction	Black	White, non-Latino	White/Black
USA	12%	45%	33%
Texas	18%	60%	41%

The *Benchmark* for male Black students for 8th Grade Reading is Connecticut, with 19% of male Black students scoring at or above Proficient. The *Benchmark* for 8th Grade Mathematics is Massachusetts, with 26% of male Black students scoring at or above Proficient.

Discipline Inequities

The U.S. Department of Education's Office for Civil Rights has not yet made out-of-school suspension data disaggregated by gender available at the state level for 2009/10. The Center for Civil Rights Remedies at The Civil Rights Project has calculated *combined* male and female percentages from the OCR samples.[75]

State	Black	White, non-Latino	Black/White Ratio
Texas	15.4	3.2	4.8

Dallas

Inequities in Graduation Rates

Male Black students in Dallas graduated at a higher rate than in 2009/10, below the state and national averages for the group. Male White, non-Latino, students also graduated at a higher rate than in 2009/10, a rate lower than the state and national averages for that group.

The *Benchmark* for graduation rates of male Black students for school districts enrolling more than 10,000 male Black students is 73% (Montgomery County, MD).

	Male Graduation Rate: 2010/11		Male Graduation Rate: 2009/10	
Jurisdiction	Black	White, non-Latino	Black	White, non-Latino
USA	53%	77%	52%	78%
Texas	54%	*76%*	53%	*75%*
Dallas	*37%*	*53%*	*35%*	*50%*

National Assessment of Educational Progress (NAEP)

NAEP 8th Grade Reading results for Dallas are below those for the state and the nation as a whole for male Black students.

Percentages of Male Black and Male White, Non-Latino, Students at or Above Proficient
Reading, Grade 8, 2011

	Percent at or Above Proficient		Gap
Jurisdiction	Black	White, non-Latino	White/Black
USA	10%	35%	25%
Texas	12%	41%	*29%*
Dallas	*7%*	‡	-

NAEP 8th Grade Mathematics results for Dallas are slightly below both state and national averages for male Black students.

[75] From: Losen, Daniel J. and Jonathan Gillispie. Opportunities Suspended: The Disparate Impact of Disciplinary Exclusion from School. The Center for Civil Rights Remedies at The Civil Rights Project, August 2012. *Source:* CRDC, 2009-2010 (numbers from national sample rounded to one decimal).

Percentages of Male Black and Male White, Non-Latino, Students at or Above Proficient Mathematics, Grade 8, 2011

	Percent at or Above Proficient		Gap
Jurisdiction	Black	White, non-Latino	White/Black
USA	12%	45%	33%
Texas	18%	60%	*41%*
Dallas	*9%*	‡[76]	-

The *Benchmark* for male Black students for 8th Grade Reading is Connecticut, with 19% of male Black students scoring at or above Proficient. The *Benchmark* for 8th Grade Mathematics is Massachusetts, with 26% of male Black students scoring at or above Proficient.

Discipline and Advanced Placement Inequities

Out-of-school suspension ratios are a measure of the extent to which disparate application of school discipline policies affect students from different racial and ethnic groups. Male Black students with disabilities were twice as likely to receive out-of-school suspensions as were male White, non-Latino, students. Female Black students with disabilities were nearly three times as likely to receive out-of-school suspensions as were male White, non-Latino, students. Male Black students without disabilities were nearly three times as likely to receive out-of-school suspensions as were male White, non-Latino, students. Female Black students without disabilities were more than four times as likely to receive out-of-school suspensions as were female White, non-Latino, students.

Enrollment ratios in Advanced Placement Mathematics are an indicator of the differing opportunities to learn that may be provided to students on the basis of race and ethnicity. Black students were enrolled in AP Mathematics at approximately a quarter of the rate of White, non-Latino, students.

Fort Bend

Inequities in Graduation Rates

Male Black students in Fort Bend graduated at a lower rate in 2010/11 than in 2009/10, below the state and national averages for the group. Male White, non-Latino, students graduated at a lower rate in 2010/11 than in 2009/10, a rate lower than the state and national averages for that group.

The *Benchmark* for graduation rates of male Black students for school districts enrolling more than 10,000 male Black students is 73% (Montgomery County, MD).

	Male Graduation Rate: 2010/11		Male Graduation Rate: 2009/10	
Jurisdiction	Black	White, non-Latino	Black	White, non-Latino
USA	53%	77%	52%	78%
Texas	54%	*76%*	53%	*75%*
Fort Bend	*44%*	*65%*	60%	83%

Discipline and Advanced Placement Inequities

Out-of-school suspension ratios are a measure of the extent to which disparate application of school discipline policies affect students from different racial and ethnic groups. Black students with disabilities were two and a half times as likely to receive out-of-school suspensions than were White, non-Latino, students. Male Black students without disabilities were nearly four and a half times as likely to receive out-of-school suspensions as

[76] Indicates insufficient sample size.

were male White, non-Latino, students. Female Black students without disabilities were six and a half times as likely to receive out-of-school suspensions as were female White, non-Latino, students.

Enrollment ratios in Advanced Placement Mathematics are an indicator of the differing opportunities to learn that may be provided to students on the basis of race and ethnicity. Male Black students were enrolled in AP Mathematics at one-fifth of the rate of White, non-Latino, students. Female Black students were enrolled in AP Mathematics at just over one quarter of the rate of White, non-Latino, students.

Houston

Inequities in Graduation Rates

Male Black students in Houston graduated at a slightly higher rate in 2010/11 than in 2009/10, below the state and national averages for the group. Male White, non-Latino, students graduated at a lower rate in 2010/11 than in 2009/10, a rate lower than the state and national averages for that group.

The *Benchmark* for graduation rates of male Black students for school districts enrolling more than 10,000 male Black students is 73% (Montgomery County, MD).

	Male Graduation Rate: 2010/11		Male Graduation Rate: 2009/10	
Jurisdiction	Black	White, non-Latino	Black	White, non-Latino
USA	53%	77%	52%	78%
Texas	54%	*76%*	53%	*75%*
Houston	*41%*	*69%*	*40%*	*73%*

National Assessment of Educational Progress (NAEP)

NAEP 8th Grade Reading results for Houston are below those for the state and the nation as a whole for male Black students and above state and national averages for male White, non-Latino, students.

Percentages of Male Black and Male White, Non-Latino, Students at or Above Proficient
Reading, Grade 8, 2011

	Percent at or Above Proficient		Gap
Jurisdiction	Black	White, non-Latino	White/Black
USA	10%	35%	25%
Texas	12%	41%	*29%*
Houston	*9%*	50%	*40%*

NAEP 8th Grade Mathematics results for Houston are above those for the nation as a whole but below those for the state for male White, non-Latino, students and below state, but above national averages for male Black students..

Percentages of Male Black and Male White, Non-Latino, Students at or Above Proficient
Mathematics, Grade 8, 2011

	Percent at or Above Proficient		Gap
Jurisdiction	Black	White, non-Latino	White/Black
USA	12%	45%	33%
Texas	18%	60%	*41%*
Houston	15%	70%	*55%*

The *Benchmark* for male Black students for 8th Grade Reading is Connecticut, with 19% of male Black students scoring at or above Proficient. The *Benchmark* for 8th Grade Mathematics is Massachusetts, with 26% of male Black students scoring at or above Proficient.

Discipline and Advanced Placement Inequities

Out-of-school suspension ratios are a measure of the extent to which disparate application of school discipline policies affect students from different racial and ethnic groups. Male Black students with disabilities received out-of-school suspensions at a rate more than four times higher than that for male White, non-Hispanic, students with disabilities. Female Black students with disabilities received out-of-school suspensions at a rate nearly ten times as high as that for female White, non-Hispanic, students with disabilities. Male Black students without disabilities were nearly four times as likely to receive out-of-school suspensions as were male White, non-Latino, students. Female Black students without disabilities were more than seven times as likely to receive out-of-school suspensions as were female White, non-Latino, students.

Enrollment ratios in Advanced Placement Mathematics are an indicator of the differing opportunities to learn that may be provided to students on the basis of race and ethnicity. Male Black students were enrolled in AP Mathematics at less than one-fifth of the rate of male White, non-Latino, students. Female Black students were enrolled in AP Mathematics at just over one-quarter of the rate of female White, non-Latino, students.

UTAH

Inequities in Graduation Rates

The few male Black students in Utah graduated at a lower rate in 2010/11 than in 2009/10, still above the national average for the group. Male White, non-Latino, students graduated at a lower rate in 2010/11 than in 2009/10, a rate just higher than the national average for that group.

The *Benchmark* for graduation rates of male Black students for states enrolling more than 10,000 Black male students is 77% (Arizona). The *Benchmark* for states with at least one district enrolling more than 10,000 Black male students is New Jersey (73%).

	Male Graduation Rate: 2010/11		Male Graduation Rate: 2009/10	
Jurisdiction	Black	White, non-Latino	Black	White, non-Latino
USA	53%	77%	52%	78%
Utah	64%	79%	76%	84%

Comparison of Estimated Graduation Rates by Gender: 2010/11

The gender gap for Black students in Utah is a reversed three points, while that for White, non-Latino, students is no points.

	Male Graduation Rate		Female Graduation Rate	
Jurisdiction	Black	White, non-Latino	Black	White, non-Latino
USA	53%	77%	63%	81%
Utah	64%	79%	*61%*	*79%*

National Assessment of Educational Progress (NAEP)

NAEP 8th Grade Reading results for Utah are below national averages for White, non-Latino, students.

Percentages of Male Black and Male White, Non-Latino, Students at or Above Proficient
Reading, Grade 8, 2011

	Percent at or Above Proficient		Gap
Jurisdiction	Black	White, non-Latino	White/Black
USA	10%	35%	25%
Utah	‡[77]	*34%*	-

NAEP 8th Grade Mathematics results for Utah are below national averages for White, non-Latino, students.

Percentages of Male Black and Male White, Non-Latino, Students at or Above Proficient
Mathematics, Grade 8, 2011

	Percent at or Above Proficient		Gap
Jurisdiction	Black	White, non-Latino	White/Black
USA	12%	45%	33%
Utah	‡	*43%*	-

[77] Indicates insufficient sample size.

The *Benchmark* for male Black students for 8th Grade Reading is Connecticut, with 19% of male Black students scoring at or above Proficient. The *Benchmark* for 8th Grade Mathematics is Massachusetts, with 26% of male Black students scoring at or above Proficient.

Discipline Inequities

The U.S. Department of Education's Office for Civil Rights has not yet made out-of-school suspension data disaggregated by gender available at the state level for 2009/10. The Center for Civil Rights Remedies at The Civil Rights Project has calculated *combined* male and female percentages from the OCR samples.[78]

State	Black	White, non-Latino	Black/White Ratio
Utah	6.2	2.1	3.0

[78] From: Losen, Daniel J. and Jonathan Gillispie. Opportunities Suspended: The Disparate Impact of Disciplinary Exclusion from School. The Center for Civil Rights Remedies at The Civil Rights Project, August 2012. *Source:* CRDC, 2009-2010 (numbers from national sample rounded to one decimal).

VERMONT

Inequities in Graduation Rates

The very few male Black students in Vermont graduated at a slightly lower rate in 2010/11 than in 2009/10, yet still significantly above the national average for the group. Male White, non-Latino, students graduated at a slightly lower rate in 2010/11 than in 2009/10, a rate higher than the national average for that group.

The *Benchmark* for graduation rates of male Black students for states enrolling more than 10,000 Black male students is 77% (Arizona). The *Benchmark* for states with at least one district enrolling more than 10,000 Black male students is New Jersey (73%).

	Male Graduation Rate: 2010/11		Male Graduation Rate: 2009/10	
Jurisdiction	Black	White, non-Latino	Black	White, non-Latino
USA	53%	77%	52%	78%
Vermont	72%	80%	82%	81%

Comparison of Estimated Graduation Rates by Gender: 2010/11

The gender gap for Black students in Vermont is thirteen points, while that for White, non-Latino, students is one point.

	Male Graduation Rate		Female Graduation Rate	
Jurisdiction	Black	White, non-Latino	Black	White, non-Latino
USA	53%	77%	63%	81%
Vermont	72%	80%	85%	81%

National Assessment of Educational Progress (NAEP)

NAEP 8th Grade Reading results for Vermont are above the national average for male White, non-Latino, students.

Percentages of Male Black and Male White, Non-Latino, Students at or Above Proficient
Reading, Grade 8, 2011

	Percent at or Above Proficient		Gap
Jurisdiction	Black	White, non-Latino	White/Black
USA	10%	35%	25%
Vermont	‡[79]	37%	-

NAEP 8th Grade Mathematics results for Vermont are above the national average for male White, non-Latino, students.

Percentages of Male Black and Male White, Non-Latino, Students at or Above Proficient
Mathematics, Grade 8, 2011

	Percent at or Above Proficient		Gap
Jurisdiction	Black	White, non-Latino	White/Black
USA	12%	45%	33%
Vermont	‡	46%	-

[79] Indicates insufficient sample size.

The *Benchmark* for male Black students for 8th Grade Reading is Connecticut, with 19% of male Black students scoring at or above Proficient. The *Benchmark* for 8th Grade Mathematics is Massachusetts, with 26% of male Black students scoring at or above Proficient.

Discipline Inequities

The U.S. Department of Education's Office for Civil Rights has not yet made out-of-school suspension data disaggregated by gender available at the state level for 2009/10. The Center for Civil Rights Remedies at The Civil Rights Project has calculated *combined* male and female percentages from the OCR samples.[80]

State	Black	White, non-Latino	Black/White Ratio
Vermont	6.5	4.4	1.5

[80] From: Losen, Daniel J. and Jonathan Gillispie. Opportunities Suspended: The Disparate Impact of Disciplinary Exclusion from School. The Center for Civil Rights Remedies at The Civil Rights Project, August 2012. *Source:* CRDC, 2009-2010 (numbers from national sample rounded to one decimal).

VIRGINIA

Inequities in Graduation Rates

Male Black students in Virginia graduated at a slightly higher rate in 2010/11 than in 2009/10, slightly above the national average for the group. Male White, non-Latino, students graduated at a slightly higher rate in 2010/11 than in 2009/10, a rate just under the national average for that group.

The *Benchmark* for graduation rates of male Black students for states enrolling more than 10,000 Black male students is 77% (Arizona). The *Benchmark* for states with at least one district enrolling more than 10,000 Black male students is New Jersey (73%).

	Male Graduation Rate: 2010/11		Male Graduation Rate: 2009/10	
Jurisdiction	Black	White, non-Latino	Black	White, non-Latino
USA	53%	77%	52%	78%
Virginia	55%	*76%*	54%	*77%*

Comparison of Estimated Graduation Rates by Gender: 2010/11

The gender gap for Black students in Virginia is thirteen points, while that for White, non-Latino, students is eight points.

	Male Graduation Rate		Female Graduation Rate	
Jurisdiction	Black	White, non-Latino	Black	White, non-Latino
USA	53%	77%	63%	81%
Virginia	55%	*76%*	68%	84%

National Assessment of Educational Progress (NAEP)

NAEP 8th Grade Reading results for Virginia are above those for the nation as a whole for both groups of male students.

Percentages of Male Black and Male White, Non-Latino, Students at or Above Proficient
Reading, Grade 8, 2011

	Percent at or Above Proficient		Gap
Jurisdiction	Black	White, non-Latino	White/Black
USA	10%	35%	25%
Virginia	11%	37%	*26%*

NAEP 8th Grade Mathematics results for Virginia are above those for the nation as a whole for both groups of male students.

Percentages of Male Black and Male White, Non-Latino, Students at or Above Proficient
Mathematics, Grade 8, 2011

	Percent at or Above Proficient		Gap
Jurisdiction	Black	White, non-Latino	White/Black
USA	12%	45%	33%
Virginia	16%	49%	33%

The *Benchmark* for male Black students for 8th Grade Reading is Connecticut, with 19% of male Black students scoring at or above Proficient. The *Benchmark* for 8th Grade Mathematics is Massachusetts, with 26% of male Black students scoring at or above Proficient.

Discipline Inequities

The U.S. Department of Education's Office for Civil Rights has not yet made out-of-school suspension data disaggregated by gender available at the state level for 2009/10. The Center for Civil Rights Remedies at The Civil Rights Project has calculated *combined* male and female percentages from the OCR samples.[81]

State	Black	White, non-Latino	Black/White Ratio
Virginia	16.6	5	3.3

Norfolk

Inequities in Graduation Rates

Male Black students in Norfolk graduated at a slightly higher rate in 2010/11 than in 2009/10, but substantially below the state and national averages for the group. Male White, non-Latino, students graduated at a lower rate in 2010/11 than in 2009/10, also at a rate under the state and national averages for that group.

The *Benchmark* for graduation rates of male Black students for school districts enrolling more than 10,000 male Black students is 73% (Montgomery County, MD).

	Male Graduation Rate: 2010/11		Male Graduation Rate: 2009/10	
Jurisdiction	Black	White, non-Latino	Black	White, non-Latino
USA	53%	77%	52%	78%
Virginia	55%	*76%*	54%	*77%*
Norfolk	*34%*	*45%*	*32%*	*52%*

Discipline and Advanced Placement Inequities

Out-of-school suspension ratios are a measure of the extent to which disparate application of school discipline policies affect students from different racial and ethnic groups. Male Black students with disabilities were nearly two and a half times as likely to receive out-of-school suspensions than were male White, non-Latino, students. Female Black students with disabilities were more than four times as likely to receive out-of-school suspensions than were female White, non-Latino, students. Male Black students without disabilities were twice as likely to receive out-of-school suspensions as were male White, non-Latino, students. Female Black students without disabilities were more than three times as likely to receive out-of-school suspensions as were female White, non-Latino, students.

Enrollment ratios in Advanced Placement Mathematics are an indicator of the differing opportunities to learn that may be provided to students on the basis of race and ethnicity. Male Black students were enrolled in AP Mathematics at one-fifth of the rate of male White, non-Latino, students. Female Black students were enrolled in AP Mathematics at just over one quarter of the rate of female White, non-Latino, students.

[81] From: Losen, Daniel J. and Jonathan Gillispie. Opportunities Suspended: The Disparate Impact of Disciplinary Exclusion from School. The Center for Civil Rights Remedies at The Civil Rights Project, August 2012. *Source:* CRDC, 2009-2010 (numbers from national sample rounded to one decimal).

Virginia Beach

Inequities in Graduation Rates

Male Black students in Virginia Beach graduated at the same rate in 2010/11 as in 2009/10, slightly below the state average and slightly above national averages for the group. Male White, non-Latino, students graduated at a lower rate in 2010/11 than in 2009/10, a rate below the state and national averages for that group.

The *Benchmark* for graduation rates of male Black students for school districts enrolling more than 10,000 male Black students is 73% (Montgomery County, MD).

	Male Graduation Rate: 2010/11		Male Graduation Rate: 2009/10	
Jurisdiction	Black	White, non-Latino	Black	White, non-Latino
USA	53%	77%	52%	78%
Virginia	55%	*76%*	54%	*77%*
Virginia Beach	*54%*	*58%*	54%	*72%*

Discipline and Advanced Placement Inequities

Out-of-school suspension ratios are a measure of the extent to which disparate application of school discipline policies affect students from different racial and ethnic groups. Black students with disabilities were nearly twice as likely to receive out-of-school suspensions than were White, non-Latino, students. Male Black students without disabilities were nearly two and a half times as likely to receive out-of-school suspensions as were male White, non-Latino, students. Female Black students without disabilities were more than three and a half times as likely to receive out-of-school suspensions as were female White, non-Latino, students.

Enrollment ratios in Advanced Placement Mathematics are an indicator of the differing opportunities to learn that may be provided to students on the basis of race and ethnicity. Black students were enrolled in AP Mathematics at one-third of the rate of White, non-Latino, students.

WASHINGTON

Inequities in Graduation Rates

Male Black students in Washington graduated at a lower rate in 2010/11 than in 2009/10, below the national average for the group. Male White, non-Latino, students also graduated at a lower rate in 2010/11 than in 2009/10, also below the national average for that group.

The *Benchmark* for graduation rates of male Black students for states enrolling more than 10,000 Black male students is 77% (Arizona). The *Benchmark* for states with at least one district enrolling more than 10,000 Black male students is New Jersey (73%).

	Male Graduation Rate: 2010/11		Male Graduation Rate: 2009/10	
Jurisdiction	Black	White, non-Latino	Black	White, non-Latino
USA	53%	77%	52%	78%
Washington	*50%*	*71%*	55%	*74%*

Comparison of Estimated Graduation Rates by Gender: 2010/11

The gender gap for Black students in Washington is a reversed two points, while that for White, non-Latino, students is one point.

	Male Graduation Rate		Female Graduation Rate	
Jurisdiction	Black	White, non-Latino	Black	White, non-Latino
USA	53%	77%	63%	81%
Washington	*50%*	*71%*	*48%*	*72%*

National Assessment of Educational Progress (NAEP)

NAEP 8th Grade Reading results for Washington are above the national average for male Black students and at the national average for male White, non-Latino, students.

Percentages of Male Black and Male White, Non-Latino, Students at or Above Proficient
Reading, Grade 8, 2011

	Percent at or Above Proficient		Gap
Jurisdiction	Black	White, non-Latino	White/Black
USA	10%	35%	25%
Washington	12%	35%	22%

NAEP 8th Grade Mathematics results for are slightly below the national average for male Black students and slightly above the national averages for White, non-Latino, students.

Percentages of Male Black and Male White, Non-Latino, Students at or Above Proficient
Mathematics, Grade 8, 2011

	Percent at or Above Proficient		Gap
Jurisdiction	Black	White, non-Latino	White/Black
USA	12%	45%	33%
Washington	*11%*	47%	*36%*

The *Benchmark* for male Black students for 8th Grade Reading is Connecticut, with 19% of male Black students scoring at or above Proficient. The *Benchmark* for 8th Grade Mathematics is Massachusetts, with 26% of male Black students scoring at or above Proficient.

Discipline Inequities

The U.S. Department of Education's Office for Civil Rights has not yet made out-of-school suspension data disaggregated by gender available at the state level for 2009/10. The Center for Civil Rights Remedies at The Civil Rights Project has calculated *combined* male and female percentages from the OCR samples.[82]

State	Black	White, non-Latino	Black/White Ratio
Washington	13.6	5.8	2.3

[82] From: Losen, Daniel J. and Jonathan Gillispie. Opportunities Suspended: The Disparate Impact of Disciplinary Exclusion from School. The Center for Civil Rights Remedies at The Civil Rights Project, August 2012. *Source:* CRDC, 2009-2010 (numbers from national sample rounded to one decimal).

WEST VIRGINIA

Inequities in Graduation Rates

Male Black students in West Virginia graduated at a higher rate in 2010/11 than in 2009/10, but still above the national average for the group. Male White, non-Latino, students also graduated at a slightly higher rate in 2010/11 than in 2009/10, a rate lower than the national average for that group.

The *Benchmark* for graduation rates of male Black students for states enrolling more than 10,000 Black male students is 77% (Arizona). The *Benchmark* for states with at least one district enrolling more than 10,000 Black male students is New Jersey (73%).

	Male Graduation Rate: 2010/11		Male Graduation Rate: 2009/10	
Jurisdiction	Black	White, non-Latino	Black	White, non-Latino
USA	53%	77%	52%	78%
West Virginia	65%	*70%*	62%	*69%*

Comparison of Estimated Graduation Rates by Gender: 2010/11

The gender gap for Black students in West Virginia is three points, while that for White, non-Latino, students is four points.

	Male Graduation Rate		Female Graduation Rate	
Jurisdiction	Black	White, non-Latino	Black	White, non-Latino
USA	53%	77%	63%	81%
West Virginia	65%	*70%*	68%	*74%*

National Assessment of Educational Progress (NAEP)

NAEP 8th Grade Reading results for West Virginia are above the national average for male Black students and considerably below the national average for male White, non-Latino, students.

Percentages of Male Black and Male White, Non-Latino, Students at or Above Proficient
Reading, Grade 8, 2011

	Percent at or Above Proficient		Gap
Jurisdiction	Black	White, non-Latino	White/Black
USA	10%	35%	25%
West Virginia	13%	19%	5%

NAEP 8th Grade Mathematics results for West Virginia are above average for Black males, but substantially below average for White, non-Latino males.

Percentages of Male Black and Male White, Non-Latino, Students at or Above Proficient
Mathematics, Grade 8, 2011

	Percent at or Above Proficient		Gap
Jurisdiction	Black	White, non-Latino	White/Black
USA	12%	45%	33%
West Virginia	15%	*23%*	8%

The *Benchmark* for male Black students for 8th Grade Reading is Connecticut, with 19% of male Black students scoring at or above Proficient. The *Benchmark* for 8th Grade Mathematics is Massachusetts, with 26% of male Black students scoring at or above Proficient.

Discipline Inequities

The U.S. Department of Education's Office for Civil Rights has not yet made out-of-school suspension data disaggregated by gender available at the state level for 2009/10. The Center for Civil Rights Remedies at The Civil Rights Project has calculated *combined* male and female percentages from the OCR samples.[83]

State	Black	White, non-Latino	Black/White Ratio
West Virginia	18.6	8.7	2.1

[83] From: Losen, Daniel J. and Jonathan Gillispie. Opportunities Suspended: The Disparate Impact of Disciplinary Exclusion from School. The Center for Civil Rights Remedies at The Civil Rights Project, August 2012. *Source:* CRDC, 2009-2010 (numbers from national sample rounded to one decimal).

WISCONSIN

Inequities in Graduation Rates

Male Black students in Wisconsin graduated at a lower rate in 2010/11 than in 2009/10, below the national average for the group. Male White, non-Latino, students graduated at a lower rate in 2010/11 than in 2009/10..

The *Benchmark* for graduation rates of male Black students for states enrolling more than 10,000 Black male students is 77% (Arizona). The *Benchmark* for states with at least one district enrolling more than 10,000 Black male students is New Jersey (73%).

	Male Graduation Rate: 2010/11		Male Graduation Rate: 2009/10	
Jurisdiction	Black	White, non-Latino	Black	White, non-Latino
USA	53%	77%	52%	78%
Wisconsin	*47%*	89%	55%	92%

Comparison of Estimated Graduation Rates by Gender: 2010/11

The gender gap for Black students in Wisconsin is three points, while that for White, non-Latino, students is four points.

	Male Graduation Rate		Female Graduation Rate	
Jurisdiction	Black	White, non-Latino	Black	White, non-Latino
USA	53%	77%	63%	81%
Wisconsin	*47%*	89%	*50%*	89%

National Assessment of Educational Progress (NAEP)

NAEP 8th Grade Reading results for Wisconsin are below those for the nation as a whole for both groups of male students.

Percentages of Male Black and Male White, Non-Latino, Students at or Above Proficient
Reading, Grade 8, 2011

	Percent at or Above Proficient		Gap
Jurisdiction	Black	White, non-Latino	White/Black
USA	10%	35%	25%
Wisconsin	*9%*	*34%*	25%

NAEP 8th Grade Mathematics results for Wisconsin are below the national average for male Black students and above the national averages for male White, non-Latino, students.

Percentages of Male Black and Male White, Non-Latino, Students at or Above Proficient
Mathematics, Grade 8, 2011

	Percent at or Above Proficient		Gap
Jurisdiction	Black	White, non-Latino	White/Black
USA	12%	45%	33%
Wisconsin	*8%*	49%	*41%*

The *Benchmark* for male Black students for 8th Grade Reading is Connecticut, with 19% of male Black students scoring at or above Proficient. The *Benchmark* for 8th Grade Mathematics is Massachusetts, with 26% of male Black students scoring at or above Proficient.

Discipline Inequities

The U.S. Department of Education's Office for Civil Rights has not yet made out-of-school suspension data disaggregated by gender available at the state level for 2009/10. The Center for Civil Rights Remedies at The Civil Rights Project has calculated *combined* male and female percentages from the OCR samples.[84]

State	Black	White, non-Latino	Black/White Ratio
Wisconsin	18.5	3.2	5.8

Milwaukee

Inequities in Graduation Rates

Male Black students in Milwaukee graduated at a lower rate in 2010/11 than in 2009/10, below the state and national averages for the group. Male White, non-Latino, students graduated at a much higher rate in 2010/11 than in 2009/10, but below the state and national averages for the group.

The *Benchmark* for graduation rates of male Black students for school districts enrolling more than 10,000 male Black students is 73% (Montgomery County, MD).

	Male Graduation Rate: 2010/11		Male Graduation Rate: 2009/10	
Jurisdiction	Black	White, non-Latino	Black	White, non-Latino
USA	53%	77%	52%	78%
Wisconsin	*47%*	89%	55%	92%
Milwaukee	*37%*	*71%*	*45%*	*55%*

National Assessment of Educational Progress (NAEP)

NAEP 8th Grade Reading results for Milwaukee are below those for the state and the nation as a whole for both groups of male students.

Percentages of Male Black and Male White, Non-Latino, Students at or Above Proficient
Reading, Grade 8, 2011

	Percent at or Above Proficient		Gap
Jurisdiction	Black	White, non-Latino	White/Black
USA	10%	35%	25%
Wisconsin	*9%*	*34%*	25%
Milwaukee	*3%*	*21%*	19%

NAEP 8th Grade Mathematics results for Milwaukee are below those for the state and the nation as a whole for both groups of male students.

[84] From: Losen, Daniel J. and Jonathan Gillispie. Opportunities Suspended: The Disparate Impact of Disciplinary Exclusion from School. The Center for Civil Rights Remedies at The Civil Rights Project, August 2012. *Source:* CRDC, 2009-2010 (numbers from national sample rounded to one decimal).

Percentages of Male Black and Male White, Non-Latino, Students at or Above Proficient
Mathematics, Grade 8, 2011

Jurisdiction	Percent at or Above Proficient		Gap
	Black	White, non-Latino	White/Black
USA	12%	45%	33%
Wisconsin	*8%*	49%	*41%*
Milwaukee	*5%*	*20%*	15%

The *Benchmark* for male Black students for 8th Grade Reading is Connecticut, with 19% of male Black students scoring at or above Proficient. The *Benchmark* for 8th Grade Mathematics is Massachusetts, with 26% of male Black students scoring at or above Proficient.

Discipline and Advanced Placement Inequities

Out-of-school suspension ratios are a measure of the extent to which disparate application of school discipline policies affect students from different racial and ethnic groups. Male Black students with disabilities were twice as likely to receive out-of-school suspensions than were male White, non-Latino, students. Female Black students with disabilities were more than two and a half times as likely to receive out-of-school suspensions than were female White, non-Latino, students. Male Black students without disabilities were more than two and a half times as likely to receive out-of-school suspensions as were male White, non-Latino, students. Female Black students without disabilities were more than four times as likely to receive out-of-school suspensions as were female White, non-Latino, students.

Enrollment ratios in Advanced Placement Mathematics are an indicator of the differing opportunities to learn that may be provided to students on the basis of race and ethnicity. Male Black students were enrolled in AP Mathematics at less than one-third of the rate of White, non-Latino, students.

WYOMING

Inequities in Graduation Rates

The few male Black students in Wyoming graduated at a lower rate than in 2009/10, but above the national average for the group. Male White, non-Latino, students graduated at the same rate in 2010/11 than in 2009/10, slightly above the national average for that group.

The *Benchmark* for graduation rates of male Black students for states enrolling more than 10,000 Black male students is 77% (Arizona). The *Benchmark* for states with at least one district enrolling more than 10,000 Black male students is New Jersey (73%).

	Male Graduation Rate: 2010/11		Male Graduation Rate: 2009/10	
Jurisdiction	Black	White, non-Latino	Black	White, non-Latino
USA	53%	77%	52%	78%
Wyoming	56%	78%	59%	78%

Comparison of Estimated Graduation Rates by Gender: 2010/11

The gender gap for Black students in Wyoming is eight points, while that for White, non-Latino, students is one point.

	Male Graduation Rate		Female Graduation Rate	
Jurisdiction	Black	White, non-Latino	Black	White, non-Latino
USA	53%	77%	63%	81%
Wyoming	56%	78%	64%	79%

National Assessment of Educational Progress (NAEP)

NAEP 8th Grade Reading results for Wyoming are below the national average for male White, non-Latino, students.

Percentages of Male Black and Male White, Non-Latino, Students at or Above Proficient
Reading, Grade 8, 2011

	Percent at or Above Proficient		Gap
Jurisdiction	Black	White, non-Latino	White/Black
USA	10%	35%	25%
Wyoming	‡	*34%*	-

NAEP 8th Grade Mathematics results for Wyoming are above those for the nation as a whole for male White, non-Latino, students.

Percentages of Male Black and Male White, Non-Latino, Students at or Above Proficient
Mathematics, Grade 8, 2011

	Percent at or Above Proficient		Gap
Jurisdiction	Black	White, non-Latino	White/Black
USA	12%	45%	33%
Wyoming	‡	45%	-

The *Benchmark* for male Black students for 8th Grade Reading is Connecticut, with 19% of male Black students scoring at or above Proficient. The *Benchmark* for 8th Grade Mathematics is Massachusetts, with 26% of male Black students scoring at or above Proficient.

Discipline Inequities

The U.S. Department of Education's Office for Civil Rights has not yet made out-of-school suspension data disaggregated by gender available at the state level for 2009/10. The Center for Civil Rights Remedies at The Civil Rights Project has calculated *combined* male and female percentages from the OCR samples.[85]

State	Black	White, non-Latino	Black/White Ratio
Wyoming	13.8	10	1.4

85 From: Losen, Daniel J. and Jonathan Gillispie. Opportunities Suspended: The Disparate Impact of Disciplinary Exclusion from School. The Center for Civil Rights Remedies at The Civil Rights Project, August 2012. *Source:* CRDC, 2009-2010 (numbers from national sample rounded to one decimal).

AMERICAN INDIAN STUDENTS AND PUBLIC EDUCATION

National Summary

This section includes United States Census[86] demographic and educational achievement data, high school graduation rate estimates based on the Department of Education's National Center for Education Statistics data[87] for American Indian and White, non-Latino, students for all states. Data from the National Assessment of Educational Progress 8th Grade Reading and Mathematics 2011 tests are also included. Each section—at the risk of repetition—is designed to be self-contained for the convenience of readers interested only in specific states.

American Indians, the descendents of the original inhabitants of what is now the United States, as with African-Americans, the descendents of enslaved Africans, have historically constituted a particularly stigmatized caste. Many continue to live on reservations in poverty. Others have recently become prosperous from ownership of natural resources and gambling casinos. Still others have integrated into multi-ethnic urban communities. The American Indian poverty rate varies from 57% in South Dakota and 51% in North Dakota to 21% in Illinois and 16% in Virginia.

Educational achievement varies from North Carolina, where 32% of the adult American Indian population (primarily Cherokee) have not finished high school, to Kansas (also primarily Cherokee), where only 13% of the adult American Indian population has not finished high school. At the other end of the education spectrum, while 19% of the American Indian population in Missouri and Georgia have a BA degree or higher, only 8% of American Indians in Alaska and Idaho have a BA degree or higher (all four again primarily Cherokee). A quarter of the American Indians in the primarily Navaho groups in Arizona and New Mexico have not finished high school.

As with most other American students, gender differences in educational achievement usually are in favor of female students. The estimated American Indian graduation rates are 65% for males and 72% for females. The graduation rates are particularly low in the Dakotas, where, on average, only about one-third of American Indian students in grade nine graduate four years later.

[86] American Community Survey table DP02.
[87] NCES/CCD/ELSI

American Indian Demography

American Indian Population							
American Indian Alone	Navajo	Cherokee	Sioux	Chippewa	Choctaw	Pueblo	Apache
2,022,516	143,960	301,380	111,334	106,941	85,569	56,275	53,509

The population of the United States in 2011 was 312 million, of whom 231 million were listed as "White alone," 52 million as "Latino," 39 million as "Black or African American alone" and 14 million as "Asian alone." As with Asian-Americans, American Indians are a highly disparate group. Most are of mixed ancestry. The principal tribes (identified as, e.g., "Cherokee Alone," by the Census) are Navajo, Cherokee, Sioux, Chippewa, Choctaw, Pueblo and Apache (in that order). Among the states, California has the largest American Indian population (723,225), followed by Oklahoma (482,760), and Arizona (353,386). The Navajo are highly concentrated in their Arizona/New Mexico reservation. The Chippewa are similarly concentrated in Minnesota and Michigan and the Sioux in the Dakotas.

American Indian Populations[88]

Sorted by State[89]

State	American Indian Alone	Navajo	Cherokee	Sioux	Chippewa	Choctaw	Pueblo	Apache
Alabama	21,755		9,402			2,515		
Alaska	5,259		951	365	455	254		
Arizona	265,436	129.426	3,641	2,161	959	1,362	9,899	23,539
Arkansas	16,421		8,442	328		2,224		
California	214,811	7,900	28,812	5,834	3,499	7,877	4,061	9,170
Colorado	36,116	5,269	4,303	3,237	1,020	729	806	2,166
Connecticut	5,841		675					
Delaware	2,317		468					
Florida	43,145	471	11,017	947	1,423	1,063		689
Georgia	16,969		6,785	509		629		393
Hawaii	2,298		395					
Idaho	16,015	557	1,358	504	400	247		
Illinois	17,107	444	4,431	989	1,332	504		588
Indiana	11,221		4,087	563	695			
Iowa	7,670		996	1,477	444			
Kansas	20,679	605	6,299	923	250	870		431
Kentucky	7,194		3,290					
Louisiana	21,597		2,643			1,682		
Maine	5,653		431					
Maryland	11,854		2,823					
Massachusetts	8,442		1,028					
Michigan	44,360		5,904	696	23,271	424		529
Minnesota	47,386		632	5,776	33,233			
Mississippi	11,908		1,203			6,702		
Missouri	18,270	469	9,941	893	486	806		390
Montana	56,309	303	629	5,602	2,872			
Nebraska	13,040	196	608	4,075				
Nevada	24,052	1,042	2,064	587	465			593
New								

[88] American Indian Alone (DP02) 2010 5-year estimates; Tribal Demography, Census, DP-1, 2000.

[89] The District of Columbia is not included in this section due to the very small number of American Indians in that jurisdiction.

Hampshire								
New Jersey	12,442		1,596					
New Mexico	181,352	106,334	1,472	865	353	532	38,404	6,847
New York	47,728		3,821	524	513		388	350
North Carolina	90,521	396	14,284	500	506	385		420
North Dakota	32,268			8,910	13,557			
Ohio	16,423	330	7,813	719	1,213			408
Oklahoma	244,890	982	98,605	956		43,434	514	1,738
Oregon	51,181	534	4,548	1,699		1,086		575
Pennsylvania	12,299		3,290	628	407			307
Rhode Island	3,223							
South Carolina	10,950		3,579					
South Dakota	64,097			53,671	672			
Tennessee	11,948		6,592			447		
Texas	86,211	1,741	18,742	1,614	956	10,393	1,580	3,108
Utah	28,289	14,456	832	626			296	373
Vermont	1,499							
Virginia	18,112	375	4,648	511	405	486		
Washington	75,738	1,079	5,389	3,111	3,143	918	327	895
West Virginia	2,418		1,287					
Wisconsin	44,142		1,163	705	14,412			
Wyoming	11,714	348	461	829				
USA	2,022,516	143,960	301,380	111,334	106,941	85,569	56,275	53,509

American Indian Demography[90]

Sorted by American Indian Alone Population

American Indians are concentrated in four states: Arizona, Oklahoma, California and New Mexico. In each of those states the American Indian population is dominated by a single tribe: Navajo in Arizona and New Mexico. Cherokee in Oklahoma and California. Other states in which the American Indian population is dominated by a single tribe include North Carolina and Texas (Cherokee); South Dakota (Sioux); Minnesota, Michigan, and Wisconsin (Chippewa); Utah (Navajo). Some states have comparatively large American Indian populations made up of tribes, such as the Blackfeet in Montana or the various localized tribes in the Pacific coast states, not included in the table of the seven largest tribes in the United States. Others have large urbanized populations without dominant tribal groups.

State	American Indian Alone	Cherokee	Navajo	Sioux	Chippewa	Choctaw	Pueblo	Apache
Arizona	265,436	3,641	129.426	2,161	959	1,362	9,899	23,539
Oklahoma	244,890	98,605	982	956		43,434	514	1,738
California	214,811	28,812	7,900	5,834	3,499	7,877	4,061	9,170
New Mexico	181,352	1,472	106,334	865	353	532	38,404	6,847
North Carolina	90,521	14,284	396	500	506	385		420
Texas	86,211	18,742	1,741	1,614	956	10,393	1,580	3,108
Washington	75,738	5,389	1,079	3,111	3,143	918	327	895
South Dakota	64,097			53,671	672			
Montana	56,309	629	303	5,602	2,872			
Oregon	51,181	4,548	534	1,699		1,086		575
New York	47,728	3,821		524	513		388	350
Minnesota	47,386	632		5,776	33,233			
Michigan	44,360	5,904		696	23,271	424		529
Wisconsin	44,142	1,163		705	14,412			
Florida	43,145	11,017	471	947	1,423	1,063		689
Colorado	36,116	4,303	5,269	3,237	1,020	729	806	2,166
North Dakota	32,268			8,910	13,557			
Utah	28,289	832	14,456	626			296	373
Nevada	24,052	2,064	1,042	587	465			593
Alabama	21,755	9,402				2,515		
Louisiana	21,597	2,643				1,682		
Kansas	20,679	6,299	605	923	250	870		431

[90] American Indian Alone (DP02) 2010 5-year estimates; Tribal Demography, Census, DP-1, 2000.

Missouri	18,270	9,941	469	893	486	806		390
Virginia	18,112	4,648	375	511	405	486		
Illinois	17,107	4,431	444	989	1,332	504		588
Georgia	16,969	6,785		509		629		393
Ohio	16,423	7,813	330	719	1,213			408
Arkansas	16,421	8,442		328		2,224		
Idaho	16,015	1,358	557	504	400	247		
Nebraska	13,040	608	196	4,075				
New Jersey	12,442	1,596						
Pennsylvania	12,299	3,290		628	407			307
Tennessee	11,948	6,592				447		
Mississippi	11,908	1,203				6,702		
Maryland	11,854	2,823						
Wyoming	11,714	461	348	829				
Indiana	11,221	4,087		563	695			
South Carolina	10,950	3,579						
Massachusetts	8,442	1,028						
Iowa	7,670	996		1,477	444			
Kentucky	7,194	3,290						
Connecticut	5,841	675						
Maine	5,653	431						
Alaska	5,259	951		365	455	254		
Rhode Island	3,223							
West Virginia	2,418	1,287						
Delaware	2,317	468						
Hawaii	2,298	395						
New Hampshire	1,946							
Vermont	1,499							
USA	2,022,516	301,380	143,960	111,334	106,941	85,569	56,275	53,509

American Indian Poverty Rates

Families with Related Children under 18 Years[91]

Sorted by State

State	American Indian Alone	Cherokee	Navajo	Sioux	Chippewa	Choctaw	Pueblo	Apache
Alabama	24%	34%				25%		
Alaska	23%	42%						
Arizona	34%	24%	33%			5%		35%
Arkansas	27%	23%				27%		
California	22%	15%	7%	31%	17%	21%		31%
Colorado	26%	20%	20%	21%				16%
Connecticut	18%	30%						
Delaware	39%							
Florida	25%	18%				2%		
Georgia	26%	15%						
Hawaii	14%	20%						
Idaho	34%	7%	29%					
Illinois	20%	22%						
Indiana	24%	34%						
Iowa	29%	18%						
Kansas	27%	27%	24%			20%		
Kentucky	29%	36%						
Louisiana	23%	8%				11%		
Maine	46%							
Maryland	17%	9%						
Massachusetts	28%	42%						
Michigan	29%	39%			30%			
Minnesota	45%	18%		83%	57%			
Mississippi	28%	11%				26%		
Missouri	26%	33%				24%		
Montana	39%	63%	50%	43%	43%			
Nebraska	44%			26%				
Nevada	18%	14%	20%					

[91] American Indian Alone (DP03) 2010 5-year estimates.

New Hampshire	18%							
New Jersey	20%	23%						
New Mexico	34%	7%	38%			9%	29%	60%
New York	25%	41%						
North Carolina	32%	35%						
North Dakota	46%			60%	40%			
Ohio	37%	49%						
Oklahoma	26%	24%	20%	54%		21%		68%
Oregon	30%	30%	39%			11%		
Pennsylvania	27%	30%						
Rhode Island	35%							
South Carolina	28%	32%						
South Dakota	48%			69%				
Tennessee	38%	23%				24%		
Texas	24%	23%	28%	49%		15%		15%
Utah	31%		35%					
Vermont	29%							
Virginia	15%	27%						
Washington	30%	11%	18%	20%	20%	9%		
West Virginia	36%	56%						
Wisconsin	35%	21%			49%			
Wyoming	29%							
USA	29%	25%	33%	38%	35%	20%	27%	30%

American Indian Poverty Rates

Families with Related Children under 18 Years[92]

Sorted by Poverty Rates

State	American Indian Alone	Cherokee	Navajo	Sioux	Chippewa	Choctaw	Pueblo	Apache
Hawaii	14%	20%						
Virginia	15%	27%						
Maryland	17%	9%						
Connecticut	18%	30%						
Nevada	18%	14%	20%					
New Hampshire	18%							
Illinois	20%	22%						
New Jersey	20%	23%						
California	22%	15%	7%	31%	17%	21%		31%
Alaska	23%	42%						
Louisiana	23%	8%				11%		
Alabama	24%	34%				25%		
Indiana	24%	34%						
Texas	24%	23%	28%	49%		15%		15%
Florida	25%	18%				2%		
New York	25%	41%						
Colorado	26%	20%	20%	21%				16%
Georgia	26%	15%						
Missouri	26%	33%				24%		
Oklahoma	26%	24%	20%	54%		21%		68%
Arkansas	27%	23%				27%		
Kansas	27%	27%	24%			20%		
Pennsylvania	27%	30%						
Massachusetts	28%	42%						
Mississippi	28%	11%				26%		
South Carolina	28%	32%						
Iowa	29%	18%						
Kentucky	29%	36%						

92 American Indian Alone (DP03) 2010 5-year estimates.

Michigan	29%	39%			30%			
Vermont	29%							
Wyoming	29%							
Oregon	30%	30%	39%			11%		
Washington	30%	11%	18%	20%	20%	9%		
Utah	31%		35%					
North Carolina	32%	35%						
Arizona	34%	24%	33%			5%		35%
Idaho	34%	7%	29%					
New Mexico	34%	7%	38%			9%	29%	60%
Rhode Island	35%							
Wisconsin	35%	21%			49%			
West Virginia	36%	56%						
Ohio	37%	49%						
Tennessee	38%	23%				24%		
Delaware	39%							
Montana	39%	63%	50%	43%	43%			
Nebraska	44%			26%				
Minnesota	45%	18%		83%	57%			
Maine	46%							
North Dakota	46%			60%	40%			
South Dakota	48%			69%				
USA	29%	25%	33%	38%	35%	20%	27%	30%

American Indian Educational Achievement

Estimated High School Graduation Rates

Sorted by State

American Indian high school graduation rates vary widely among the states: from 40% to 86%. In most cases Asian-American graduation rates are lower than the comparative rates for Asian-American, White, non-Latino, and Latino students, but higher that those for Black students. Factors affecting high school graduation rates for American Indian students are difficult to determine, given the relatively small number of students involved. There appear to be negative effects where large American Indian populations are on reservations and positive effects in states with higher quality schools systems, but in some cases the opposite is true.

State	American Indian	Asian	Latino	Black	White, non-Latino
Alabama	78%	*77%*	*59%*	58%	*73%*
Alaska	*54%*	*87%*	*62%*	65%	*77%*
Arizona	*61%*	*87%*	67%	75%	80%
Arkansas	69%	91%	77%	69%	*77%*
California	69%	92%	68%	59%	84%
Colorado	*54%*	*72%*	*60%*	58%	*77%*
Connecticut	*45%*	-	*58%*	64%	87%
Delaware	-	93%	66%	65%	*76%*
Florida	65%	*84%*	68%	*54%*	*68%*
Georgia	65%	90%	*58%*	*55%*	*70%*
Hawaii	62%	*67%*	*47%*	75%	*51%*
Idaho	*54%*	90%	74%	70%	79%
Illinois	*46%*	90%	66%	*53%*	81%
Indiana	*60%*	97%	74%	60%	*78%*
Iowa	67%	*86%*	81%	61%	87%
Kansas	64%	*81%*	72%	63%	83%
Kentucky	-	-	80%	65%	*75%*
Louisiana	69%	99%	*52%*	*57%*	*71%*
Maine	86%	*88%*	-	63%	97%
Maryland	69%	92%	73%	66%	81%
Massachusetts	69%	89%	*54%*	63%	85%
Michigan	*61%*	92%	66%	*53%*	79%
Minnesota	63%	92%	*63%*	65%	94%
Mississippi	-	*77%*	*57%*	*57%*	*66%*
Missouri	74%	92%	82%	62%	83%
Montana	*58%*	-	89%	100%	81%
Nebraska	*49%*	93%	74%	*42%*	86%
Nevada	*40%*	*73%*	*53%*	*45%*	*68%*
New Hampshire	-	-	-	-	82%
New Jersey	80%	-	77%	75%	90%
New Mexico	*53%*	*79%*	*60%*	*57%*	*69%*
New York	*55%*	89%	*47%*	*45%*	*74%*

North Carolina	*60%*	*80%*	*53%*	67%	*77%*
North Dakota	*51%*	-	-	-	92%
Ohio	76%	93%	69%	*51%*	83%
Oklahoma	74%	-	75%	66%	79%
Oregon	74%	*82%*	78%	65%	*78%*
Pennsylvania	65%	98%	66%	64%	88%
Rhode Island	-	*65%*	*62%*	59%	*77%*
South Carolina	*50%*	*39%*	*50%*	*54%*	*67%*
South Dakota	*43%*	99%	69%	73%	84%
Tennessee	*58%*	95%	69%	71%	82%
Texas	68%	*80%*	*56%*	*46%*	*63%*
Utah	*54%*	*84%*	*55%*	62%	79%
Vermont	-	-	70%	78%	80%
Virginia	67%	95%	82%	62%	80%
Washington	*51%*	*79%*	*53%*	*49%*	*72%*
West Virginia	-	91%	79%	67%	*72%*
Wisconsin	69%	95%	67%	*48%*	89%
Wyoming	*42%*	*87%*	78%	60%	79%
USA	62%	89%	65%	58%	79%

Italics indicate below national average for group.

American Indian Enrollment and Estimated High School Graduation Rates*

Sorted by State

The relatively small numbers of American Indian students make estimated graduation rates by gender unreliable.

State Name	Total Students	American Indian Students	American Indian Estimated Graduation Rates
Alabama	755,552	6,102	78%
Alaska	132,104	30,433	*54%*
Arizona	1,071,751	55,312	*61%*
Arkansas	482,114	3,369	69%
California	6,289,578	43,546	69%
Colorado	843,316	7,452	*54%*
Connecticut	560,546	2,100	*45%*
Delaware	129,403	635	-
Florida	2,643,347	10,493	65%
Georgia	1,677,067	3,959	65%
Hawaii	179,601	1,071	62%
Idaho	275,859	3,846	*54%*
Illinois	2,091,654	6,846	*46%*
Indiana	1,047,232	3,376	*60%*
Iowa	495,775	2,362	67%
Kansas	483,701	6,184	64%
Kentucky	673,128	941	-
Louisiana	696,558	6,585	69%
Maine	189,077	1,385	86%
Maryland	852,211	3,047	69%
Massachusetts	955,563	2,382	69%
Michigan	1,587,067	13,003	*61%*
Minnesota	838,037	16,296	63%
Mississippi	490,526	930	-
Missouri	918,710	4,341	74%
Montana	141,693	15,734	*58%*
Nebraska	298,500	4,413	*49%*
Nevada	437,149	5,705	*40%*
New Hampshire	194,711	653	-
New Jersey	1,402,548	1,864	80%
New Mexico	338,122	34,530	*53%*
New York	2,734,955	14,541	*55%*
North Carolina	1,490,605	22,199	*60%*
North Dakota	96,323	8,789	*51%*
Ohio	1,754,191	2,519	76%
Oklahoma	659,911	116,597	74%
Oregon	570,720	10,406	74%
Pennsylvania	1,793,284	2,892	65%
Rhode Island	143,793	951	-
South Carolina	725,838	2,111	*50%*

South Dakota	126,128	14,683	*43%*
Tennessee	987,422	1,902	*58%*
Texas	4,935,715	23,607	68%
Utah	585,552	7,816	*54%*
Vermont	96,858	268	-
Virginia	1,251,440	4,251	67%
Washington	1,043,788	17,570	*51%*
West Virginia	282,879	338	-
Wisconsin	872,286	11,625	69%
Wyoming	89,009	2,937	*42%*
USA	49,484,181	564,949	62%

Italics indicate below national average.

* Graduation rates for states with fewer than 1,000 American Indian students are not calculated.

American Indian Enrollment and Estimated High School Graduation Rates*

Sorted by Estimated Graduation Rates

State Name	Total Students	American Indian Students	American Indian Estimated Graduation Rates
Maine	189,077	1,385	86%
New Jersey	1,402,548	1,864	80%
Alabama	755,552	6,102	78%
Ohio	1,754,191	2,519	76%
Oklahoma	659,911	116,597	74%
Oregon	570,720	10,406	74%
Missouri	918,710	4,341	74%
California	6,289,578	43,546	69%
Wisconsin	872,286	11,625	69%
Louisiana	696,558	6,585	69%
Arkansas	482,114	3,369	69%
Maryland	852,211	3,047	69%
Massachusetts	955,563	2,382	69%
Texas	4,935,715	23,607	68%
Virginia	1,251,440	4,251	67%
Iowa	495,775	2,362	67%
Florida	2,643,347	10,493	65%
Georgia	1,677,067	3,959	65%
Pennsylvania	1,793,284	2,892	65%
Kansas	483,701	6,184	64%
Minnesota	838,037	16,296	63%
Hawaii	179,601	1,071	62%
Arizona	1,071,751	55,312	*61%*
Michigan	1,587,067	13,003	*61%*
North Carolina	1,490,605	22,199	*60%*
Indiana	1,047,232	3,376	*60%*
Montana	141,693	15,734	*58%*
Tennessee	987,422	1,902	*58%*
New York	2,734,955	14,541	*55%*
Alaska	132,104	30,433	*54%*
Utah	585,552	7,816	*54%*
Colorado	843,316	7,452	*54%*
Idaho	275,859	3,846	*54%*
New Mexico	338,122	34,530	*53%*
Washington	1,043,788	17,570	*51%*
North Dakota	96,323	8,789	*51%*
South Carolina	725,838	2,111	*50%*
Nebraska	298,500	4,413	*49%*
Illinois	2,091,654	6,846	*46%*
Connecticut	560,546	2,100	*45%*
South Dakota	126,128	14,683	*43%*
Wyoming	89,009	2,937	*42%*

Nevada	437,149	5,705	*40%*
Rhode Island	143,793	951	-
Kentucky	673,128	941	-
Mississippi	490,526	930	-
New Hampshire	194,711	653	-
Delaware	129,403	635	-
West Virginia	282,879	338	-
Vermont	96,858	268	-
USA	49,484,181	564,949	62%

Italics indicate below national average.

* Graduation rates for states with fewer than 1,000 are not calculated.

American Indian Educational Attainment

Percent High School Graduate or Higher

Data on educational attainment is from the United States Census Bureau, Selected Social Characteristics in the United States (DP02) American Community Survey (ACS) three- and five-year estimates. Educational attainment is self-reported for the population 25 years and over. The High School Graduate or Higher category includes people whose highest degree was a high school diploma or its equivalent, people who attended college but did not receive a degree, and people who received an associate's, bachelor's, master's, or professional or doctorate degree. People who reported completing the 12th grade but not receiving a diploma are not included. It has been pointed out that data from this category may be deceptive, given, for example, varying proportions of people receiving GED or other alternative to high school diplomas.

Total Population and Other Groups					
Total Population	White Alone	Black Alone	Latino	Asian	American Indian
85%	87%	81%	62%	86%	77%

Educational attainment reported by American Indians is lower than that of the total U.S. population and lower than that of subgroups other than those classifying themselves as Latinos, who may be of any race.

Race/Ethnicity Comparative Educational Attainment

High School Diploma or Higher, Age 25 and Over

Sorted by State

State	Total Population	Asian Alone	White Alone	Black Alone	Latino	American Indian
Alabama	*81%*	*85%*	*83%*	*77%*	*56%*	*74%*
Alaska	91%	*79%*	94%	91%	77%	90%
Arizona	85%	89%	87%	88%	62%	*72%*
Arkansas	*82%*	*82%*	*84%*	*77%*	*49%*	81%
California	*81%*	86%	*84%*	87%	*57%*	*76%*
Colorado	89%	86%	91%	87%	65%	80%
Connecticut	88%	88%	91%	81%	68%	78%
Delaware	87%	91%	89%	84%	*58%*	79%
Florida	85%	86%	87%	*78%*	74%	78%
Georgia	*84%*	86%	*86%*	81%	*56%*	77%
Hawaii	90%	86%	95%	96%	87%	88%
Idaho	88%	86%	89%	83%	*53%*	80%
Illinois	86%	91%	89%	82%	*60%*	79%
Indiana	86%	89%	87%	82%	*61%*	79%
Iowa	90%	*81%*	91%	*80%*	*56%*	79%
Kansas	89%	*81%*	91%	85%	*59%*	86%
Kentucky	*81%*	88%	*81%*	81%	63%	79%
Louisiana	*81%*	*77%*	*85%*	*74%*	69%	*69%*
Maine	90%	*85%*	90%	84%	82%	81%
Maryland	88%	90%	90%	86%	62%	80%
Massachusetts	89%	*83%*	91%	82%	65%	85%
Michigan	88%	88%	90%	82%	67%	82%
Minnesota	91%	*80%*	93%	81%	*61%*	81%
Mississippi	*80%*	*76%*	*84%*	*72%*	*57%*	*67%*
Missouri	86%	86%	87%	81%	66%	84%
Montana	91%	*84%*	92%	90%	83%	80%
Nebraska	90%	*84%*	91%	84%	*52%*	79%
Nevada	*84%*	89%	*85%*	87%	*58%*	84%
New Hampshire	91%	90%	91%	86%	80%	81%
New Jersey	87%	92%	89%	83%	70%	*71%*
New Mexico	*83%*	88%	*85%*	87%	70%	*75%*
New York	*84%*	*78%*	89%	*80%*	65%	79%
North Carolina	*84%*	*84%*	*86%*	*80%*	*53%*	*67%*
North Dakota	89%	86%	90%	84%	77%	83%
Ohio	87%	89%	88%	81%	71%	81%
Oklahoma	85%	*82%*	87%	84%	*56%*	83%

Oregon	89%	86%	90%	86%	*55%*	*66%*
Pennsylvania	87%	*83%*	89%	81%	66%	83%
Rhode Island	*84%*	*79%*	*86%*	*75%*	*60%*	78%
South Carolina	*83%*	86%	*86%*	*76%*	*59%*	*73%*
South Dakota	89%	86%	90%	82%	69%	79%
Tennessee	*83%*	86%	*83%*	*80%*	*57%*	80%
Texas	*80%*	87%	*82%*	84%	*58%*	79%
Utah	91%	86%	92%	85%	64%	78%
Vermont	91%	*83%*	91%	86%	91%	*75%*
Virginia	86%	89%	88%	*80%*	68%	79%
Washington	90%	*85%*	92%	87%	*59%*	81%
West Virginia	*82%*	90%	*82%*	84%	73%	80%
Wisconsin	89%	*81%*	91%	*78%*	62%	84%
Wyoming	91%	90%	92%	89%	74%	85%
USA	85%	86%	87%	81%	62%	77%

Italics indicate below national average.

American Indian Educational Attainment[93]

Sorted by State

State Name	Less than High School Diploma	High School Graduate	Some College	BA or Higher
Alabama	24%	33%	29%	14%
Alaska	20%	41%	32%	8%
Arizona	26%	32%	33%	9%
Arkansas	21%	31%	32%	16%
California	25%	26%	35%	13%
Colorado	20%	29%	38%	14%
Connecticut	25%	34%	26%	16%
Delaware	22%	30%	35%	14%
Florida	26%	28%	31%	15%
Georgia	23%	26%	32%	19%
Hawaii	13%	26%	40%	21%
Idaho	21%	34%	37%	8%
Illinois	21%	28%	34%	17%
Indiana	22%	33%	29%	15%
Iowa	22%	30%	34%	13%
Kansas	13%	32%	37%	18%
Kentucky	22%	31%	33%	14%
Louisiana	32%	36%	23%	9%
Maine	22%	29%	35%	14%
Maryland	21%	27%	32%	21%
Massachusetts	21%	30%	27%	22%
Michigan	18%	34%	35%	12%
Minnesota	19%	33%	36%	12%
Mississippi	32%	27%	30%	12%
Missouri	15%	35%	31%	19%
Montana	18%	32%	37%	13%
Nebraska	25%	30%	34%	10%
Nevada	15%	35%	41%	9%
New Hampshire	21%	28%	28%	23%
New Jersey	26%	28%	28%	17%
New Mexico	24%	34%	33%	9%
New York	26%	29%	28%	17%
North Carolina	32%	29%	27%	12%
North Dakota	19%	26%	42%	13%
Ohio	20%	32%	30%	18%
Oklahoma	16%	36%	33%	16%
Oregon	18%	28%	41%	13%
Pennsylvania	20%	32%	31%	18%
Rhode Island	27%	36%	26%	11%
South Carolina	29%	32%	29%	10%
South Dakota	22%	30%	36%	12%

[93] Census, S0201, 2011 ACS 3-year estimates and DP02, 2006-2010 ACS American Indian and Alaska Native Tribes

Tennessee	22%	30%	33%	15%
Texas	25%	25%	33%	18%
Utah	20%	34%	35%	10%
Vermont	22%	38%	25%	15%
Virginia	18%	30%	33%	13%
Washington	18%	30%	38%	13%
West Virginia	20%	38%	32%	8%
Wisconsin	15%	34%	40%	11%
Wyoming	15%	32%	42%	10%

American Indian Educational Attainment[94]

Sorted by Less than High School Diploma

The percentage of American Indians ages 25 and above reporting that they have less education than a high school diploma (or GED) varies from 13% in Hawaii and Kansas to 32% in Louisiana, Mississippi and North Carolina. Many adults in this category may have significant literacy difficulties.

State Name	Less than High School Diploma	High School Graduate	Some College	BA or Higher
Hawaii	13%	26%	40%	21%
Kansas	13%	32%	37%	18%
Missouri	15%	35%	31%	19%
Nevada	15%	35%	41%	9%
Wisconsin	15%	34%	40%	11%
Wyoming	15%	32%	42%	10%
Oklahoma	16%	36%	33%	16%
Michigan	18%	34%	35%	12%
Montana	18%	32%	37%	13%
Oregon	18%	28%	41%	13%
Virginia	18%	30%	33%	13%
Washington	18%	30%	38%	13%
Minnesota	19%	33%	36%	12%
North Dakota	19%	26%	42%	13%
Alaska	20%	41%	32%	8%
Colorado	20%	29%	38%	14%
Ohio	20%	32%	30%	18%
Pennsylvania	20%	32%	31%	18%
Utah	20%	34%	35%	10%
West Virginia	20%	38%	32%	8%
Arkansas	21%	31%	32%	16%
Idaho	21%	34%	37%	8%
Illinois	21%	28%	34%	17%
Maryland	21%	27%	32%	21%
Massachusetts	21%	30%	27%	22%
New Hampshire	21%	28%	28%	23%
Delaware	22%	30%	35%	14%
Indiana	22%	33%	29%	15%
Iowa	22%	30%	34%	13%
Kentucky	22%	31%	33%	14%
Maine	22%	29%	35%	14%
South Dakota	22%	30%	36%	12%
Tennessee	22%	30%	33%	15%
Vermont	22%	38%	25%	15%
Georgia	23%	26%	32%	19%
Alabama	24%	33%	29%	14%
New Mexico	24%	34%	33%	9%

[94] Census, S0201, 2011 ACS 3-year estimates and DP02, 2006-2010 ACS American Indian and Alaska Native Tribes

California	25%	26%	35%	13%
Connecticut	25%	34%	26%	16%
Nebraska	25%	30%	34%	10%
Texas	25%	25%	33%	18%
Arizona	26%	32%	33%	9%
Florida	26%	28%	31%	15%
New Jersey	26%	28%	28%	17%
New York	26%	29%	28%	17%
Rhode Island	27%	36%	26%	11%
South Carolina	29%	32%	29%	10%
Louisiana	32%	36%	23%	9%
Mississippi	32%	27%	30%	12%
North Carolina	32%	29%	27%	12%

American Indian Educational Attainment[95]

Sorted by BA or Higher

The percentage of American Indians ages 25 and above reporting that they have a BA degree or higher varies from 23% in New Hampshire and 22% in Massachusetts to 8% in Alaska, West Virginia and Idaho. The low levels of educational attainment by this measure in New Mexico and Arizona point to significant issues for the Navajo, Pueblo and Apache tribes.

State Name	Less than High School Diploma	High School Graduate	Some College	BA or Higher
New Hampshire	21%	28%	28%	23%
Massachusetts	21%	30%	27%	22%
Hawaii	13%	26%	40%	21%
Maryland	21%	27%	32%	21%
Missouri	15%	35%	31%	19%
Georgia	23%	26%	32%	19%
Kansas	13%	32%	37%	18%
Ohio	20%	32%	30%	18%
Pennsylvania	20%	32%	31%	18%
Texas	25%	25%	33%	18%
Illinois	21%	28%	34%	17%
New Jersey	26%	28%	28%	17%
New York	26%	29%	28%	17%
Oklahoma	16%	36%	33%	16%
Arkansas	21%	31%	32%	16%
Connecticut	25%	34%	26%	16%
Indiana	22%	33%	29%	15%
Tennessee	22%	30%	33%	15%
Vermont	22%	38%	25%	15%
Florida	26%	28%	31%	15%
Colorado	20%	29%	38%	14%
Delaware	22%	30%	35%	14%
Kentucky	22%	31%	33%	14%
Maine	22%	29%	35%	14%
Alabama	24%	33%	29%	14%
Montana	18%	32%	37%	13%
Oregon	18%	28%	41%	13%
Virginia	18%	30%	33%	13%
Washington	18%	30%	38%	13%
North Dakota	19%	26%	42%	13%
Iowa	22%	30%	34%	13%
California	25%	26%	35%	13%
Michigan	18%	34%	35%	12%
Minnesota	19%	33%	36%	12%
South Dakota	22%	30%	36%	12%
Mississippi	32%	27%	30%	12%
North Carolina	32%	29%	27%	12%

[95] Census, S0201, 2011 ACS 3-year estimates and DP02, 2006-2010 ACS American Indian and Alaska Native Tribes

Wisconsin	15%	34%	40%	11%
Rhode Island	27%	36%	26%	11%
Wyoming	15%	32%	42%	10%
Utah	20%	34%	35%	10%
Nebraska	25%	30%	34%	10%
South Carolina	29%	32%	29%	10%
Nevada	15%	35%	41%	9%
New Mexico	24%	34%	33%	9%
Arizona	26%	32%	33%	9%
Louisiana	32%	36%	23%	9%
Alaska	20%	41%	32%	8%
West Virginia	20%	38%	32%	8%
Idaho	21%	34%	37%	8%

National Assessment of Educational Progress (NAEP)

NAEP Grade 8 Reading: 2011

Percentage at or Above Proficient

Sorted by State

State	White, non-Latino	American Indian	Gap
Alabama	*34*	22	12
Alaska	42	‡	-
Arizona	41	*10*	*31*
Arkansas	*35*	*15*	*20*
California	*35*	‡	-
Colorado	49	‡	-
Connecticut	54	‡	-
Delaware	42	‡	-
Florida	*38*	‡	-
Georgia	*38*	‡	-
Hawaii	41	‡	-
Idaho	*37*	‡	-
Illinois	44	‡	-
Indiana	*36*	‡	-
Iowa	*35*	‡	-
Kansas	41	‡	-
Kentucky	*39*	‡	-
Louisiana	*31*	‡	-
Maine	*39*	‡	-
Maryland	52	‡	-
Massachusetts	53	‡	-
Michigan	*36*	‡	-
Minnesota	44	30	14
Mississippi	*33*	‡	-
Missouri	*40*	‡	-
Montana	44	25	19
Nebraska	*39*	‡	-
Nevada	*37*	‡	-
New Hampshire	41	‡	-
New Jersey	56	‡	-
New Mexico	*36*	*16*	*20*
New York	46	‡	-
North Carolina	*40*	*16*	*24*
North Dakota	*37*	*13*	*24*
Ohio	43	‡	-
Oklahoma	*32*	23	9
Oregon	*37*	30	7

Pennsylvania	46	‡	-
Rhode Island	41	‡	-
South Carolina	*37*	‡	-
South Dakota	*39*	*14*	*25*
Tennessee	*31*	‡	-
Texas	42	‡	-
Utah	*40*	*18*	*22*
Vermont	45	‡	-
Virginia	43	‡	-
Washington	42	24	18
West Virginia	*24*	‡	-
Wisconsin	*40*	‡	-
Wyoming	*40*	‡	-
National Public	41	22	19

Italics indicate below national average.

NAEP Grade 8 Reading: 2011

Percentage at or Above Proficient

Sorted by American Indian

State	White, non-Latino	American Indian	Gap
Minnesota	44	30	14
Oregon	*37*	30	7
Montana	44	25	19
Washington	42	24	18
Oklahoma	*32*	23	9
Alabama	*34*	22	12
Utah	*40*	*18*	*22*
New Mexico	*36*	*16*	*20*
North Carolina	*40*	*16*	*24*
Arkansas	*35*	*15*	*20*
South Dakota	*39*	*14*	*25*
North Dakota	*37*	*13*	*24*
Arizona	41	*10*	*31*
Alaska	42	‡	-
California	*35*	‡	-
Colorado	49	‡	-
Connecticut	54	‡	-
Delaware	42	‡	-
Florida	*38*	‡	-
Georgia	*38*	‡	-
Hawaii	41	‡	-
Idaho	*37*	‡	-
Illinois	44	‡	-
Indiana	*36*	‡	-
Iowa	*35*	‡	-
Kansas	41	‡	-
Kentucky	*39*	‡	-
Louisiana	*31*	‡	-
Maine	*39*	‡	-
Maryland	52	‡	-
Massachusetts	53	‡	-
Michigan	*36*	‡	-
Mississippi	*33*	‡	-
Missouri	*40*	‡	-
Nebraska	*39*	‡	-
Nevada	*37*	‡	-
New Hampshire	41	‡	-
New Jersey	56	‡	-
New York	46	‡	-
Ohio	43	‡	-
Pennsylvania	46	‡	-
Rhode Island	41	‡	-

South Carolina	*37*	‡	-
Tennessee	*31*	‡	-
Texas	42	‡	-
Vermont	45	‡	-
Virginia	43	‡	-
West Virginia	*24*	‡	-
Wisconsin	*40*	‡	-
Wyoming	*40*	‡	-
National public	41	48	7

Italics indicate below national average.

NAEP Grade 8 Reading: 2011

Percentage at or Above Proficient:

Sorted by Gap

State	White, non-Latino	American Indian	Gap
Arizona	41	*10*	*31*
South Dakota	*39*	*14*	*25*
North Carolina	*40*	*16*	*24*
North Dakota	*37*	*13*	*24*
Utah	*40*	*18*	*22*
New Mexico	*36*	*16*	*20*
Arkansas	*35*	*15*	*20*
Montana	44	25	19
Washington	42	24	18
Minnesota	44	30	14
Alabama	*34*	22	12
Oklahoma	*32*	23	9
Oregon	*37*	30	7
Alaska	42	‡	-
California	*35*	‡	-
Colorado	49	‡	-
Connecticut	54	‡	-
Delaware	42	‡	-
Florida	*38*	‡	-
Georgia	*38*	‡	-
Hawaii	41	‡	-
Idaho	*37*	‡	-
Illinois	44	‡	-
Indiana	*36*	‡	-
Iowa	*35*	‡	-
Kansas	41	‡	-
Kentucky	*39*	‡	-
Louisiana	*31*	‡	-
Maine	*39*	‡	-
Maryland	52	‡	-
Massachusetts	53	‡	-
Michigan	*36*	‡	-
Mississippi	*33*	‡	-
Missouri	*40*	‡	-
Nebraska	*39*	‡	-
Nevada	*37*	‡	-
New Hampshire	41	‡	-
New Jersey	56	‡	-
New York	46	‡	-
Ohio	43	‡	-
Pennsylvania	46	‡	-
Rhode Island	41	‡	-

South Carolina	*37*	‡	-
Tennessee	*31*	‡	-
Texas	42	‡	-
Vermont	45	‡	-
Virginia	43	‡	-
West Virginia	*24*	‡	-
Wisconsin	*40*	‡	-
Wyoming	*40*	‡	-
National Public	41	48	7

Italics indicate below national average.

NAEP Grade 8 Mathematics: 2011

Percentage at or Above Proficient:

Sorted by State

State	White, non-Latino	American Indian	Gap
Alabama	*28*	17	*11*
Alaska	47	‡	-
Arizona	46	*15*	31
Arkansas	*37*	*12*	*25*
California	*41*	‡	-
Colorado	55	‡	-
Connecticut	48	‡	-
Delaware	43	‡	-
Florida	*37*	‡	-
Georgia	*40*	‡	-
Hawaii	*41*	‡	-
Idaho	*41*	‡	-
Illinois	44	‡	-
Indiana	*40*	‡	-
Iowa	*37*	‡	-
Kansas	47	‡	-
Kentucky	*33*	‡	-
Louisiana	*31*	‡	-
Maine	*40*	‡	-
Maryland	56	‡	-
Massachusetts	58	‡	-
Michigan	*35*	‡	-
Minnesota	55	*11*	44
Mississippi	*30*	‡	-
Missouri	*36*	‡	-
Montana	49	‡	-
Nebraska	*39*	‡	-
Nevada	43	‡	-
New Hampshire	45	‡	-
New Jersey	59	‡	-
New Mexico	*40*	‡	-
New York	*40*	‡	-
North Carolina	48	22	26
North Dakota	47	*15*	32
Ohio	46	‡	-
Oklahoma	*34*	21	*13*
Oregon	*37*	*16*	*21*
Pennsylvania	47	‡	-
Rhode Island	*42*	‡	-
South Carolina	43	‡	-
South Dakota	47	*14*	33
Tennessee	*28*	‡	-

Texas	58	‡	-
Utah	*41*	‡	-
Vermont	47	‡	-
Virginia	48	‡	-
Washington	46	*12*	34
West Virginia	*22*	‡	-
Wisconsin	47	‡	-
Wyoming	*41*	‡	-
National Public	43	17	26

Italics indicate below national average.

NAEP Grade 8 Mathematics: 2011

Percentage at or Above Proficient

Sorted by American Indian

State	White, non-Latino	American Indian	Gap
North Carolina	48	22	26
Oklahoma	*34*	21	*13*
Alabama	*28*	17	*11*
Alabama	*28*	17	*11*
Oregon	*37*	*16*	*21*
Arizona	46	*15*	31
North Dakota	47	*15*	32
South Dakota	47	*14*	33
Arkansas	*37*	*12*	*25*
Washington	46	*12*	34
Minnesota	55	*11*	44
Alaska	47	‡	-
California	*41*	‡	-
Colorado	55	‡	-
Connecticut	48	‡	-
Delaware	43	‡	-
Florida	*37*	‡	-
Georgia	*40*	‡	-
Hawaii	*41*	‡	-
Idaho	*41*	‡	-
Illinois	44	‡	-
Indiana	*40*	‡	-
Iowa	*37*	‡	-
Kansas	47	‡	-
Kentucky	*33*	‡	-
Louisiana	*31*	‡	-
Maine	*40*	‡	-
Maryland	56	‡	-
Massachusetts	58	‡	-
Michigan	*35*	‡	-
Mississippi	*30*	‡	-
Missouri	*36*	‡	-
Montana	49	‡	-
Nebraska	*39*	‡	-
Nevada	43	‡	-
New Hampshire	45	‡	-
New Jersey	59	‡	-
New Mexico	*40*	‡	-
New York	*40*	‡	-
Ohio	46	‡	-
Pennsylvania	47	‡	-
Rhode Island	*42*	‡	-

South Carolina	43	‡	-
Tennessee	*28*	‡	-
Texas	58	‡	-
Utah	*41*	‡	-
Vermont	47	‡	-
Virginia	48	‡	-
West Virginia	*22*	‡	-
Wisconsin	47	‡	-
Wyoming	*41*	‡	-
National Public	43	17	26

Italics indicate below national average.

NAEP Grade 8 Mathematics: 2011

Percentage at or Above Proficient

Sorted by Gap

State	White, non-Latino	American Indian	Gap
Minnesota	55	*11*	44
Washington	46	*12*	34
South Dakota	47	*14*	33
North Dakota	47	*15*	32
Arizona	46	*15*	31
North Carolina	48	22	26
Arkansas	*37*	*12*	*25*
Oregon	*37*	*16*	*21*
Oklahoma	*34*	21	*13*
Alabama	*28*	17	*11*
Alabama	*28*	17	*11*
Alaska	47	‡	-
California	*41*	‡	-
Colorado	55	‡	-
Connecticut	48	‡	-
Delaware	43	‡	-
Florida	*37*	‡	-
Georgia	*40*	‡	-
Hawaii	*41*	‡	-
Idaho	*41*	‡	-
Illinois	44	‡	-
Indiana	*40*	‡	-
Iowa	*37*	‡	-
Kansas	47	‡	-
Kentucky	*33*	‡	-
Louisiana	*31*	‡	-
Maine	*40*	‡	-
Maryland	56	‡	-
Massachusetts	58	‡	-
Michigan	*35*	‡	-
Mississippi	*30*	‡	-
Missouri	*36*	‡	-
Montana	49	‡	-
Nebraska	*39*	‡	-
Nevada	43	‡	-
New Hampshire	45	‡	-
New Jersey	59	‡	-
New Mexico	*40*	‡	-
New York	*40*	‡	-
Ohio	46	‡	-
Pennsylvania	47	‡	-
Rhode Island	*42*	‡	-

South Carolina	43	‡	-
Tennessee	*28*	‡	-
Texas	58	‡	-
Utah	*41*	‡	-
Vermont	47	‡	-
Virginia	48	‡	-
West Virginia	*22*	‡	-
Wisconsin	47	‡	-
Wyoming	*41*	‡	-
National Public	43	17	26

Italics indicate below national average.

Individual State Reports

This section includes United States Department of Education's National Center for Education Statistics, state data for American Indian and White, non-Latino, students.

Certain types of data are *Benchmarked* at the highest level obtained by one of the states or districts included. It is assumed that the goal in each case is to close the racial and gender achievement gaps. Each section—at the risk of repetition—is designed to be self-contained for the convenience of readers interested only in specific districts or states.

ALABAMA

American Indian Demography

State	American Indian Alone	Navajo	Cherokee	Sioux	Chippewa	Choctaw	Pueblo	Apache
Alabama	21,755		9,402			2,515		

The state has significant Creek and Muscogee populations.

Educational Attainment: Percent High School Graduate or Higher

State	Total Population	Asian Alone	White Alone	Black Alone	Latino	American Indian
USA	85%	86%	87%	81%	62%	77%
Alabama	*81%*	*85%*	*83%*	*77%*	*56%*	*74%*

Educational attainment for American Indians in Alabama is lower than that for the total population, Asian, White, non-Latino and Black residents but higher than that of Latino residents of the state.

Estimated High School Graduation Rates

State	American Indian	Asian	Latino	Black	White, non-Latino
USA	62%	89%	65%	58%	79%
Alabama	78%	*77%*	*59%*	58%	*73%*

American Indian students in the state graduate at higher rates than their counterparts.

National Assessment of Educational Progress (NAEP)

NAEP 8th Grade Reading results for the state's White, non-Latino, students are below national averages. The results for American Indian students are below those for White, non-Latino, students and at the national average for the group.

Percentages of American Indian and White, Non-Latino, Students
Reading, Grade 8, 2011

	Percent at or Above Proficient		Gap
	White, non-Latino	American Indian	American Indian/White
USA	41	22	19
Alabama	*34*	22	12

NAEP 8th Grade Mathematics results for the state's White, non-Latino, students are below national averages. The results for American Indian students are below those for White, non-Latino, students and at the national average for the group.

Percentages of American Indian and White, Non-Latino, Students
Mathematics, Grade 8, 2011

	Percent at or Above Proficient		Gap
	White, non-Latino	American Indian	American Indian/White
USA	43	17	26
Alabama	*28*	17	11

The *Benchmark* for American Indian students in 8th Grade Reading is achieved by Minnesota and Oregon, with 30% of American Indian students scoring at or above Proficient. The *Benchmark* for 8th Grade Mathematics is North Carolina, with 22% of American Indian students scoring at or above Proficient.

ALASKA

American Indian Demography

State	American Indian Alone	Navajo	Cherokee	Sioux	Chippewa	Choctaw	Pueblo	Apache
Alaska	5,259		951	365	455	254		

The state has significant unique American Indian and Alaska Native populations.

Educational Attainment: Percent High School Graduate or Higher

State	Total Population	Asian Alone	White Alone	Black Alone	Latino	American Indian
USA	85%	86%	87%	81%	62%	77%
Alaska	91%	*79%*	94%	91%	77%	90%

Educational attainment for American Indians and Alaska Natives is slightly lower than that for the total population, White, non-Latino and Black residents, but higher than that of White, non-Latino, and Latino residents of the state.

Estimated High School Graduation Rates

State	American Indian	Asian	Latino	Black	White, non-Latino
USA	62%	89%	65%	58%	79%
Alaska	54%	*87%*	*62%*	65%	*77%*

American Indian and Alaska Native students in the state graduate at lower rates than their counterparts and at rates lower than the national average.

National Assessment of Educational Progress (NAEP)

There are too few American Indian students in the state for the purposes of the NAEP estimates.

Percentages of American Indian and White, Non-Latino, Students
Reading, Grade 8, 2011

	Percent at or Above Proficient		Gap
	White, non-Latino	American Indian	American Indian/White
USA	41	22	19
Alaska	42	‡	-

There are too few American Indian students in the state for the purposes of the NAEP estimates.

Percentages of American Indian and White, Non-Latino, Students
Mathematics, Grade 8, 2011

	Percent at or Above Proficient		Gap
	White, non-Latino	American Indian	American Indian/White
USA	43	17	26
Alaska	47	‡	-

The *Benchmark* for American Indian students in 8th Grade Reading is achieved by Minnesota and Oregon, with 30% of American Indian students scoring at or above Proficient. The *Benchmark* for 8th Grade Mathematics is North Carolina, with 22% of American Indian students scoring at or above Proficient.

ARIZONA

American Indian Demography

State	American Indian Alone	Navajo	Cherokee	Sioux	Chippewa	Choctaw	Pueblo	Apache
Arizona	265,436	129.426	3,641	2,161	959	1,362	9,899	23,539

Educational Attainment: Percent High School Graduate or Higher

State	Total Population	Asian Alone	White Alone	Black Alone	Latino	American Indian
USA	85%	86%	87%	81%	62%	77%
Arizona	85%	89%	87%	88%	62%	*72%*

Educational attainment for American Indians is lower than that for the total population and all other subgroups other than Latino residents of the state.

Estimated High School Graduation Rates

State	American Indian	Asian	Latino	Black	White, non-Latino
USA	62%	89%	65%	58%	79%
Arizona	*61%*	*87%*	67%	75%	80%

American Indian students in the state graduate at lower rates than their counterparts and at rates lower than the national average.

National Assessment of Educational Progress (NAEP)

Results for American Indian students in the state are below those for White, non-Latino, students and below national averages for the group.

Percentages of American Indian and White, Non-Latino, Students
Reading, Grade 8, 2011

	Percent at or Above Proficient		Gap
	White, non-Latino	American Indian	American Indian/White
USA	41	22	19
Arizona	41	*10*	*31*

NAEP 8th Grade Mathematics results for the state's White, non-Latino, students are above national averages. The results for American Indian students are below those for White, non-Latino, students and below the national average for the group.

Percentages of American Indian and White, Non-Latino, Students
Mathematics, Grade 8, 2011

	Percent at or Above Proficient		Gap
	White, non-Latino	American Indian	American Indian/White
USA	43	17	26
Arizona	46	*15*	*31*

The *Benchmark* for American Indian students in 8th Grade Reading is achieved by Minnesota and Oregon, with 30% of American Indian students scoring at or above Proficient. The *Benchmark* for 8th Grade Mathematics is North Carolina, with 22% of American Indian students scoring at or above Proficient.

ARKANSAS

American Indian Demography

State	American Indian Alone	Navajo	Cherokee	Sioux	Chippewa	Choctaw	Pueblo	Apache
Arkansas	16,421		8,442	328		2,224		

Educational Attainment: Percent High School Graduate or Higher

State	Total Population	Asian Alone	White Alone	Black Alone	Latino	American Indian
USA	85%	86%	87%	81%	62%	77%
Arkansas	*82%*	*82%*	*84%*	*77%*	*49%*	81%

Educational attainment for American Indians is slightly lower than that for the total population and lower than Asian and White, non-Latino, residents of the state but higher than that of Black and Latino residents.

Estimated High School Graduation Rates

State	American Indian	Asian	Latino	Black	White, non-Latino
USA	62%	89%	65%	58%	79%
Arkansas	69%	91%	77%	69%	*77%*

American Indian students in the state graduate at lower rates than their Asian, Latino, and White, non-Latino, counterparts, at the same rate as the state's Black students and at rates higher than the national average for the group.

National Assessment of Educational Progress (NAEP)

Results for American Indian students in the state are below those for White, non-Latino, students and below national averages for the group.

Percentages of American Indian and White, Non-Latino, Students
Reading, Grade 8, 2011

	Percent at or Above Proficient		Gap
	White, non-Latino	American Indian	American Indian/White
USA	41	22	19
Arkansas	35	15	20

NAEP 8th Grade Mathematics results for the state's White, non-Latino, students are below national averages. The results for American Indian students are below those for White, non-Latino, students and below the national average for the group.

Percentages of American Indian and White, Non-Latino, Students
Mathematics, Grade 8, 2011

	Percent at or Above Proficient		Gap
	White, non-Latino	American Indian	American Indian/White
USA	43	17	26
Arkansas	37	12	25

The *Benchmark* for American Indian students in 8th Grade Reading is achieved by Minnesota and Oregon, with 30% of American Indian students scoring at or above Proficient. The *Benchmark* for 8th Grade Mathematics is North Carolina, with 22% of American Indian students scoring at or above Proficient.

CALIFORNIA

American Indian Demography

State	American Indian Alone	Navajo	Cherokee	Sioux	Chippewa	Choctaw	Pueblo	Apache
California	214,811	7,900	28,812	5,834	3,499	7,877	4,061	9,170

The state has a large number of small local American Indian and Mexican Indian tribes.

Educational Attainment: Percent High School Graduate or Higher

State	Total Population	Asian Alone	White Alone	Black Alone	Latino	American Indian
USA	85%	86%	87%	81%	62%	77%
California	*81%*	86%	*84%*	87%	*57%*	*76%*

Educational attainment for American Indians is lower than that for the total population and lower than that for most other sub-groups, but higher than that of Latino residents.

Estimated High School Graduation Rates

State	American Indian	Asian	Latino	Black	White, non-Latino
USA	62%	89%	65%	58%	79%
California	69%	92%	68%	59%	84%

American Indian students in the state graduate at lower rates than their Asian and White, non-Latino, counterparts, at a higher rate than the state's Black and Latino students and at rates higher than the national average for the group.

National Assessment of Educational Progress (NAEP)

There are too few American Indian students in the state for the purposes of the NAEP estimates.

Percentages of American Indian and White, Non-Latino, Students
Reading, Grade 8, 2011

	Percent at or Above Proficient		Gap
	White, non-Latino	American Indian	American Indian/White
USA	41	22	19
California	*35*	‡	-

NAEP 8th Grade Mathematics results for the state's White, non-Latino, students are below national averages. There are too few American Indian students in the state for the purposes of the NAEP estimates.

Percentages of American Indian and White, Non-Latino, Students
Mathematics, Grade 8, 2011

	Percent at or Above Proficient		Gap
	White, non-Latino	American Indian	American Indian/White
USA	43	17	26
California	*41*	‡	-

The *Benchmark* for American Indian students in 8th Grade Reading is achieved by Minnesota and Oregon, with 30% of American Indian students scoring at or above Proficient. The *Benchmark* for 8th Grade Mathematics is North Carolina, with 22% of American Indian students scoring at or above Proficient.

COLORADO

American Indian Demography

State	American Indian Alone	Navajo	Cherokee	Sioux	Chippewa	Choctaw	Pueblo	Apache
Colorado	36,116	5,269	4,303	3,237	1,020	729	806	2,166

The state has a significant Ute population.

Educational Attainment: Percent High School Graduate or Higher

State	Total Population	Asian Alone	White Alone	Black Alone	Latino	American Indian
USA	85%	86%	87%	81%	62%	77%
Colorado	89%	86%	91%	87%	65%	80%

Educational attainment for American Indians is lower than that for the total population and lower than that for other sub-groups, but higher than that of Latino residents.

Estimated High School Graduation Rates

State	American Indian	Asian	Latino	Black	White, non-Latino
USA	62%	89%	65%	58%	79%
Colorado	*54%*	*72%*	60%	58%	*77%*

American Indian students in the state graduate at lower rates than their counterparts and than the national average for the group.

National Assessment of Educational Progress (NAEP)

There are too few American Indian students in the state for the purposes of the NAEP estimates.

Percentages of American Indian and White, Non-Latino, Students
Reading, Grade 8, 2011

	Percent at or Above Proficient		Gap
	White, non-Latino	American Indian	American Indian/White
USA	41	22	19
Colorado	49	‡	-

NAEP 8th Grade Mathematics results for the state's White, non-Latino, students are above national averages. There are too few American Indian students in the state for the purposes of the NAEP estimates.

Percentages of American Indian and White, Non-Latino, Students
Mathematics, Grade 8, 2011

	Percent at or Above Proficient		Gap
	White, non-Latino	American Indian	American Indian/White
USA	43	17	26
Colorado	55	‡	-

The *Benchmark* for American Indian students in 8th Grade Reading is achieved by Minnesota and Oregon, with 30% of American Indian students scoring at or above Proficient. The *Benchmark* for 8th Grade Mathematics is North Carolina, with 22% of American Indian students scoring at or above Proficient.

CONNECTICUT

American Indian Demography

State	American Indian Alone	Navajo	Cherokee	Sioux	Chippewa	Choctaw	Pueblo	Apache
Connecticut	5,841		675					

The state has significant Mashantucket Pequot and Mohegan populations.

Educational Attainment: Percent High School Graduate or Higher

State	Total Population	Asian Alone	White Alone	Black Alone	Latino	American Indian
USA	85%	86%	87%	81%	62%	77%
Connecticut	88%	88%	91%	81%	68%	78%

Educational attainment for American Indians is lower than that for the total population and lower than that for most other sub-groups, but higher than that of Latino residents.

Estimated High School Graduation Rates

State	American Indian	Asian	Latino	Black	White, non-Latino
USA	62%	89%	65%	58%	79%
Connecticut	*45%*	-	*58%*	64%	87%

American Indian students in the state graduate at lower rates than their counterparts and than the national average for the group.

National Assessment of Educational Progress (NAEP)

There are too few American Indian students in the state for the purposes of the NAEP estimates.

Percentages of American Indian and White, Non-Latino, Students
Reading, Grade 8, 2011

	Percent at or Above Proficient		Gap
	White, non-Latino	American Indian	American Indian/White
USA	41	22	19
Connecticut	54	‡	-

NAEP 8th Grade Mathematics results for the state's White, non-Latino, students are above national averages. There are too few American Indian students in the state for the purposes of the NAEP estimates.

Percentages of American Indian and White, Non-Latino, Students
Mathematics, Grade 8, 2011

	Percent at or Above Proficient		Gap
	White, non-Latino	American Indian	American Indian/White
USA	43	17	26
Connecticut	48	‡	-

The *Benchmark* for American Indian students in 8th Grade Reading is achieved by Minnesota and Oregon, with 30% of American Indian students scoring at or above Proficient. The *Benchmark* for 8th Grade Mathematics is North Carolina, with 22% of American Indian students scoring at or above Proficient.

DELAWARE

American Indian Demography

State	American Indian Alone	Navajo	Cherokee	Sioux	Chippewa	Choctaw	Pueblo	Apache
Delaware	2,317		468					

Educational Attainment: Percent High School Graduate or Higher

State	Total Population	Asian Alone	White Alone	Black Alone	Latino	American Indian
USA	85%	86%	87%	81%	62%	77%
Delaware	87%	91%	89%	84%	*58%*	79%

Educational attainment for American Indians is lower than that for the total population and lower than that for other sub-groups, but higher than that of Latino residents.

Estimated High School Graduation Rates

State	American Indian	Asian	Latino	Black	White, non-Latino
USA	62%	89%	65%	58%	79%
Delaware	-	93%	66%	65%	*76%*

There are too few American Indian students in the state to meaningfully estimate graduation rates.

National Assessment of Educational Progress (NAEP)

There are too few American Indian students in the state for the purposes of the NAEP estimates.

Percentages of American Indian and White, Non-Latino, Students
Reading, Grade 8, 2011

	Percent at or Above Proficient		Gap
	White, non-Latino	American Indian	American Indian/White
USA	41	22	19
Delaware	42	‡	-

NAEP 8th Grade Mathematics results for the state's White, non-Latino, students are at national averages. There are too few American Indian students in the state for the purposes of the NAEP estimates.

Percentages of American Indian and White, Non-Latino, Students
Mathematics, Grade 8, 2011

	Percent at or Above Proficient		Gap
	White, non-Latino	American Indian	American Indian/White
USA	43	17	26
Delaware	43	‡	-

The *Benchmark* for American Indian students in 8th Grade Reading is achieved by Minnesota and Oregon, with 30% of American Indian students scoring at or above Proficient. The *Benchmark* for 8th Grade Mathematics is North Carolina, with 22% of American Indian students scoring at or above Proficient.

FLORIDA

American Indian Demography

State	American Indian Alone	Navajo	Cherokee	Sioux	Chippewa	Choctaw	Pueblo	Apache
Florida	43,145	471	11,017	947	1,423	1,063		689

The state has significant Seminole, Miccosukee and Creek populations.

Educational Attainment: Percent High School Graduate or Higher

State	Total Population	Asian Alone	White Alone	Black Alone	Latino	American Indian
USA	85%	86%	87%	81%	62%	77%
Florida	85%	86%	87%	*78%*	74%	78%

Educational attainment for American Indians is lower than that for the total population, lower than that for Asian and White, non-Latino, residents, the same as that for Black residents, but higher than that of Latino residents.

Estimated High School Graduation Rates

State	American Indian	Asian	Latino	Black	White, non-Latino
USA	62%	89%	65%	58%	79%
Florida	65%	84%	68%	*54%*	*68%*

American Indian students in the state graduate at lower rates than their counterparts, other than Black students, and at a higher average than the national average for the group.

National Assessment of Educational Progress (NAEP)

There are too few American Indian students in the state for the purposes of the NAEP estimates.

Percentages of American Indian and White, Non-Latino, Students
Reading, Grade 8, 2011

	Percent at or Above Proficient		Gap
	White, non-Latino	American Indian	American Indian/White
USA	41	22	19
Florida	*38*	‡	-

NAEP 8th Grade Mathematics results for the state's White, non-Latino, students are below national averages. There are too few American Indian students in the state for the purposes of the NAEP estimates.

Percentages of American Indian and White, Non-Latino, Students
Mathematics, Grade 8, 2011

	Percent at or Above Proficient		Gap
	White, non-Latino	American Indian	American Indian/White
USA	43	17	26
Florida	*37*	‡	-

The *Benchmark* for American Indian students in 8th Grade Reading is achieved by Minnesota and Oregon, with 30% of American Indian students scoring at or above Proficient. The *Benchmark* for 8th Grade Mathematics is North Carolina, with 22% of American Indian students scoring at or above Proficient.

GEORGIA

American Indian Demography

State	American Indian Alone	Navajo	Cherokee	Sioux	Chippewa	Choctaw	Pueblo	Apache
Georgia	16,969		6,785	509		629		393

Educational Attainment: Percent High School Graduate or Higher

State	Total Population	Asian Alone	White Alone	Black Alone	Latino	American Indian
USA	85%	86%	87%	81%	62%	77%
Georgia	84%	86%	*86%*	81%	*56%*	77%

Educational attainment for American Indians is lower than that for the total population, lower than that for other sub-groups, but higher than that of Latino residents.

Estimated High School Graduation Rates

State	American Indian	Asian	Latino	Black	White, non-Latino
USA	62%	89%	65%	58%	79%
Georgia	65%	90%	*58%*	*55%*	*70%*

American Indian students in the state graduate at higher rates than their Black and Latino counterparts, lower rates than the state's Asian and White, non-Latino, students, and at a higher rate than the national average for the group.

National Assessment of Educational Progress (NAEP)

There are too few American Indian students in the state for the purposes of the NAEP estimates.

Percentages of American Indian and White, Non-Latino, Students
Reading, Grade 8, 2011

	Percent at or Above Proficient		Gap
	White, non-Latino	American Indian	American Indian/White
USA	41	22	19
Georgia	*38*	‡	-

NAEP 8th Grade Mathematics results for the state's White, non-Latino, students are below national averages. There are too few American Indian students in the state for the purposes of the NAEP estimates.

Percentages of American Indian and White, Non-Latino, Students
Mathematics, Grade 8, 2011

	Percent at or Above Proficient		Gap
	White, non-Latino	American Indian	American Indian/White
USA	43	17	26
Georgia	*40*	‡	-

The *Benchmark* for American Indian students in 8th Grade Reading is achieved by Minnesota and Oregon, with 30% of American Indian students scoring at or above Proficient. The *Benchmark* for 8th Grade Mathematics is North Carolina, with 22% of American Indian students scoring at or above Proficient.

HAWAII

American Indian Demography

State	American Indian Alone	Navajo	Cherokee	Sioux	Chippewa	Choctaw	Pueblo	Apache
Hawaii	2,298		395					

Educational Attainment: Percent High School Graduate or Higher

State	Total Population	Asian Alone	White Alone	Black Alone	Latino	American Indian
USA	85%	86%	87%	81%	62%	77%
Hawaii	90%	86%	95%	96%	87%	88%

Educational attainment for American Indians is lower than that for the total population, lower than that for other sub-groups, but higher than that of Latino residents.

Estimated High School Graduation Rates

State	American Indian	Asian	Latino	Black	White, non-Latino
USA	62%	89%	65%	58%	79%
Hawaii	62%	*67%*	*47%*	75%	*51%*

American Indian students in the state graduate at higher rates than their Latino and White, non-Latino, counterparts, at lower rates than the state's Asian and Black students, and at the same rate as the national average for the group.

National Assessment of Educational Progress (NAEP)

There are too few American Indian students in the state for the purposes of the NAEP estimates.

Percentages of American Indian and White, Non-Latino, Students
Reading, Grade 8, 2011

	Percent at or Above Proficient		Gap
	White, non-Latino	American Indian	American Indian/White
USA	41	22	19
Hawaii	41	‡	-

NAEP 8th Grade Mathematics results for the state's White, non-Latino, students are below national averages. There are too few American Indian students in the state for the purposes of the NAEP estimates.

Percentages of American Indian and White, Non-Latino, Students
Mathematics, Grade 8, 2011

	Percent at or Above Proficient		Gap
	White, non-Latino	American Indian	American Indian/White
USA	43	17	26
Hawaii	*41*	‡	-

The *Benchmark* for American Indian students in 8th Grade Reading is achieved by Minnesota and Oregon, with 30% of American Indian students scoring at or above Proficient. The *Benchmark* for 8th Grade Mathematics is North Carolina, with 22% of American Indian students scoring at or above Proficient.

IDAHO

American Indian Demography

State	American Indian Alone	Navajo	Cherokee	Sioux	Chippewa	Choctaw	Pueblo	Apache
Idaho	16,015	557	1,358	504	400	247		

The state has significant Nez Perce and Shoshoni populations.

Educational Attainment: Percent High School Graduate or Higher

State	Total Population	Asian Alone	White Alone	Black Alone	Latino	American Indian
USA	85%	86%	87%	81%	62%	77%
Idaho	88%	86%	89%	83%	*53%*	80%

Educational attainment for American Indians is lower than that for the total population, lower than that for other sub-groups, but higher than that of Latino residents.

Estimated High School Graduation Rates

State	American Indian	Asian	Latino	Black	White, non-Latino
USA	62%	89%	65%	58%	79%
Idaho	*54%*	90%	74%	70%	79%

American Indian students in the state graduate at lower rates than their counterparts and at a lower rate than the national average for the group.

National Assessment of Educational Progress (NAEP)

There are too few American Indian students in the state for the purposes of the NAEP estimates.

Percentages of American Indian and White, Non-Latino, Students
Reading, Grade 8, 2011

	Percent at or Above Proficient		Gap
	White, non-Latino	American Indian	American Indian/White
USA	41	22	19
Idaho	*37*	‡	-

NAEP 8th Grade Mathematics results for the state's White, non-Latino, students are below national averages. There are too few American Indian students in the state for the purposes of the NAEP estimates.

Percentages of American Indian and White, Non-Latino, Students
Mathematics, Grade 8, 2011

	Percent at or Above Proficient		Gap
	White, non-Latino	American Indian	American Indian/White
USA	43	17	26
Idaho	*41*	‡	-

The *Benchmark* for American Indian students in 8th Grade Reading is achieved by Minnesota and Oregon, with 30% of American Indian students scoring at or above Proficient. The *Benchmark* for 8th Grade Mathematics is North Carolina, with 22% of American Indian students scoring at or above Proficient.

ILLINOIS

American Indian Demography

State	American Indian Alone	Navajo	Cherokee	Sioux	Chippewa	Choctaw	Pueblo	Apache
Illinois	17,107	444	4,431	989	1,332	504		588

Educational Attainment: Percent High School Graduate or Higher

State	Total Population	Asian Alone	White Alone	Black Alone	Latino	American Indian
USA	85%	86%	87%	81%	62%	77%
Illinois	86%	91%	89%	82%	*60%*	79%

Educational attainment for American Indians is lower than that for the total population, lower than that for other sub-groups, but higher than that of Latino residents.

Estimated High School Graduation Rates

State	American Indian	Asian	Latino	Black	White, non-Latino
USA	62%	89%	65%	58%	79%
Illinois	46%	90%	66%	53%	81%

American Indian students in the state graduate at lower rates than their counterparts and at a lower rate than the national average for the group.

National Assessment of Educational Progress (NAEP)

There are too few American Indian students in the state for the purposes of the NAEP estimates.

Percentages of American Indian and White, Non-Latino, Students
Reading, Grade 8, 2011

	Percent at or Above Proficient		Gap
	White, non-Latino	American Indian	American Indian/White
USA	41	22	19
Illinois	44	‡	-

NAEP 8th Grade Mathematics results for the state's White, non-Latino, students are above national averages. There are too few American Indian students in the state for the purposes of the NAEP estimates.

Percentages of American Indian and White, Non-Latino, Students
Mathematics, Grade 8, 2011

	Percent at or Above Proficient		Gap
	White, non-Latino	American Indian	American Indian/White
USA	43	17	26
Illinois	44	‡	-

The *Benchmark* for American Indian students in 8th Grade Reading is achieved by Minnesota and Oregon, with 30% of American Indian students scoring at or above Proficient. The *Benchmark* for 8th Grade Mathematics is North Carolina, with 22% of American Indian students scoring at or above Proficient.

INDIANA

American Indian Demography

State	American Indian Alone	Navajo	Cherokee	Sioux	Chippewa	Choctaw	Pueblo	Apache
Indiana	11,221		4,087	563	695			

The state has significant Miami and Shawnee populations.

Educational Attainment: Percent High School Graduate or Higher

State	Total Population	Asian Alone	White Alone	Black Alone	Latino	American Indian
USA	85%	86%	87%	81%	62%	77%
Indiana	86%	89%	87%	82%	*61%*	79%

Educational attainment for American Indians is lower than that for the total population, lower than that for other sub-groups, but higher than that of Latino residents.

Estimated High School Graduation Rates

State	American Indian	Asian	Latino	Black	White, non-Latino
USA	62%	89%	65%	58%	79%
Indiana	60%	97%	74%	60%	78%

American Indian students in the state graduate at lower rates than their counterparts, other than Black students, and at a lower rate than the national average for the group.

National Assessment of Educational Progress (NAEP)

There are too few American Indian students in the state for the purposes of the NAEP estimates.

Percentages of American Indian and White, Non-Latino, Students
Reading, Grade 8, 2011

	Percent at or Above Proficient		Gap
	White, non-Latino	American Indian	American Indian/White
USA	41	22	19
Indiana	*36*	‡	-

NAEP 8th Grade Mathematics results for the state's White, non-Latino, students are below national averages. There are too few American Indian students in the state for the purposes of the NAEP estimates.

Percentages of American Indian and White, Non-Latino, Students
Mathematics, Grade 8, 2011

	Percent at or Above Proficient		Gap
	White, non-Latino	American Indian	American Indian/White
USA	43	17	26
Indiana	*40*	‡	-

The *Benchmark* for American Indian students in 8th Grade Reading is achieved by Minnesota and Oregon, with 30% of American Indian students scoring at or above Proficient. The *Benchmark* for 8th Grade Mathematics is North Carolina, with 22% of American Indian students scoring at or above Proficient.

IOWA

American Indian Demography

State	American Indian Alone	Navajo	Cherokee	Sioux	Chippewa	Choctaw	Pueblo	Apache
Iowa	7,670		996	1,477	444			

Educational Attainment: Percent High School Graduate or Higher

State	Total Population	Asian Alone	White Alone	Black Alone	Latino	American Indian
USA	85%	86%	87%	81%	62%	77%
Iowa	90%	*81%*	91%	*80%*	*56%*	79%

Educational attainment for American Indians is lower than that for the total population, lower than that for other sub-groups, but higher than that of Latino residents.

Estimated High School Graduation Rates

State	American Indian	Asian	Latino	Black	White, non-Latino
USA	62%	89%	65%	58%	79%
Iowa	67%	*86%*	81%	61%	87%

American Indian students in the state graduate at lower rates than their counterparts, other than Black students, and at a higher rate than the national average for the group.

National Assessment of Educational Progress (NAEP)

There are too few American Indian students in the state for the purposes of the NAEP estimates.

Percentages of American Indian and White, Non-Latino, Students
Reading, Grade 8, 2011

	Percent at or Above Proficient		Gap
	White, non-Latino	American Indian	American Indian/White
USA	41	22	19
Iowa	*35*	‡	-

NAEP 8th Grade Mathematics results for the state's White, non-Latino, students are below national averages. There are too few American Indian students in the state for the purposes of the NAEP estimates.

Percentages of American Indian and White, Non-Latino, Students
Mathematics, Grade 8, 2011

	Percent at or Above Proficient		Gap
	White, non-Latino	American Indian	American Indian/White
USA	43	17	26
Iowa	*37*	‡	-

The *Benchmark* for American Indian students in 8th Grade Reading is achieved by Minnesota and Oregon, with 30% of American Indian students scoring at or above Proficient. The *Benchmark* for 8th Grade Mathematics is North Carolina, with 22% of American Indian students scoring at or above Proficient.

KANSAS

American Indian Demography

State	American Indian Alone	Navajo	Cherokee	Sioux	Chippewa	Choctaw	Pueblo	Apache
Kansas	20,679	605	6,299	923	250	870		431

The state has significant Kickapoo, Potawatomi, Sac & Fox populations.

Educational Attainment: Percent High School Graduate or Higher

State	Total Population	Asian Alone	White Alone	Black Alone	Latino	American Indian
USA	85%	86%	87%	81%	62%	77%
Kansas	89%	*81%*	91%	85%	*59%*	86%

Educational attainment for American Indians is lower than that for the total population, lower than that for White, non-Latino and Black residents, but higher than that of Asian and Latino residents.

Estimated High School Graduation Rates

State	American Indian	Asian	Latino	Black	White, non-Latino
USA	62%	89%	65%	58%	79%
Kansas	64%	81%	72%	63%	83%

American Indian students in the state graduate at lower rates than their counterparts, other than Black students, and at a higher rate than the national average for the group.

National Assessment of Educational Progress (NAEP)

There are too few American Indian students in the state for the purposes of the NAEP estimates.

Percentages of American Indian and White, Non-Latino, Students
Reading, Grade 8, 2011

	Percent at or Above Proficient		Gap
	White, non-Latino	American Indian	American Indian/White
USA	41	22	19
Kansas	41	‡	-

NAEP 8th Grade Mathematics results for the state's White, non-Latino, students are above national averages. There are too few American Indian students in the state for the purposes of the NAEP estimates.

Percentages of American Indian and White, Non-Latino, Students
Mathematics, Grade 8, 2011

	Percent at or Above Proficient		Gap
	White, non-Latino	American Indian	American Indian/White
USA	43	17	26
Kansas	47	‡	-

The *Benchmark* for American Indian students in 8th Grade Reading is achieved by Minnesota and Oregon, with 30% of American Indian students scoring at or above Proficient. The *Benchmark* for 8th Grade Mathematics is North Carolina, with 22% of American Indian students scoring at or above Proficient.

KENTUCKY

American Indian Demography

State	American Indian Alone	Navajo	Cherokee	Sioux	Chippewa	Choctaw	Pueblo	Apache
Kentucky	7,194		3,290					

Educational Attainment: Percent High School Graduate or Higher

State	Total Population	Asian Alone	White Alone	Black Alone	Latino	American Indian
USA	85%	86%	87%	81%	62%	77%
Kentucky	*81%*	88%	*81%*	81%	63%	79%

Educational attainment for American Indians is lower than that for the total population, lower than that for other sub-groups, but higher than that of Latino residents.

Estimated High School Graduation Rates

State	American Indian	Asian	Latino	Black	White, non-Latino
USA	62%	89%	65%	58%	79%
Kentucky	-	-	80%	65%	75%

There are too few American Indian students in the state to estimate the high school graduation rate average for the group.

National Assessment of Educational Progress (NAEP)

There are too few American Indian students in the state for the purposes of the NAEP estimates.

Percentages of American Indian and White, Non-Latino, Students
Reading, Grade 8, 2011

	Percent at or Above Proficient		Gap
	White, non-Latino	American Indian	American Indian/White
USA	41	22	19
Kentucky	*39*	‡	-

NAEP 8th Grade Mathematics results for the state's White, non-Latino, students are below national averages. There are too few American Indian students in the state for the purposes of the NAEP estimates.

Percentages of American Indian and White, Non-Latino, Students
Mathematics, Grade 8, 2011

	Percent at or Above Proficient		Gap
	White, non-Latino	American Indian	American Indian/White
USA	43	17	26
Kentucky	*33*	‡	-

The *Benchmark* for American Indian students in 8th Grade Reading is achieved by Minnesota and Oregon, with 30% of American Indian students scoring at or above Proficient. The *Benchmark* for 8th Grade Mathematics is North Carolina, with 22% of American Indian students scoring at or above Proficient.

LOUISIANA

American Indian Demography

State	American Indian Alone	Navajo	Cherokee	Sioux	Chippewa	Choctaw	Pueblo	Apache
Louisiana	21,597		2,643			1,682		

The state has significant Tunica-Biloxi, Coushatta and Chitimacha populations.

Educational Attainment: Percent High School Graduate or Higher

State	Total Population	Asian Alone	White Alone	Black Alone	Latino	American Indian
USA	85%	86%	87%	81%	62%	77%
Louisiana	*81%*	*77%*	*85%*	*74%*	69%	*69%*

Educational attainment for American Indians is lower than that for the total population, lower than that for other sub-groups, but the same as that of Latino residents.

Estimated High School Graduation Rates

State	American Indian	Asian	Latino	Black	White, non-Latino
USA	62%	89%	65%	58%	79%
Louisiana	69%	99%	52%	57%	71%

American Indian students in the state graduate at lower rates than their Asian and White, non-Latino, counterparts, at higher rates than the state's Latino and Black students, and at a higher rate than the national average for the group.

National Assessment of Educational Progress (NAEP)

There are too few American Indian students in the state for the purposes of the NAEP estimates.

Percentages of American Indian and White, Non-Latino, Students
Reading, Grade 8, 2011

	Percent at or Above Proficient		Gap
	White, non-Latino	American Indian	American Indian/White
USA	41	22	19
Louisiana	*31*	‡	-

NAEP 8th Grade Mathematics results for the state's White, non-Latino, students are below national averages. There are too few American Indian students in the state for the purposes of the NAEP estimates.

Percentages of American Indian and White, Non-Latino, Students
Mathematics, Grade 8, 2011

	Percent at or Above Proficient		Gap
	White, non-Latino	American Indian	American Indian/White
USA	43	17	26
Louisiana	*31*	‡	-

The *Benchmark* for American Indian students in 8th Grade Reading is achieved by Minnesota and Oregon, with 30% of American Indian students scoring at or above Proficient. The *Benchmark* for 8th Grade Mathematics is North Carolina, with 22% of American Indian students scoring at or above Proficient.

MAINE

American Indian Demography

State	American Indian Alone	Navajo	Cherokee	Sioux	Chippewa	Choctaw	Pueblo	Apache
Maine	5,653		431					

The state has significant Micmac, Maliseet, Penobscot and Passamaquoddy populations.

Educational Attainment: Percent High School Graduate or Higher

State	Total Population	Asian Alone	White Alone	Black Alone	Latino	American Indian
USA	85%	86%	87%	81%	62%	77%
Maine	90%	*85%*	90%	84%	82%	81%

Educational attainment for American Indians is lower than that for the total population, land ower than that for all other sub-groups.

Estimated High School Graduation Rates

State	American Indian	Asian	Latino	Black	White, non-Latino
USA	62%	89%	65%	58%	79%
Maine	86%	88%	-	63%	97%

American Indian students in the state graduate at lower rates than their Asian and White, non-Latino, counterparts, at higher rates than the state's Black students, and at a much higher rate than the national average for the group.

National Assessment of Educational Progress (NAEP)

There are too few American Indian students in the state for the purposes of the NAEP estimates.

Percentages of American Indian and White, Non-Latino, Students
Reading, Grade 8, 2011

	Percent at or Above Proficient		Gap
	White, non-Latino	American Indian	American Indian/White
USA	41	22	19
Maine	*39*	‡	-

NAEP 8th Grade Mathematics results for the state's White, non-Latino, students are below national averages. There are too few American Indian students in the state for the purposes of the NAEP estimates.

Percentages of American Indian and White, Non-Latino, Students
Mathematics, Grade 8, 2011

	Percent at or Above Proficient		Gap
	White, non-Latino	American Indian	American Indian/White
USA	43	17	26
Maine	*40*	‡	-

The *Benchmark* for American Indian students in 8th Grade Reading is achieved by Minnesota and Oregon, with 30% of American Indian students scoring at or above Proficient. The *Benchmark* for 8th Grade Mathematics is North Carolina, with 22% of American Indian students scoring at or above Proficient.

MARYLAND

American Indian Demography

State	American Indian Alone	Navajo	Cherokee	Sioux	Chippewa	Choctaw	Pueblo	Apache
Maryland	11,854		2,823					

The state has a significant Piscataway population.

Educational Attainment: Percent High School Graduate or Higher

State	Total Population	Asian Alone	White Alone	Black Alone	Latino	American Indian
USA	85%	86%	87%	81%	62%	77%
Maryland	88%	90%	90%	86%	62%	80%

Educational attainment for American Indians is lower than that for the total population, lower than that for other sub-groups, but higher than that of Latino residents.

Estimated High School Graduation Rates

State	American Indian	Asian	Latino	Black	White, non-Latino
USA	62%	89%	65%	58%	79%
Maryland	69%	92%	73%	66%	82%

American Indian students in the state graduate at lower rates than their Asian, Latino and White, non-Latino, counterparts, at higher rates than the state's Black students, and at a higher rate than the national average for the group.

National Assessment of Educational Progress (NAEP)

There are too few American Indian students in the state for the purposes of the NAEP estimates.

Percentages of American Indian and White, Non-Latino, Students
Reading, Grade 8, 2011

	Percent at or Above Proficient		Gap
	White, non-Latino	American Indian	American Indian/White
USA	41	22	19
Maryland	52	‡	-

NAEP 8th Grade Mathematics results for the state's White, non-Latino, students are above national averages. There are too few American Indian students in the state for the purposes of the NAEP estimates.

Percentages of American Indian and White, Non-Latino, Students
Mathematics, Grade 8, 2011

	Percent at or Above Proficient		Gap
	White, non-Latino	American Indian	American Indian/White
USA	43	17	26
Maryland	56	‡	-

The *Benchmark* for American Indian students in 8th Grade Reading is achieved by Minnesota and Oregon, with 30% of American Indian students scoring at or above Proficient. The *Benchmark* for 8th Grade Mathematics is North Carolina, with 22% of American Indian students scoring at or above Proficient.

MASSACHUSETTS

American Indian Demography

State	American Indian Alone	Navajo	Cherokee	Sioux	Chippewa	Choctaw	Pueblo	Apache
Massachusetts	8,442		1,028					

The state has a significant Wampanoag population.

Educational Attainment: Percent High School Graduate or Higher

State	Total Population	Asian Alone	White Alone	Black Alone	Latino	American Indian
USA	85%	86%	87%	81%	62%	77%
Massachusetts	89%	*83%*	91%	82%	65%	85%

Educational attainment for American Indians is lower than that for the total population, lower than that for White, non-Latino residents, but higher than that for other sub-groups.

Estimated High School Graduation Rates

State	American Indian	Asian	Latino	Black	White, non-Latino
USA	62%	89%	65%	58%	79%
Massachusetts	69%	89%	*54%*	63%	85%

American Indian students in the state graduate at lower rates than their Asian and White, non-Latino, counterparts, at higher rates than the state's Latino and Black students, and at a higher rate than the national average for the group.

National Assessment of Educational Progress (NAEP)
There are too few American Indian students in the state for the purposes of the NAEP estimates.

Percentages of American Indian and White, Non-Latino, Students
Reading, Grade 8, 2011

	Percent at or Above Proficient		Gap
	White, non-Latino	American Indian	American Indian/White
USA	41	22	19
Massachusetts	53	‡	-

NAEP 8th Grade Mathematics results for the state's White, non-Latino, students are above national averages. There are too few American Indian students in the state for the purposes of the NAEP estimates.

Percentages of American Indian and White, Non-Latino, Students
Mathematics, Grade 8, 2011

	Percent at or Above Proficient		Gap
	White, non-Latino	American Indian	American Indian/White
USA	43	17	26
Massachusetts	58	‡	-

The *Benchmark* for American Indian students in 8th Grade Reading is achieved by Minnesota and Oregon, with 30% of American Indian students scoring at or above Proficient. The *Benchmark* for 8th Grade Mathematics is North Carolina, with 22% of American Indian students scoring at or above Proficient.

MICHIGAN

American Indian Demography

State	American Indian Alone	Navajo	Cherokee	Sioux	Chippewa	Choctaw	Pueblo	Apache
Michigan	44,360		5,904	696	23,271	424		529

Educational Attainment: Percent High School Graduate or Higher

State	Total Population	Asian Alone	White Alone	Black Alone	Latino	American Indian
USA	85%	86%	87%	81%	62%	77%
Michigan	88%	88%	90%	82%	67%	82%

Educational attainment for American Indians is lower than that for the total population, lower than that for other sub-groups (except the same as that for Black residents), but higher than that of Latino residents.

Estimated High School Graduation Rates

State	American Indian	Asian	Latino	Black	White, non-Latino
USA	62%	89%	65%	58%	79%
Michigan	61%	92%	66%	53%	79%

American Indian students in the state graduate at lower rates than their Asian, Latino and White, non-Latino, counterparts, at higher rates than the state's Black students, and at a slightly lower rate than the national average for the group.

National Assessment of Educational Progress (NAEP)

There are too few American Indian students in the state for the purposes of the NAEP estimates.

Percentages of American Indian and White, Non-Latino, Students
Reading, Grade 8, 2011

	Percent at or Above Proficient		Gap
	White, non-Latino	American Indian	American Indian/White
USA	41	22	19
Michigan	*36*	‡	-

NAEP 8th Grade Mathematics results for the state's White, non-Latino, students are below national averages. There are too few American Indian students in the state for the purposes of the NAEP estimates.

Percentages of American Indian and White, Non-Latino, Students
Mathematics, Grade 8, 2011

	Percent at or Above Proficient		Gap
	White, non-Latino	American Indian	American Indian/White
USA	43	17	26
Michigan	*35*	‡	-

The *Benchmark* for American Indian students in 8th Grade Reading is achieved by Minnesota and Oregon, with 30% of American Indian students scoring at or above Proficient. The *Benchmark* for 8th Grade Mathematics is North Carolina, with 22% of American Indian students scoring at or above Proficient.

MINNESOTA

American Indian Demography

State	American Indian Alone	Navajo	Cherokee	Sioux	Chippewa	Choctaw	Pueblo	Apache
Minnesota	47,386		632	5,776	33,233			

Educational Attainment: Percent High School Graduate or Higher

State	Total Population	Asian Alone	White Alone	Black Alone	Latino	American Indian
USA	85%	86%	87%	81%	62%	77%
Minnesota	91%	*80%*	93%	81%	*61%*	81%

Educational attainment for American Indians is lower than that for the total population, lower than that for White, non-Latinos, but the same as or higher than that of Asian, Black and Latino residents.

Estimated High School Graduation Rates

State	American Indian	Asian	Latino	Black	White, non-Latino
USA	62%	89%	65%	58%	79%
Minnesota	63%	92%	*63%*	65%	94%

American Indian students in the state graduate at lower rates than their Asian, Black and White, non-Latino, counterparts, at the same rate as Latino students and at a slightly higher rate than the national average for the group.

National Assessment of Educational Progress (NAEP)

American Indian students in the state score below their White, non-Latino, counterparts but above the national average for the group.

Percentages of American Indian and White, Non-Latino, Students
Reading, Grade 8, 2011

	Percent at or Above Proficient		Gap
	White, non-Latino	American Indian	American Indian/White
USA	41	22	19
Minnesota	44	30	14

NAEP 8th Grade Mathematics results for the state's White, non-Latino, students are above national averages. The state's American Indian student results were below those of White, non-Latino, students and the national average for the group.

Percentages of American Indian and White, Non-Latino, Students
Mathematics, Grade 8, 2011

	Percent at or Above Proficient		Gap
	White, non-Latino	American Indian	American Indian/White
USA	43	17	26
Minnesota	55	*11*	*44*

The *Benchmark* for American Indian students in 8th Grade Reading is achieved by Minnesota and Oregon, with 30% of American Indian students scoring at or above Proficient. The *Benchmark* for 8th Grade Mathematics is North Carolina, with 22% of American Indian students scoring at or above Proficient.

MISSISSIPPI

American Indian Demography

State	American Indian Alone	Navajo	Cherokee	Sioux	Chippewa	Choctaw	Pueblo	Apache
Mississippi	11,908		1,203			6,702		

Educational Attainment: Percent High School Graduate or Higher

State	Total Population	Asian Alone	White Alone	Black Alone	Latino	American Indian
USA	85%	86%	87%	81%	62%	77%
Mississippi	*80%*	*76%*	*84%*	*72%*	*57%*	*67%*

Educational attainment for American Indians is lower than that for the total population, lower than that for other sub-groups, but higher than that of Latino residents.

Estimated High School Graduation Rates

State	American Indian	Asian	Latino	Black	White, non-Latino
USA	62%	89%	65%	58%	79%
Mississippi	-	*77%*	*57%*	*57%*	*66%*

There are too few American Indian students in the state to estimate the average high school graduation rate for the group.

National Assessment of Educational Progress (NAEP)

There are too few American Indian students in the state for the purposes of the NAEP estimates.

Percentages of American Indian and White, Non-Latino, Students
Reading, Grade 8, 2011

	Percent at or Above Proficient		Gap
	White, non-Latino	American Indian	American Indian/White
USA	41	22	19
Mississippi	*33*	‡	-

NAEP 8th Grade Mathematics results for the state's White, non-Latino, students are below national averages. There are too few American Indian students in the state for the purposes of the NAEP estimates.

Percentages of American Indian and White, Non-Latino, Students
Mathematics, Grade 8, 2011

	Percent at or Above Proficient		Gap
	White, non-Latino	American Indian	American Indian/White
USA	43	17	26
Mississippi	*30*	‡	-

The *Benchmark* for American Indian students in 8th Grade Reading is achieved by Minnesota and Oregon, with 30% of American Indian students scoring at or above Proficient. The *Benchmark* for 8th Grade Mathematics is North Carolina, with 22% of American Indian students scoring at or above Proficient.

MISSOURI

American Indian Demography

State	American Indian Alone	Navajo	Cherokee	Sioux	Chippewa	Choctaw	Pueblo	Apache
Missouri	18,270	469	9,941	893	486	806		390

The state has a significant Shawnee population.

Educational Attainment: Percent High School Graduate or Higher

State	Total Population	Asian Alone	White Alone	Black Alone	Latino	American Indian
USA	85%	86%	87%	81%	62%	77%
Missouri	86%	86%	87%	81%	66%	84%

Educational attainment for American Indians is lower than that for the total population, White, non-Latino and Asian residents, but higher than that of Black and Latino residents.

Estimated High School Graduation Rates

State	American Indian	Asian	Latino	Black	White, non-Latino
USA	62%	89%	65%	58%	79%
Missouri	74%	92%	82%	62%	83%

American Indian students in the state graduate at lower rates than their Asian, Latino and White, non-Latino, counterparts, at a higher rate than Black students and at a higher rate than the national average for the group.

National Assessment of Educational Progress (NAEP)

There are too few American Indian students in the state for the purposes of the NAEP estimates.

Percentages of American Indian and White, Non-Latino, Students
Reading, Grade 8, 2011

	Percent at or Above Proficient		Gap
	White, non-Latino	American Indian	American Indian/White
USA	41	22	19
Missouri	*40*	‡	-

NAEP 8th Grade Mathematics results for the state's White, non-Latino, students are below national averages. There are too few American Indian students in the state for the purposes of the NAEP estimates.

Percentages of American Indian and White, Non-Latino, Students
Mathematics, Grade 8, 2011

	Percent at or Above Proficient		Gap
	White, non-Latino	American Indian	American Indian/White
USA	43	17	26
Missouri	*36*	‡	-

The *Benchmark* for American Indian students in 8th Grade Reading is achieved by Minnesota and Oregon, with 30% of American Indian students scoring at or above Proficient. The *Benchmark* for 8th Grade Mathematics is North Carolina, with 22% of American Indian students scoring at or above Proficient.

MONTANA

American Indian Demography

State	American Indian Alone	Navajo	Cherokee	Sioux	Chippewa	Choctaw	Pueblo	Apache
Montana	56,309	303	629	5,602	2,872			

The state has significant Blackfoot and Crow populations.

Educational Attainment: Percent High School Graduate or Higher

State	Total Population	Asian Alone	White Alone	Black Alone	Latino	American Indian
USA	85%	86%	87%	81%	62%	77%
Montana	91%	*84%*	92%	90%	83%	80%

Educational attainment for American Indians is lower than that for the total population and all other sub-groups.

Estimated High School Graduation Rates

State	American Indian	Asian	Latino	Black	White, non-Latino
USA	62%	89%	65%	58%	79%
Montana	*58%*	-	89%	100%	81%

American Indian students in the state graduate at lower rates than their counterparts and than the national average for the group.

National Assessment of Educational Progress (NAEP)

American Indian students in the state score below the results for their White, non-Latino, counterparts, but above the national average for the group.

Percentages of American Indian and White, Non-Latino, Students
Reading, Grade 8, 2011

	Percent at or Above Proficient		Gap
	White, non-Latino	American Indian	American Indian/White
USA	41	22	19
Montana	44	25	19

NAEP 8th Grade Mathematics results for the state's White, non-Latino, students are above national averages. There are too few American Indian students in the state for the purposes of the NAEP estimates.

Percentages of American Indian and White, Non-Latino, Students
Mathematics, Grade 8, 2011

	Percent at or Above Proficient		Gap
	White, non-Latino	American Indian	American Indian/White
USA	43	17	26
Montana	49	‡	-

The *Benchmark* for American Indian students in 8th Grade Reading is achieved by Minnesota and Oregon, with 30% of American Indian students scoring at or above Proficient. The *Benchmark* for 8th Grade Mathematics is North Carolina, with 22% of American Indian students scoring at or above Proficient.

NEBRASKA

American Indian Demography

State	American Indian Alone	Navajo	Cherokee	Sioux	Chippewa	Choctaw	Pueblo	Apache
Nebraska	13,040	196	608	4,075				

The state has significant Ponca, Omaha and Winnebago populations.

Educational Attainment: Percent High School Graduate or Higher

State	Total Population	Asian Alone	White Alone	Black Alone	Latino	American Indian
USA	85%	86%	87%	81%	62%	77%
Nebraska	90%	*84%*	91%	84%	*52%*	79%

Educational attainment for American Indians is lower than that for the total population and all sub-groups other than Latino.

Estimated High School Graduation Rates

State	American Indian	Asian	Latino	Black	White, non-Latino
USA	62%	89%	65%	58%	79%
Nebraska	*49%*	93%	74%	*42%*	86%

American Indian students in the state graduate at lower rates than their counterparts and than the national average for the group.

National Assessment of Educational Progress (NAEP)

There are too few American Indian students in the state for the purposes of the NAEP estimates.

Percentages of American Indian and White, Non-Latino, Students
Reading, Grade 8, 2011

	Percent at or Above Proficient		Gap
	White, non-Latino	American Indian	American Indian/White
USA	41	22	19
Nebraska	*39*	‡	-

NAEP 8th Grade Mathematics results for the state's White, non-Latino, students are below national averages. There are too few American Indian students in the state for the purposes of the NAEP estimates.

Percentages of American Indian and White, Non-Latino, Students
Mathematics, Grade 8, 2011

	Percent at or Above Proficient		Gap
	White, non-Latino	American Indian	American Indian/White
USA	43	17	26
Nebraska	*39*	‡	-

The *Benchmark* for American Indian students in 8th Grade Reading is achieved by Minnesota and Oregon, with 30% of American Indian students scoring at or above Proficient. The *Benchmark* for 8th Grade Mathematics is North Carolina, with 22% of American Indian students scoring at or above Proficient.

NEVADA

American Indian Demography

State	American Indian Alone	Navajo	Cherokee	Sioux	Chippewa	Choctaw	Pueblo	Apache
Nevada	24,052	1,042	2,064	587	465			593

The state has significant Paiute, Shoshone and Washoe populations.

Educational Attainment: Percent High School Graduate or Higher

State	Total Population	Asian Alone	White Alone	Black Alone	Latino	American Indian
USA	85%	86%	87%	81%	62%	77%
Nevada	*84%*	89%	*85%*	87%	*58%*	84%

Educational attainment for American Indians is the same as that for the total population, lower than that of Asian, White, non-Latino, and Black residents and higher than that for Latinos.

Estimated High School Graduation Rates

State	American Indian	Asian	Latino	Black	White, non-Latino
USA	62%	89%	65%	58%	79%
Nevada	*40%*	*73%*	*53%*	*45%*	*68%*

American Indian students in the state graduate at lower rates than their counterparts and than the national average for the group.

National Assessment of Educational Progress (NAEP)

There are too few American Indian students in the state for the purposes of the NAEP estimates.

Percentages of American Indian and White, Non-Latino, Students
Reading, Grade 8, 2011

	Percent at or Above Proficient		Gap
	White, non-Latino	American Indian	American Indian/White
USA	41	22	19
Nevada	*37*	‡	-

NAEP 8th Grade Mathematics results for the state's White, non-Latino, students are at national averages. There are too few American Indian students in the state for the purposes of the NAEP estimates.

Percentages of American Indian and White, Non-Latino, Students
Mathematics, Grade 8, 2011

	Percent at or Above Proficient		Gap
	White, non-Latino	American Indian	American Indian/White
USA	43	17	26
Nevada	43	‡	-

The *Benchmark* for American Indian students in 8th Grade Reading is achieved by Minnesota and Oregon, with 30% of American Indian students scoring at or above Proficient. The *Benchmark* for 8th Grade Mathematics is North Carolina, with 22% of American Indian students scoring at or above Proficient.

NEW HAMPSHIRE

American Indian Demography

State	American Indian Alone	Navajo	Cherokee	Sioux	Chippewa	Choctaw	Pueblo	Apache
New Hampshire	1,946							

Educational Attainment: Percent High School Graduate or Higher

State	Total Population	Asian Alone	White Alone	Black Alone	Latino	American Indian
USA	85%	86%	87%	81%	62%	77%
New Hampshire	91%	90%	91%	86%	80%	81%

Educational attainment for American Indians is lower than that for the total population and all sub-groups other than Latino.

Estimated High School Graduation Rates

State	American Indian	Asian	Latino	Black	White, non-Latino
USA	62%	89%	65%	58%	79%
New Hampshire	-	-	-	-	82%

There are too few American Indian students in the state to estimate high school graduation rates for the group.

National Assessment of Educational Progress (NAEP)

There are too few American Indian students in the state for the purposes of the NAEP estimates.

Percentages of American Indian and White, Non-Latino, Students
Reading, Grade 8, 2011

	Percent at or Above Proficient		Gap
	White, non-Latino	American Indian	American Indian/White
USA	41	22	19
New Hampshire	41	‡	-

NAEP 8th Grade Mathematics results for the state's White, non-Latino, students are above national averages. There are too few American Indian students in the state for the purposes of the NAEP estimates.

Percentages of American Indian and White, Non-Latino, Students
Mathematics, Grade 8, 2011

	Percent at or Above Proficient		Gap
	White, non-Latino	American Indian	American Indian/White
USA	43	17	26
New Hampshire	45	‡	-

The *Benchmark* for American Indian students in 8th Grade Reading is achieved by Minnesota and Oregon, with 30% of American Indian students scoring at or above Proficient. The *Benchmark* for 8th Grade Mathematics is North Carolina, with 22% of American Indian students scoring at or above Proficient.

NEW JERSEY

American Indian Demography

State	American Indian Alone	Navajo	Cherokee	Sioux	Chippewa	Choctaw	Pueblo	Apache
New Jersey	12,442		1,596					

The state has a significant Lenape (Delaware) population.

Educational Attainment: Percent High School Graduate or Higher

State	Total Population	Asian Alone	White Alone	Black Alone	Latino	American Indian
USA	85%	86%	87%	81%	62%	77%
New Jersey	87%	92%	89%	83%	70%	*71%*

Educational attainment for American Indians is lower than that for the total population and all sub-groups other than Latino.

Estimated High School Graduation Rates

State	American Indian	Asian	Latino	Black	White, non-Latino
USA	62%	89%	65%	58%	79%
New Jersey	80%	-	77%	75%	90%

American Indian students in the state graduate at higher rates than their Black and Latino counterparts, lower rates than White, non-Latino, students and higher rates than the national average for the group.

National Assessment of Educational Progress (NAEP)

There are too few American Indian students in the state for the purposes of the NAEP estimates.

Percentages of American Indian and White, Non-Latino, Students
Reading, Grade 8, 2011

	Percent at or Above Proficient		Gap
	White, non-Latino	American Indian	American Indian/White
USA	41	22	19
New Jersey	56	‡	-

NAEP 8th Grade Mathematics results for the state's White, non-Latino, students are above national averages. There are too few American Indian students in the state for the purposes of the NAEP estimates.

Percentages of American Indian and White, Non-Latino, Students
Mathematics, Grade 8, 2011

	Percent at or Above Proficient		Gap
	White, non-Latino	American Indian	American Indian/White
USA	43	17	26
New Jersey	59	‡	-

The *Benchmark* for American Indian students in 8th Grade Reading is achieved by Minnesota and Oregon, with 30% of American Indian students scoring at or above Proficient. The *Benchmark* for 8th Grade Mathematics is North Carolina, with 22% of American Indian students scoring at or above Proficient.

NEW MEXICO

American Indian Demography

State	American Indian Alone	Navajo	Cherokee	Sioux	Chippewa	Choctaw	Pueblo	Apache
New Mexico	181,352	106,334	1,472	865	353	532	38,404	6,847

Educational Attainment: Percent High School Graduate or Higher

State	Total Population	Asian Alone	White Alone	Black Alone	Latino	American Indian
USA	85%	86%	87%	81%	62%	77%
New Mexico	*83%*	88%	*85%*	87%	70%	*75%*

Educational attainment for American Indians is lower than that for the total population and all sub-groups other than Latino.

Estimated High School Graduation Rates

State	American Indian	Asian	Latino	Black	White, non-Latino
USA	62%	89%	65%	58%	79%
New Mexico	*53%*	*79%*	*60%*	*57%*	*69%*

American Indian students in the state graduate at lower rates than their counterparts and than the national average for the group.

National Assessment of Educational Progress (NAEP)

American Indian students in the state score below the results for their White, non-Latino, counterparts and below the national average for the group.

Percentages of American Indian and White, Non-Latino, Students
Reading, Grade 8, 2011

	Percent at or Above Proficient		Gap
	White, non-Latino	American Indian	American Indian/White
USA	41	22	19
New Mexico	*36*	*16*	*20*

NAEP 8th Grade Mathematics results for the state's White, non-Latino, students are below national averages. There are too few American Indian students in the state for the purposes of the NAEP estimates.

Percentages of American Indian and White, Non-Latino, Students
Mathematics, Grade 8, 2011

	Percent at or Above Proficient		Gap
	White, non-Latino	American Indian	American Indian/White
USA	43	17	26
New Mexico	*40*	‡	-

The *Benchmark* for American Indian students in 8th Grade Reading is achieved by Minnesota and Oregon, with 30% of American Indian students scoring at or above Proficient. The *Benchmark* for 8th Grade Mathematics is North Carolina, with 22% of American Indian students scoring at or above Proficient.

NEW YORK

American Indian Demography

State	American Indian Alone	Navajo	Cherokee	Sioux	Chippewa	Choctaw	Pueblo	Apache
New York	47,728		3,821	524	513		388	350

The state has significant Tuscarora, Oneida, Mohawk, Onondaga, Seneca and Cayuga populations.

Educational Attainment: Percent High School Graduate or Higher

State	Total Population	Asian Alone	White Alone	Black Alone	Latino	American Indian
USA	85%	86%	87%	81%	62%	77%
New York	*84%*	*78%*	89%	*80%*	65%	79%

Educational attainment for American Indians is lower than that for the total population and all sub-groups other than Asian and Latino.

Estimated High School Graduation Rates

State	American Indian	Asian	Latino	Black	White, non-Latino
USA	62%	89%	65%	58%	79%
New York	*55%*	89%	*47%*	*45%*	*74%*

American Indian students in the state graduate at lower rates than their Asian and White, non-Latino, counterparts, higher rates than Latino and Black students, and lower rates than the national average for the group.

National Assessment of Educational Progress (NAEP)

There are too few American Indian students in the state for the purposes of the NAEP estimates.

Percentages of American Indian and White, Non-Latino, Students
Reading, Grade 8, 2011

	Percent at or Above Proficient		Gap
	White, non-Latino	American Indian	American Indian/White
USA	41	22	19
New York	46	‡	-

NAEP 8th Grade Mathematics results for the state's White, non-Latino, students are below national averages. There are too few American Indian students in the state for the purposes of the NAEP estimates.

Percentages of American Indian and White, Non-Latino, Students
Mathematics, Grade 8, 2011

	Percent at or Above Proficient		Gap
	White, non-Latino	American Indian	American Indian/White
USA	43	17	26
New York	*40*	‡	-

The *Benchmark* for American Indian students in 8th Grade Reading is achieved by Minnesota and Oregon, with 30% of American Indian students scoring at or above Proficient. The *Benchmark* for 8th Grade Mathematics is North Carolina, with 22% of American Indian students scoring at or above Proficient.

NORTH CAROLINA

American Indian Demography

State	American Indian Alone	Navajo	Cherokee	Sioux	Chippewa	Choctaw	Pueblo	Apache
North Carolina	90,521	396	14,284	500	506	385		420

Educational Attainment: Percent High School Graduate or Higher

State	Total Population	Asian Alone	White Alone	Black Alone	Latino	American Indian
USA	85%	86%	87%	81%	62%	77%
North Carolina	*84%*	*84%*	*86%*	*80%*	*53%*	*67%*

Educational attainment for American Indians is lower than that for the total population and all sub-groups other than Latino.

Estimated High School Graduation Rates

State	American Indian	Asian	Latino	Black	White, non-Latino
USA	62%	89%	65%	58%	79%
North Carolina	*60%*	*80%*	*53%*	67%	*77%*

American Indian students in the state graduate at lower rates than their Asian, Black and White, non-Latino, counterparts, higher rates than Latino students, and lower rates than the national average for the group.

National Assessment of Educational Progress (NAEP)

American Indian students in the state score below the results for their White, non-Latino, counterparts and below the national average for the group.

Percentages of American Indian and White, Non-Latino, Students
Reading, Grade 8, 2011

	Percent at or Above Proficient		Gap
	White, non-Latino	American Indian	American Indian/White
USA	41	22	19
North Carolina	*40*	*16*	*24*

NAEP 8th Grade Mathematics results for the state's White, non-Latino, students are above national averages. Results for American Indian students in the state are below those for White, non-Latino, students and above those of the national average for the group.

Percentages of American Indian and White, Non-Latino, Students
Mathematics, Grade 8, 2011

	Percent at or Above Proficient		Gap
	White, non-Latino	American Indian	American Indian/White
USA	43	17	26
North Carolina	48	22	26

The *Benchmark* for American Indian students in 8th Grade Reading is achieved by Minnesota and Oregon, with 30% of American Indian students scoring at or above Proficient. The *Benchmark* for 8th Grade Mathematics is North Carolina, with 22% of American Indian students scoring at or above Proficient.

NORTH DAKOTA

American Indian Demography

State	American Indian Alone	Navajo	Cherokee	Sioux	Chippewa	Choctaw	Pueblo	Apache
North Dakota	32,268			8,910	13,557			

Educational Attainment: Percent High School Graduate or Higher

State	Total Population	Asian Alone	White Alone	Black Alone	Latino	American Indian
USA	85%	86%	87%	81%	62%	77%
North Dakota	89%	86%	90%	84%	77%	83%

Educational attainment for American Indians is lower than that for the total population and all sub-groups other than Latino.

Estimated High School Graduation Rates

State	American Indian	Asian	Latino	Black	White, non-Latino
USA	62%	89%	65%	58%	79%
North Dakota	*51%*	-	-	-	92%

American Indian students in the state graduate at lower rates than their White, non-Latino, counterparts and lower rates than the national average for the group.

National Assessment of Educational Progress (NAEP)

American Indian students in the state score below the results for their White, non-Latino, counterparts and below the national average for the group.

Percentages of American Indian and White, Non-Latino, Students
Reading, Grade 8, 2011

	Percent at or Above Proficient		Gap
	White, non-Latino	American Indian	American Indian/White
USA	41	22	19
North Dakota	*37*	*13*	*24*

NAEP 8th Grade Mathematics results for the state's White, non-Latino, students are above national averages. Results for American Indian students in the state are below those for White, non-Latino, students and below those of the national average for the group.

Percentages of American Indian and White, Non-Latino, Students
Mathematics, Grade 8, 2011

	Percent at or Above Proficient		Gap
	White, non-Latino	American Indian	American Indian/White
USA	43	17	26
North Dakota	47	*15*	*32*

The *Benchmark* for American Indian students in 8th Grade Reading is achieved by Minnesota and Oregon, with 30% of American Indian students scoring at or above Proficient. The *Benchmark* for 8th Grade Mathematics is North Carolina, with 22% of American Indian students scoring at or above Proficient.

OHIO

American Indian Demography

State	American Indian Alone	Navajo	Cherokee	Sioux	Chippewa	Choctaw	Pueblo	Apache
Ohio	16,423	330	7,813	719	1,213			408

The state has significant Alleghenny, Shawnee and Piqua populations.

Educational Attainment: Percent High School Graduate or Higher

State	Total Population	Asian Alone	White Alone	Black Alone	Latino	American Indian
USA	85%	86%	87%	81%	62%	77%
Ohio	87%	89%	88%	81%	71%	81%

Educational attainment for American Indians is lower than that for the total population and Asian and White, non-Latino, residents, the same as that for Black residents and higher than that of Latinos.

Estimated High School Graduation Rates

State	American Indian	Asian	Latino	Black	White, non-Latino
USA	62%	89%	65%	58%	79%
Ohio	76%	93%	69%	*51%*	83%

American Indian students in the state graduate at lower rates than their Asian and White, non-Latino, counterparts, higher rates than Latino and Black students and than the national average for the group.

National Assessment of Educational Progress (NAEP)

There are too few American Indian students in the state for the purposes of the NAEP estimates.

Percentages of American Indian and White, Non-Latino, Students
Reading, Grade 8, 2011

	Percent at or Above Proficient		Gap
	White, non-Latino	American Indian	American Indian/White
USA	41	22	19
Ohio	43	‡	-

NAEP 8th Grade Mathematics results for the state's White, non-Latino, students are above national averages. There are too few American Indian students in the state for the purposes of the NAEP estimates.

Percentages of American Indian and White, Non-Latino, Students
Mathematics, Grade 8, 2011

	Percent at or Above Proficient		Gap
	White, non-Latino	American Indian	American Indian/White
USA	43	17	26
Ohio	46	‡	-

The *Benchmark* for American Indian students in 8th Grade Reading is achieved by Minnesota and Oregon, with 30% of American Indian students scoring at or above Proficient. The *Benchmark* for 8th Grade Mathematics is North Carolina, with 22% of American Indian students scoring at or above Proficient.

OKLAHOMA

American Indian Demography

State	American Indian Alone	Navajo	Cherokee	Sioux	Chippewa	Choctaw	Pueblo	Apache
Oklahoma	244,890	982	98,605	956		43,434	514	1,738

Educational Attainment: Percent High School Graduate or Higher

State	Total Population	Asian Alone	White Alone	Black Alone	Latino	American Indian
USA	85%	86%	87%	81%	62%	77%
Oklahoma	85%	*82%*	87%	84%	*56%*	83%

Educational attainment for American Indians is lower than that for the total population, White, non-Latino, and Black residents, and higher than that of Asians and Latinos.

Estimated High School Graduation Rates

State	American Indian	Asian	Latino	Black	White, non-Latino
USA	62%	89%	65%	58%	79%
Oklahoma	74%	-	75%	66%	79%

American Indian students in the state graduate at lower rates than their Latino and White, non-Latino, counterparts, higher rates than Black students and than the national average for the group.

National Assessment of Educational Progress (NAEP)

American Indian students in the state score below the results for their White, non-Latino, counterparts and above the national average for the group.

Percentages of American Indian and White, Non-Latino, Students
Reading, Grade 8, 2011

	Percent at or Above Proficient		Gap
	White, non-Latino	American Indian	American Indian/White
USA	41	22	19
Oklahoma	*32*	23	9

NAEP 8th Grade Mathematics results for the state's White, non-Latino, students are below national averages. Results for American Indian students in the state are below those for White, non-Latino, students and above those of the national average for the group.

Percentages of American Indian and White, Non-Latino, Students
Mathematics, Grade 8, 2011

	Percent at or Above Proficient		Gap
	White, non-Latino	American Indian	American Indian/White
USA	43	17	26
Oklahoma	*34*	21	13

The *Benchmark* for American Indian students in 8th Grade Reading is achieved by Minnesota and Oregon, with 30% of American Indian students scoring at or above Proficient. The *Benchmark* for 8th Grade Mathematics is North Carolina, with 22% of American Indian students scoring at or above Proficient.

OREGON

American Indian Demography

State	American Indian Alone	Navajo	Cherokee	Sioux	Chippewa	Choctaw	Pueblo	Apache
Oregon	51,181	534	4,548	1,699		1,086		575

The state has significant populations of localized tribes.

Educational Attainment: Percent High School Graduate or Higher

State	Total Population	Asian Alone	White Alone	Black Alone	Latino	American Indian
USA	85%	86%	87%	81%	62%	77%
Oregon	89%	86%	90%	86%	*55%*	*66%*

Educational attainment for American Indians is lower than that for the total population and all sub-groups other than Latinos.

Estimated High School Graduation Rates

State	American Indian	Asian	Latino	Black	White, non-Latino
USA	62%	89%	65%	58%	79%
Oregon	74%	*82%*	78%	65%	*78%*

American Indian students in the state graduate at lower rates than their Asian, Latino and White, non-Latino, counterparts, higher rates than Black students and higher rates than the national average for the group.

National Assessment of Educational Progress (NAEP)

American Indian students in the state score below the results for their White, non-Latino, counterparts and above the national average for the group.

Percentages of American Indian and White, Non-Latino, Students
Reading, Grade 8, 2011

	Percent at or Above Proficient		Gap
	White, non-Latino	American Indian	American Indian/White
USA	41	22	19
Oregon	*37*	30	7

NAEP 8th Grade Mathematics results for the state's White, non-Latino, students are below national averages. Results for American Indian students in the state are below those for White, non-Latino, students and below those of the national average for the group.

Percentages of American Indian and White, Non-Latino, Students
Mathematics, Grade 8, 2011

	Percent at or Above Proficient		Gap
	White, non-Latino	American Indian	American Indian/White
USA	43	17	26
Oregon	*37*	*16*	21

The *Benchmark* for American Indian students in 8th Grade Reading is achieved by Minnesota and Oregon, with 30% of American Indian students scoring at or above Proficient. The *Benchmark* for 8th Grade Mathematics is North Carolina, with 22% of American Indian students scoring at or above Proficient.

PENNSYLVANIA

American Indian Demography

State	American Indian Alone	Navajo	Cherokee	Sioux	Chippewa	Choctaw	Pueblo	Apache
Pennsylvania	12,299		3,290	628	407			307

Educational Attainment: Percent High School Graduate or Higher

State	Total Population	Asian Alone	White Alone	Black Alone	Latino	American Indian
USA	85%	86%	87%	81%	62%	77%
Pennsylvania	87%	*83%*	89%	81%	66%	83%

Educational attainment for American Indians is lower than that for the total population and White, non-Latinos, the same as Asians and higher than that of Black and Latino residents.

Estimated High School Graduation Rates

State	American Indian	Asian	Latino	Black	White, non-Latino
USA	62%	89%	65%	58%	79%
Pennsylvania	65%	98%	66%	64%	88%

American Indian students in the state graduate at lower rates than their Asian, Latino and White, non-Latino, counterparts, higher rates than Black students and higher rates than the national average for the group.

National Assessment of Educational Progress (NAEP)

There are too few American Indian students in the state for the purposes of the NAEP estimates.

Percentages of American Indian and White, Non-Latino, Students
Reading, Grade 8, 2011

	Percent at or Above Proficient		Gap
	White, non-Latino	American Indian	American Indian/White
USA	41	22	19
Pennsylvania	46	‡	-

NAEP 8th Grade Mathematics results for the state's White, non-Latino, students are above national averages. There are too few American Indian students in the state for the purposes of the NAEP estimates.

Percentages of American Indian and White, Non-Latino, Students
Mathematics, Grade 8, 2011

	Percent at or Above Proficient		Gap
	White, non-Latino	American Indian	American Indian/White
USA	43	17	26
Pennsylvania	47	‡	-

The *Benchmark* for American Indian students in 8th Grade Reading is achieved by Minnesota and Oregon, with 30% of American Indian students scoring at or above Proficient. The *Benchmark* for 8th Grade Mathematics is North Carolina, with 22% of American Indian students scoring at or above Proficient.

RHODE ISLAND

American Indian Demography

State	American Indian Alone	Navajo	Cherokee	Sioux	Chippewa	Choctaw	Pueblo	Apache
Rhode Island	3,223							

The state has a significant Narragansett population.

Educational Attainment: Percent High School Graduate or Higher

State	Total Population	Asian Alone	White Alone	Black Alone	Latino	American Indian
USA	85%	86%	87%	81%	62%	77%
Rhode Island	*84%*	*79%*	*86%*	*75%*	*60%*	78%

Educational attainment for American Indians is lower than that for the total population, Asian and White, non- Latinos, and higher than that of Black and Latino residents.

Estimated High School Graduation Rates

State	American Indian	Asian	Latino	Black	White, non-Latino
USA	62%	89%	65%	58%	79%
Rhode Island	-	*65%*	*62%*	59%	*77%*

There are too few American Indian students in the state to estimate the high school graduation rate for the group.

National Assessment of Educational Progress (NAEP)
There are too few American Indian students in the state for the purposes of the NAEP estimates.

Percentages of American Indian and White, Non-Latino, Students
Reading, Grade 8, 2011

	Percent at or Above Proficient		Gap
	White, non-Latino	American Indian	American Indian/White
USA	41	22	19
Rhode Island	41	‡	-

NAEP 8th Grade Mathematics results for the state's White, non-Latino, students are below national averages. There are too few American Indian students in the state for the purposes of the NAEP estimates.

Percentages of American Indian and White, Non-Latino, Students
Mathematics, Grade 8, 2011

	Percent at or Above Proficient		Gap
	White, non-Latino	American Indian	American Indian/White
USA	43	17	26
Rhode Island	*42*	‡	-

The *Benchmark* for American Indian students in 8th Grade Reading is achieved by Minnesota and Oregon, with 30% of American Indian students scoring at or above Proficient. The *Benchmark* for 8th Grade Mathematics is North Carolina, with 22% of American Indian students scoring at or above Proficient.

SOUTH CAROLINA

American Indian Demography

State	American Indian Alone	Navajo	Cherokee	Sioux	Chippewa	Choctaw	Pueblo	Apache
South Carolina	10,950		3,579					

The state has significant Cawtawba and Edisto populations.

Educational Attainment: Percent High School Graduate or Higher

State	Total Population	Asian Alone	White Alone	Black Alone	Latino	American Indian
USA	85%	86%	87%	81%	62%	77%
South Carolina	*83%*	86%	*86%*	*76%*	*59%*	*73%*

Educational attainment for American Indians is lower than that for the total population and other sub-groups, but higher than that of Latino residents.

Estimated High School Graduation Rates

State	American Indian	Asian	Latino	Black	White, non-Latino
USA	62%	89%	65%	58%	79%
South Carolina	*50%*	*39%*	*50%*	*54%*	*67%*

American Indian students in the state graduate at lower rates than their Black and White, non-Latino, counterparts, higher rates than Asian students, the same rate as Latino students and lower rates than the national average for the group.

National Assessment of Educational Progress (NAEP)

There are too few American Indian students in the state for the purposes of the NAEP estimates.

Percentages of American Indian and White, Non-Latino, Students
Reading, Grade 8, 2011

	Percent at or Above Proficient		Gap
	White, non-Latino	American Indian	American Indian/White
USA	41	22	19
South Carolina	*37*	‡	-

NAEP 8th Grade Mathematics results for the state's White, non-Latino, students are at national averages. There are too few American Indian students in the state for the purposes of the NAEP estimates.

Percentages of American Indian and White, Non-Latino, Students
Mathematics, Grade 8, 2011

	Percent at or Above Proficient		Gap
	White, non-Latino	American Indian	American Indian/White
USA	43	17	26
South Carolina	43	‡	-

The *Benchmark* for American Indian students in 8th Grade Reading is achieved by Minnesota and Oregon, with 30% of American Indian students scoring at or above Proficient. The *Benchmark* for 8th Grade Mathematics is North Carolina, with 22% of American Indian students scoring at or above Proficient.

SOUTH DAKOTA

American Indian Demography

State	American Indian Alone	Navajo	Cherokee	Sioux	Chippewa	Choctaw	Pueblo	Apache
South Dakota	64,097			53,671	672			

Educational Attainment: Percent High School Graduate or Higher

State	Total Population	Asian Alone	White Alone	Black Alone	Latino	American Indian
USA	85%	86%	87%	81%	62%	77%
South Dakota	89%	86%	90%	82%	69%	79%

Educational attainment for American Indians is lower than that for the total population, White, non-Latino, Black, and Asian residents, but higher than that of Latino residents.

Estimated High School Graduation Rates

State	American Indian	Asian	Latino	Black	White, non-Latino
USA	62%	89%	65%	58%	79%
South Dakota	*43%*	99%	69%	73%	84%

American Indian students in the state graduate at lower rates than their counterparts and than the national average for the group.

National Assessment of Educational Progress (NAEP)

American Indian students in the state score below the results of their White, non-Latino, counterparts and below the national average for the group.

Percentages of American Indian and White, Non-Latino, Students
Reading, Grade 8, 2011

	Percent at or Above Proficient		Gap
	White, non-Latino	American Indian	American Indian/White
USA	41	22	19
South Dakota	*39*	*14*	*25*

NAEP 8th Grade Mathematics results for the state's White, non-Latino, students are above national averages. Results for American Indian students in the state are below those for White, non-Latino, students and below those of the national average for the group.

Percentages of American Indian and White, Non-Latino, Students
Mathematics, Grade 8, 2011

	Percent at or Above Proficient		Gap
	White, non-Latino	American Indian	American Indian/White
USA	43	17	26
South Dakota	47	*14*	*33*

The *Benchmark* for American Indian students in 8th Grade Reading is achieved by Minnesota and Oregon, with 30% of American Indian students scoring at or above Proficient. The *Benchmark* for 8th Grade Mathematics is North Carolina, with 22% of American Indian students scoring at or above Proficient.

TENNESSEE

American Indian Demography

State	American Indian Alone	Navajo	Cherokee	Sioux	Chippewa	Choctaw	Pueblo	Apache
Tennessee	11,948		6,592			447		

The state has a significant Creek population.

Educational Attainment: Percent High School Graduate or Higher

State	Total Population	Asian Alone	White Alone	Black Alone	Latino	American Indian
USA	85%	86%	87%	81%	62%	77%
Tennessee	*83%*	86%	*83%*	*80%*	*57%*	80%

Educational attainment for American Indians is lower than that for the total population, White, non-Latino, and Asian residents, the same as that for Black resident and higher than that of Latino residents.

Estimated High School Graduation Rates

State	American Indian	Asian	Latino	Black	White, non-Latino
USA	62%	89%	65%	58%	79%
Tennessee	*58%*	95%	69%	71%	82%

American Indian students in the state graduate at lower rates than their counterparts and than the national average for the group.

National Assessment of Educational Progress (NAEP)

There are too few American Indian students in the state for the purposes of the NAEP estimates.

Percentages of American Indian and White, Non-Latino, Students
Reading, Grade 8, 2011

	Percent at or Above Proficient		Gap
	White, non-Latino	American Indian	American Indian/White
USA	41	22	19
Tennessee	*31*	‡	-

NAEP 8th Grade Mathematics results for the state's White, non-Latino, students are below national averages. There are too few American Indian students in the state for the purposes of the NAEP estimates.

Percentages of American Indian and White, Non-Latino, Students
Mathematics, Grade 8, 2011

	Percent at or Above Proficient		Gap
	White, non-Latino	American Indian	American Indian/White
USA	43	17	26
Tennessee	*28*	‡	-

The *Benchmark* for American Indian students in 8th Grade Reading is achieved by Minnesota and Oregon, with 30% of American Indian students scoring at or above Proficient. The *Benchmark* for 8th Grade Mathematics is North Carolina, with 22% of American Indian students scoring at or above Proficient.

TEXAS

American Indian Demography

State	American Indian Alone	Navajo	Cherokee	Sioux	Chippewa	Choctaw	Pueblo	Apache
Texas	86,211	1,741	18,742	1,614	956	10,393	1,580	3,108

The state has a significant Kickapoo population.

Educational Attainment: Percent High School Graduate or Higher

State	Total Population	Asian Alone	White Alone	Black Alone	Latino	American Indian
USA	85%	86%	87%	81%	62%	77%
Texas	*80%*	87%	*82%*	84%	*58%*	79%

Educational attainment for American Indians is lower than that for the total population, but higher than that of Latino residents.

Estimated High School Graduation Rates

State	American Indian	Asian	Latino	Black	White, non-Latino
USA	62%	89%	65%	58%	79%
Texas	68%	*80%*	*56%*	*46%*	*63%*

American Indian students in the state graduate at lower rates than their Asian and White, non-Latino, counterparts and higher rates than Latino and Black students and than the national average for the group.

National Assessment of Educational Progress (NAEP)

There are too few American Indian students in the state for the purposes of the NAEP estimates.

Percentages of American Indian and White, Non-Latino, Students
Reading, Grade 8, 2011

	Percent at or Above Proficient		Gap
	White, non-Latino	American Indian	American Indian/White
USA	41	22	19
Texas	42	‡	-

NAEP 8th Grade Mathematics results for the state's White, non-Latino, students are above national averages. There are too few American Indian students in the state for the purposes of the NAEP estimates.

Percentages of American Indian and White, Non-Latino, Students
Mathematics, Grade 8, 2011

	Percent at or Above Proficient		Gap
	White, non-Latino	American Indian	American Indian/White
USA	43	17	26
Texas	58	‡	-

The *Benchmark* for American Indian students in 8th Grade Reading is achieved by Minnesota and Oregon, with 30% of American Indian students scoring at or above Proficient. The *Benchmark* for 8th Grade Mathematics is North Carolina, with 22% of American Indian students scoring at or above Proficient.

UTAH

American Indian Demography

State	American Indian Alone	Navajo	Cherokee	Sioux	Chippewa	Choctaw	Pueblo	Apache
Utah	28,289	14,456	832	626			296	373

The state has significant Unitah, Ouray, Shoshone, Ute and Paiute populations.

Educational Attainment: Percent High School Graduate or Higher

State	Total Population	Asian Alone	White Alone	Black Alone	Latino	American Indian
USA	85%	86%	87%	81%	62%	77%
Utah	91%	86%	92%	85%	64%	78%

Educational attainment for American Indians is lower than that for the total population, but higher than that of Latino residents.

Estimated High School Graduation Rates

State	American Indian	Asian	Latino	Black	White, non-Latino
USA	62%	89%	65%	58%	79%
Utah	*54%*	*84%*	*55%*	62%	79%

American Indian students in the state graduate at lower rates than their counterparts and than the national average for the group.

National Assessment of Educational Progress (NAEP)

American Indian students in the state scored below the results for their White, non-Latino, counterparts and below the national average for the group.

Percentages of American Indian and White, Non-Latino, Students
Reading, Grade 8, 2011

	Percent at or Above Proficient		Gap
	White, non-Latino	American Indian	American Indian/White
USA	41	22	19
Utah	*40*	*18*	*22*

NAEP 8th Grade Mathematics results for the state's White, non-Latino, students are below national averages. There are too few American Indian students in the state for the purposes of the NAEP estimates.

Percentages of American Indian and White, Non-Latino, Students
Mathematics, Grade 8, 2011

	Percent at or Above Proficient		Gap
	White, non-Latino	American Indian	American Indian/White
USA	43	17	26
Utah	*41*	‡	-

The *Benchmark* for American Indian students in 8th Grade Reading is achieved by Minnesota and Oregon, with 30% of American Indian students scoring at or above Proficient. The Benchmark for 8th Grade Mathematics is North Carolina, with 22% of American Indian students scoring at or above Proficient.

VERMONT

American Indian Demography

State	American Indian Alone	Navajo	Cherokee	Sioux	Chippewa	Choctaw	Pueblo	Apache
Vermont	1,499							

The state has a significant Abenaki population.

Educational Attainment: Percent High School Graduate or Higher

State	Total Population	Asian Alone	White Alone	Black Alone	Latino	American Indian
USA	85%	86%	87%	81%	62%	77%
Vermont	91%	*83%*	91%	86%	91%	*75%*

Educational attainment for American Indians is lower than that for the total population and each sub-group.

Estimated High School Graduation Rates

State	American Indian	Asian	Latino	Black	White, non-Latino
USA	62%	89%	65%	58%	79%
Vermont	-	-	70%	78%	80%

There are too few American Indian students in the state to estimate the high school graduation rate for the group.

National Assessment of Educational Progress (NAEP)

There are too few American Indian students in the state for the purposes of the NAEP estimates.

Percentages of American Indian and White, Non-Latino, Students
Reading, Grade 8, 2011

	Percent at or Above Proficient		Gap
	White, non-Latino	American Indian	American Indian/White
USA	41	22	19
Vermont	45	‡	-

NAEP 8th Grade Mathematics results for the state's White, non-Latino, students are above national averages. There are too few American Indian students in the state for the purposes of the NAEP estimates.

Percentages of American Indian and White, Non-Latino, Students
Mathematics, Grade 8, 2011

	Percent at or Above Proficient		Gap
	White, non-Latino	American Indian	American Indian/White
USA	43	17	26
Vermont	47	‡	-

The *Benchmark* for American Indian students in 8th Grade Reading is achieved by Minnesota and Oregon, with 30% of American Indian students scoring at or above Proficient. The *Benchmark* for 8th Grade Mathematics is North Carolina, with 22% of American Indian students scoring at or above Proficient.

VIRGINIA

American Indian Demography

State	American Indian Alone	Navajo	Cherokee	Sioux	Chippewa	Choctaw	Pueblo	Apache
Virginia	18,112	375	4,648	511	405	486		

The state has a significant Chickahominy population.

Educational Attainment: Percent High School Graduate or Higher

State	Total Population	Asian Alone	White Alone	Black Alone	Latino	American Indian
USA	85%	86%	87%	81%	62%	77%
Virginia	86%	89%	88%	*80%*	68%	79%

Educational attainment for American Indians is lower than that for the total population and each sub-group except Latino residents.

Estimated High School Graduation Rates

State	American Indian	Asian	Latino	Black	White, non-Latino
USA	62%	89%	65%	58%	79%
Virginia	67%	95%	82%	62%	80%

American Indian students in the state graduate at lower rates than their Asian, Latino and White, non-Latino, counterparts and at higher rates than Black students and than the national average for the group.

National Assessment of Educational Progress (NAEP)

There are too few American Indian students in the state for the purposes of the NAEP estimates.

Percentages of American Indian and White, Non-Latino, Students
Reading, Grade 8, 2011

	Percent at or Above Proficient		Gap
	White, non-Latino	American Indian	American Indian/White
USA	41	22	19
Virginia	43	‡	-

NAEP 8th Grade Mathematics results for the state's White, non-Latino, students are above national averages. There are too few American Indian students in the state for the purposes of the NAEP estimates.

Percentages of American Indian and White, Non-Latino, Students
Mathematics, Grade 8, 2011

	Percent at or Above Proficient		Gap
	White, non-Latino	American Indian	American Indian/White
USA	43	17	26
Virginia	48	‡	-

The *Benchmark* for American Indian students in 8th Grade Reading is achieved by Minnesota and Oregon, with 30% of American Indian students scoring at or above Proficient. The *Benchmark* for 8th Grade Mathematics is North Carolina, with 22% of American Indian students scoring at or above Proficient.

WASHINGTON

American Indian Demography

State	American Indian Alone	Navajo	Cherokee	Sioux	Chippewa	Choctaw	Pueblo	Apache
Washington	75,738	1,079	5,389	3,111	3,143	918	327	895

As with Oregon and California, the state has significant localized tribal populations.

Educational Attainment: Percent High School Graduate or Higher

State	Total Population	Asian Alone	White Alone	Black Alone	Latino	American Indian
USA	85%	86%	87%	81%	62%	77%
Washington	90%	*85%*	92%	87%	*59%*	81%

Educational attainment for American Indians is lower than that for the total population and each sub-group except Latino residents.

Estimated High School Graduation Rates

State	American Indian	Asian	Latino	Black	White, non-Latino
USA	62%	89%	65%	58%	79%
Washington	*51%*	*79%*	*53%*	*49%*	*72%*

American Indian students in the state graduate at lower rates than their Asian, Latino and White, non-Latino, counterparts, at higher rates than Black students and than a lower rate than the national average for the group.

National Assessment of Educational Progress (NAEP)

American Indian students in the state scored below the results for their White, non-Latino, counterparts and above the national average of the group.

Percentages of American Indian and White, Non-Latino, Students
Reading, Grade 8, 2011

	Percent at or Above Proficient		Gap
	White, non-Latino	American Indian	American Indian/White
USA	41	22	19
Washington	42	24	18

NAEP 8th Grade Mathematics results for the state's White, non-Latino, students are above national averages. Results for American Indian students in the state are below those for White, non-Latino, students and below those of the national average for the group.

Percentages of American Indian and White, Non-Latino, Students
Mathematics, Grade 8, 2011

	Percent at or Above Proficient		Gap
	White, non-Latino	American Indian	American Indian/White
USA	43	17	26
Washington	46	*12*	34

The *Benchmark* for American Indian students in 8th Grade Reading is achieved by Minnesota and Oregon, with 30% of American Indian students scoring at or above Proficient. The *Benchmark* for 8th Grade Mathematics is North Carolina, with 22% of American Indian students scoring at or above Proficient.

WEST VIRGINIA

American Indian Demography

State	American Indian Alone	Navajo	Cherokee	Sioux	Chippewa	Choctaw	Pueblo	Apache
West Virginia	2,418		1,287					

Educational Attainment: Percent High School Graduate or Higher

State	Total Population	Asian Alone	White Alone	Black Alone	Latino	American Indian
USA	85%	86%	87%	81%	62%	77%
West Virginia	*82%*	90%	*82%*	84%	73%	80%

Educational attainment for American Indians is lower than that for the total population and each sub-group except Latino residents.

Estimated High School Graduation Rates

State	American Indian	Asian	Latino	Black	White, non-Latino
USA	62%	89%	65%	58%	79%
West Virginia	-	91%	79%	67%	*72%*

There are too few American Indian students in the state to estimate the high school graduation rate for the group.

National Assessment of Educational Progress (NAEP)

There are too few American Indian students in the state for the purposes of the NAEP estimates.

Percentages of American Indian and White, Non-Latino, Students
Reading, Grade 8, 2011

	Percent at or Above Proficient		Gap
	White, non-Latino	American Indian	American Indian/White
USA	41	22	19
West Virginia	*24*	‡	-

NAEP 8th Grade Mathematics results for the state's White, non-Latino, students are below national averages. There are too few American Indian students in the state for the purposes of the NAEP estimates.

Percentages of American Indian and White, Non-Latino, Students
Mathematics, Grade 8, 2011

	Percent at or Above Proficient		Gap
	White, non-Latino	American Indian	American Indian/White
USA	43	17	26
West Virginia	*22*	‡	-

The *Benchmark* for American Indian students in 8th Grade Reading is achieved by Minnesota and Oregon, with 30% of American Indian students scoring at or above Proficient. The *Benchmark* for 8th Grade Mathematics is North Carolina, with 22% of American Indian students scoring at or above Proficient.

WISCONSIN

American Indian Demography

State	American Indian Alone	Navajo	Cherokee	Sioux	Chippewa	Choctaw	Pueblo	Apache
Wisconsin	44,142		1,163	705	14,412			

Educational Attainment: Percent High School Graduate or Higher

State	Total Population	Asian Alone	White Alone	Black Alone	Latino	American Indian
USA	85%	86%	87%	81%	62%	77%
Wisconsin	89%	*81%*	91%	*78%*	62%	84%

Educational attainment for American Indians is lower than that for the total population and White, non-Latino residents, but higher than that of the other sub-groups.

Estimated High School Graduation Rates

State	American Indian	Asian	Latino	Black	White, non-Latino
USA	62%	89%	65%	58%	79%
Wisconsin	69%	95%	67%	*48%*	89%

American Indian students in the state graduate at lower rates than their Asian and White, non-Latino, counterparts, at higher rates than Latino and Black students and at a higher rate than the national average for the group.

National Assessment of Educational Progress (NAEP)

There are too few American Indian students in the state for the purposes of the NAEP estimates.

Percentages of American Indian and White, Non-Latino, Students
Reading, Grade 8, 2011

	Percent at or Above Proficient		Gap
	White, non-Latino	American Indian	American Indian/White
USA	41	22	19
Wisconsin	*40*	‡	-

NAEP 8th Grade Mathematics results for the state's White, non-Latino, students are above national averages. There are too few American Indian students in the state for the purposes of the NAEP estimates.

Percentages of American Indian and White, Non-Latino, Students
Mathematics, Grade 8, 2011

	Percent at or Above Proficient		Gap
	White, non-Latino	American Indian	American Indian/White
USA	43	17	26
Wisconsin	47	‡	-

The *Benchmark* for American Indian students in 8th Grade Reading is achieved by Minnesota and Oregon, with 30% of American Indian students scoring at or above Proficient. The *Benchmark* for 8th Grade Mathematics is North Carolina, with 22% of American Indian students scoring at or above Proficient.

WYOMING

American Indian Demography

State	American Indian Alone	Navajo	Cherokee	Sioux	Chippewa	Choctaw	Pueblo	Apache
Wyoming	11,714	348	461	829				

The state has significant Arapahoe and Shoshone populations.

Educational Attainment: Percent High School Graduate or Higher

State	Total Population	Asian Alone	White Alone	Black Alone	Latino	American Indian
USA	85%	86%	87%	81%	62%	77%
Wyoming	91%	90%	92%	89%	74%	85%

Educational attainment for American Indians is lower than that for the total population and White, non-Latino residents, and that of the other sub-groups, aside from Latinos.

Estimated High School Graduation Rates

State	American Indian	Asian	Latino	Black	White, non-Latino
USA	62%	89%	65%	58%	79%
Wyoming	*42%*	*87%*	78%	60%	79%

American Indian students in the state graduate at lower rates than their counterparts and than the national average for the group.

National Assessment of Educational Progress (NAEP)

There are too few American Indian students in the state for the purposes of the NAEP estimates.

Percentages of American Indian and White, Non-Latino, Students
Reading, Grade 8, 2011

	Percent at or Above Proficient		Gap
	White, non-Latino	American Indian	American Indian/White
USA	41	22	19
Wyoming	*40*	‡	-

NAEP 8th Grade Mathematics results for the state's White, non-Latino, students are below national averages. There are too few American Indian students in the state for the purposes of the NAEP estimates.

Percentages of American Indian and White, Non-Latino, Students

Mathematics, Grade 8, 2011

	Percent at or Above Proficient		Gap
	White, non-Latino	American Indian	American Indian/White
USA	43	17	26
Wyoming	*41*	‡	-

The *Benchmark* for American Indian students in 8th Grade Reading is achieved by Minnesota and Oregon, with 30% of American Indian students scoring at or above Proficient. The *Benchmark* for 8th Grade Mathematics is North Carolina, with 22% of American Indian students scoring at or above Proficient.

www.ingramcontent.com/pod-product-compliance
Lightning Source LLC
Chambersburg PA
CBHW080509090426
42734CB00015B/3011

* 9 7 8 0 6 1 5 9 3 0 9 5 4 *